GENDER IN LOW- AND MIDDLE-INCOME COUNTRIES

Marc H. Bornstein, *Eunice Kennedy Shriver National Institute of Child Health and Human Development*
Diane L. Putnick, *Eunice Kennedy Shriver National Institute of Child Health and Human Development*
Jennifer E. Lansford, *Duke University*
Kirby Deater-Deckard, *Virginia Tech*
Robert H. Bradley, *Arizona State University*

WITH COMMENTARY BY

Kofi Marfo

Stafford Library
Columbia College
1001 Rogers Street
Columbia, MO 65216

Patricia J. Bauer
Series Editor

MONOGRAPHS OF THE SOCIETY FOR RESEARCH IN CHILD DEVELOPMENT

Serial No. 320, Vol. 81, No. 1, 2016

WILEY Boston, Massachusetts   Oxford, United Kingdom

EDITOR
PATRICIA J. BAUER
Emory University

MANAGING EDITOR
ADAM MARTIN
Society for Research in Child Development

EDITORIAL ASSISTANT
STEPHANIE CUSTER
Society for Research in Child Development

GENDER IN LOW- AND MIDDLE-INCOME COUNTRIES

CONTENTS

I. GENDER IN LOW- AND MIDDLE-INCOME COUNTRIES: INTRODUCTION — 7
Marc H. Bornstein, Diane L. Putnick, Robert H. Bradley, Kirby Deater-Deckard, and Jennifer E. Lansford

II. GENDER IN LOW- AND MIDDLE-INCOME COUNTRIES: GENERAL METHODS — 24
Marc H. Bornstein, Diane L. Putnick, Robert H. Bradley, Kirby Deater-Deckard, Jennifer E. Lansford, and Yumiko Ota

III. THE ROLE OF PHYSICAL CAPITAL ASSETS IN YOUNG GIRLS' AND BOYS' MORTALITY AND GROWTH IN LOW- AND MIDDLE-INCOME COUNTRIES — 33
Robert H. Bradley and Diane L. Putnick

IV. MOTHERS' AND FATHERS' PARENTING PRACTICES WITH THEIR DAUGHTERS AND SONS IN LOW- AND MIDDLE-INCOME COUNTRIES — 60
Marc H. Bornstein and Diane L. Putnick

V. DAUGHTERS' AND SONS' EXPOSURE TO CHILDREARING DISCIPLINE AND VIOLENCE IN LOW- AND MIDDLE-INCOME COUNTRIES — 78
Kirby Deater-Deckard and Jennifer E. Lansford

VI. GIRLS' AND BOYS' LABOR AND HOUSEHOLD CHORES IN LOW- AND MIDDLE-INCOME COUNTRIES — 104
Diane L. Putnick and Marc H. Bornstein

VII. GENDER IN LOW- AND MIDDLE-INCOME COUNTRIES: REFLECTIONS, LIMITATIONS, DIRECTIONS, AND IMPLICATIONS — 123
Marc H. Bornstein, Diane L. Putnick, Kirby Deater-Deckard, Jennifer E. Lansford, and Robert H. Bradley

REFERENCES — 145

ACKNOWLEDGMENTS — 171

COMMENTARY

CONTEXT AND THE ADVANCEMENT OF A GLOBAL SCIENCE   172
OF HUMAN DEVELOPMENT: A COMMENTARY
Kofi Marfo

CONTRIBUTORS   183

STATEMENT OF EDITORIAL POLICY   185

SUBJECT INDEX   187

I. GENDER IN LOW- AND MIDDLE-INCOME COUNTRIES: INTRODUCTION

Marc H. Bornstein, Diane L. Putnick, Robert H. Bradley, Kirby Deater-Deckard, and Jennifer E. Lansford

> This article is part of the issue "Gender in Low- and Middle-Income Countries," Bornstein, Putnick, Lansford, Deater-Deckard, and Bradley (Issue Authors). For a full listing of articles in this issue, see: http://onlinelibrary.wiley.com/doi/10.1111/mono.v81.1/issuetoc.

How do girls and boys in low- and middle-income countries (LMIC) in the majority world vary with respect to central indicators of child growth and mortality, parental caregiving, discipline and violence, and child labor? How do key indicators of national gender equity and economic development relate to gender similarities and differences in each of these substantive areas of child development? This monograph of the SRCD is concerned with central topics of child gender, gendered parenting, gendered environments, and gendered behaviors and socializing practices in the underresearched and underserved world of LMIC.

To examine protective and risk factors related to child gender in LMIC around the world, we used data from more than 2 million individuals in 400,000 families in 41 LMIC collected in the Multiple Indicator Cluster Survey, a household survey that includes nationally representative samples of participating countries. In the first chapter of this monograph, we describe the conceptual "gender similarities" and "bioecological" frameworks that helped guide the monograph. In the second chapter, we detail the general methodology adhered to in the substantive chapters. Then, in topical chapters, we describe the situations of girls and boys with successive foci on child growth and mortality, parental caregiving, family discipline and violence, and child labor. We conclude with a general discussion of findings from the substantive chapters in the context of gender and bioecological theories.

Across 41 LMIC and four substantive areas of child development, few major gender differences emerged. Our data support a gender similarities view and suggest that general emphases on early child gender differences may be overstated at least for the developing world of LMIC.

Corresponding author: Dr. Marc H. Bornstein, Child and Family Research, *Eunice Kennedy Shriver* National Institute of Child Health and Human Development, Suite 8030 6705 Rockledge Drive, Bethesda, MD 20892-7971; email: Marc_H_Bornstein@nih.gov
DOI: 10.1111/mono.12223
© 2015 The Society for Research in Child Development, Inc.

> *... everyone is entitled to all the rights and freedoms set forth [in the Convention on the Rights of the Child], without distinction of ... sex ....*
>
> – Preamble, Convention on the Rights of the Child
> General Assembly resolution 44/25, 20 November 1989.

In 2013, the United Nations estimated that 1.1 billion people lived in countries characterized as very high on the Human Development Index (HDI; a measure of the social and economic status of a country), and another 1.0 billion lived in countries characterized as high HDI (United Nations Development Programme, 2013). This situation contrasts with over 3.5 billion in countries listed as medium HDI and 1.3 billion in countries listed as low HDI. As it happens, the vast majority of research on gender and child development has taken place in countries in the top tier (i.e., High-Income Countries; HIC), whereas almost none has taken place in the bottom tier (i.e., Low- to Middle-Income Countries; LMIC). There are, of course, notable exceptions, such as the Six Cultures Study (Whiting, 1963) and Young Lives Study (Harpham, Huttly, De Silva, & Abramsky, 2005); however, the vast majority of what is known about how gender is implicated in children's experiences is derived from studies conducted in HIC (that is, the "minority world"). In HIC, parents tend to create gender-contrasting home environments for girls and boys, a process that may begin even prior to birth. Girls generally have more dolls and fictional characters, and boys more sports equipment, tools, and vehicles (Pomerleau, Bolduc, Malcuit, & Cossette, 1990). In the United States, for example, parents possess different ideas about their girls' and boys' emotions (Diener & Lucas, 2004 Putnam, Sanson, & Rothbart, 2002), and European American mothers and fathers talk about emotions differently with daughters than with sons (Adams, Kuebli, Boyle, & Fivush, 1995; Chodorow, 1978; Fivush, Berlin, Sales, Mennuti-Washburn, & Cassidy, 2003; Fivush, Brotman, Buckner, & Goodman, 2000). From the little that is documented about parenting in LMIC (the "majority world"), the same approach to gender differentiation appears to be operative. For example, in a study of Zinacanteco babies in Mexico, a father reported giving his son three green chilies to hold so that the boy would know to buy chili when he grew up (Greenfield, Brazelton, & Childs, 1989). In an African village, girls are given dolls to play with whereas boys are given construction vehicles and weapons (Bloch & Adler, 1994). By age 4–5, Sri Lankan village children display gender differences in play, similar to those found with British children (Prosser, Hutt, Hutt, Mahindadasa, & Goonetilleke, 1986). These important contributions to the LMIC literature on gender differences in child and parent behavior notwithstanding, there is a general dearth of multinational information on gendered child development and gender-based parenting practices for most LMICs.

Around the world, from conception onward gender is commonly believed to pervasively direct how children are reared and what roles they learn. Everywhere, it seems, adult caregivers appear primed to treat girls and boys differently so that each will follow cultural paths deemed to be gender appropriate. It is routine to attribute different beliefs and behaviors to girls and boys and to hold different expectations for them. It may be that some of these beliefs and behaviors are universal or near universal around the world. Alternatively, some may have roots only in local cultural or religious traditions or reflect situational social and economic conditions. Whatever their origins, gender differences in experiences at any point in the life course are important, but may be especially so in childhood because even small differences in patterns of development or treatment can cumulate over time, and so gender typing likely has power to fashion variations in the trajectories of children's gender development. For their part, children are exquisitely tuned to detect nuances in how they are treated by others (Williams & Best, 1982/1990). Indeed, young children seem to learn gender-appropriateness even before they can translate their ideas into words or behaviors. Children quickly come to see themselves and others in terms of gender (e.g., girls versus boys, females versus males, femininity versus masculinity), as distal influences (from national treatment of the genders to gendered occupations of adults around them) combine with more proximal ones (those beliefs and behaviors referred to earlier) to promote lifelong gendered roles.

Research interest in the intergenerational transmission of gender is longstanding (McHale, Crouter, & Whiteman, 2003). Lytton and Romney (1991) examined differential parental socialization of girls and boys through meta-analysis of the psychological and developmental literatures. They included 172 studies conducted in North America and non-North American Western societies. A clear effect to emerge from their survey was systematic encouragement of children's gender-typed activities by both mothers and fathers. Psychological socialization by family members appears to be fairly consistently gender informed, and, even in realms of development where parental socialization does not differentiate between daughters and sons, the same parental treatment may still affect girls and boys differently as girls and boys may experience their environments differently or interpret their experiences differently. According to Gurin and Markus (1989), processes of gender-based treatment that occur within the family very often are aligned with gender-based treatment and ideas emanating from numerous other sources (social exchanges with peers, interactions with other adults in the community, political climate), thus solidifying sets of perceptions and patterns of behavior observed in females and males within a society. In effect, gender is consensually acknowledged to be an important moderator in understanding many aspects of childhood and parenthood. Attributes associated with being either female or male appear early, are stable across time, and shape attitudes and actions throughout the balance of the life course (Anker, 1997).

All that said, new theory and careful re-examination of extant results are beginning to cast doubt on such facile conclusions. The findings from a worldwide survey of children's experiences in multiple domains of development reported in this monograph of the SRCD add fresh data to this cresting iconoclastic revision.

GENDER THEORY AND GENDER SIMILARITIES AND DIFFERENCES

Gender plays a role in how children are treated (Ruble, Martin, & Berenbaum, 2006; Wilcox & Kline, 2013), and it is widely believed that girls and boys are reared differently in most parts of the world. Prevailing theory buttresses past empirical observations and cultural stereotypes. Evolutionary theory, cognitive social learning theory, and sociocultural theory all devote considerable attention to gender differences. The ensuing brief overview closely follows Hyde's (2014) insightful disquisition and deconstruction. Evolutionary theory focuses on how natural selection produces a psychology of gender based on an assumption that different behaviors may be adaptive for females and males (Buss & Schmitt, 1993). A key to the evolutionary argument is parental investment, behaviors of adults that increase the offspring's chances of survival but that also cost the parent (Trivers, 1972). Given that organisms have finite amounts of time, effort, and energy to maximize fitness (the ability to both survive and reproduce), evolution optimizes females toward parenting and its associated psychological concomitants (in nurturance and safety) and males toward mating and its associated psychological concomitants (in aggression). Evolutionary psychologists emphasize cross-cultural universals in patterns of gender differences, and, broadly, daughters and sons appear to be trained in ways that relate to the evolutionary history of reproductive successes of the two genders (Low, 1989). Maternal parental investment concentrates on assuring survival of offspring, whereas paternal parental investment focuses on mating to produce offspring (Draper & Harpending, 1982; Mascaro, Hackett, & Rilling, 2013). Cognitive social learning theory, as applied to understanding the psychology of gender, asserts that child (and adult) behavior is shaped by incentives and disincentives. Thus, people imitate or model others in their environment, particularly if those others are powerful or admirable (Bussey & Bandura, 1999). Sociocultural theory, which focuses on variations across cultures in patterns of gender, contends that the psychology of gender results from accommodations or adaptations of the individual to restrictions on or opportunities for their gender in their society (Eagly & Wood, 1999; Wood & Eagly, 2012). Gender operates in social structures that define power relations in a society (Fiske & Stevens, 1993; Goodwin & Fiske, 2001; Stewart, 1998), and the more a culture or nation values gender similarities and differences, the more likely are gender similarities and differences to appear there (Oyserman & Markus, 1993).

All three theories developed at least in part to explain gender differences. The theories converge in support of the idea that gender sorts individuals into categories of female and male characteristics and circumstances that support those characteristics. The primary difference among the theories resides in the causal mechanisms responsible (i.e., biology, socialization, or context). There is also convergence in the ideas that gender relates to individual differences in women and men and gender structures social institutions within which women and men develop. In a nutshell, theory and research tend to paint gender differences as universal, inadvertently reinforcing credence in trait-like assumptions of female-male differences. To date, not surprisingly, most thinking has favored gender differences (Shields, 2007).

Although *vive la différence!* is (in some respects) supportable based on evidence produced in a wide variety of social science studies, just how large la différence is has come under serious question as biological, psychological, and sociological evidence using new methodologies and paradigms has mounted. The strong and continuing presumption of gender differences as fully penetrating the thoughts and behaviors of females and males tends to mitigate or even overlook entirely gender similarities and the large variances of many characteristics within the genders. In some sense, the gender differences perspective exaggerates, reinforces, or even creates gender differences. Females and males may differ biologically, but at the most basic level human beings are diploid organisms whose cells contain 23 matched pairs of chromosomes, one inherited from mother and one from father. Only one pair, the sex chromosomes, strictly distinguish females and males. The remaining 22 pairs of autosomes are found in females and males alike, and the approximately 25,000 genes in the human genome are passed from mothers and fathers to daughters and sons across generations and expressed equally when inherited from either parent. Moreover, biology is neither a necessary nor a sufficient cause of gender-related distinctions or differential development because biology is not determinative (Best, 2010). Gender variation in experience and expression is socially constructed (Brody, 1999; Shields, 2007)—and so may be socially constructed to be different or similar (Mead, 2001). Even domains of development under genetic, anatomical, or hormonal influence are modifiable. That is, gendered phenomena may develop from genetically, anatomically, or hormonally influenced predispositions, but their ultimate phenotypic expression is shaped by experiences with the social environment and affordances of the physical environment (Best, 2010; Wallen, 1996). Context also defines what possibilities and situations individual children can access in determining their own development. Contemporary theoretical perspectives concur that sociocultural norms help to account for gender (e.g., Brody, 1999; Durik et al., 2006; Hewlett, 2004; Shields, 2007), and that biology and experience co-influence expressions of gender and their development. Biological factors may impose restrictions and predispositions on gender in girls and boys, but contextual factors are influential determinants. Context can render gender categories salient or not, increasing or decreasing gender identification, and may or may not lead to one or another set of gendered beliefs and behaviors (Abrams, Sparkes, & Hogg, 1985; Abrams, Wetherell, Cochrane, Hogg, & Turner, 1990). Indeed, the magnitudes of a range of gender differences appear to vary impressively across cultures and nations (Lucas & Gohm, 2000; Williams & Best, 1990). Analysis of data from a small number of LMICs reveals that structural differences at the community or country level, and access to various forms of material and human capital at the household level, tend to have stronger impacts on most areas of child health and behavior than gender per se (Pells, 2010; Rendall, 2012).

Reorganization of internal structures and functional connections between components of psychobiological systems is especially likely in phylogenetically advanced organisms living in complex ecologies (Lerner, Hershberg, Hilliard, & Johnson, 2015). Human beings qualify. In some ways, it behooves such organisms to harbor somewhat offsetting tendencies so as to allow maximum flexibility in addressing the full panoply of conditions they might face over time. In effect, even as one acknowledges certain predominant biological, social, or contextual mechanisms for particular (gendered) tendencies, it is worth considering circumstances that might induce competing or compensatory tendencies. Consider, by way of illustration, some "facts of life" that might partially diminish the likelihood females and males exclusively manifest the nurturing versus mating tendencies discussed above. One fact of life is parental death. Throughout history mothers have died (in childbirth, via accident, on account of disease) leaving offspring of various ages without their "primary" nurturer. To some extent, the likelihood such offspring would survive and live to reproduce (humans take an exceptionally long time to fully mature) might be enhanced if fathers had some tendency to nurture—at least until another female could step in to enact the role. Likewise, in the case of paternal death (or even prolonged absence), it may fall to mothers to act in an aggressive manner to protect offspring—there is substantial evidence of this in some mammalian species—and in other ways (e.g., by employment) to support development. So, there might be predominant tendencies in females and males that have broad survival value and that would likely be fostered; but there are commonly experienced circumstances that might also increase the likelihood of developing offsetting tendencies and capacities (which also might be fostered). The gradual movement of humans over millennia into larger communities and constantly interacting and evolving social enterprises may further increase the likelihood that some counterpoising tendencies would be fostered—more so perhaps in some societies than others—as these new circumstances offer quite different affordances from the circumstances that typically faced humans millennia ago.

In contrast with the long-standing tradition of focusing on gender differences, the "gender similarities" hypothesis states that females and males are actually similar on many psychological measures (Hyde, 2005, 2014). Some early evidence for this hypothesis can be found in Maccoby and Jacklin's (1974) narrative review of parents' gender-differentiated socialization practices. Outside parents' reinforcing gender-typed play activities and toy choices, Maccoby and Jacklin (1974, p. 342) concluded that "the reinforcement contingencies for the two sexes appear to be remarkably similar." Even though Lytton and Romney (1991) later determined that parents systematically encourage their children's gender-typed activities based on a meta-analysis of 172 studies, most studies comparing socialization practices aimed at girls and boys tend to identify relatively small differences (with many nonsignificant findings emerging). In the last 2 decades more gender studies and more meta-analyses of putative gender differences in more domains of development have appeared. For example, Bornstein, Putnick, Bradley, Lansford, and Deater-Deckard (2015) found that maternal education (instructional capital) led to improved infant growth through availability of household resources (physical capital) in 117,881 families across a wide swath of 39 LMIC but did so equivalently for girls and boys. Likewise, attachment research shows a conspicuous absence of gender differences (Benenson, 1996). Generally, Strange Situation attachment classifications as well as maternal sensitivity ratings do not reveal gender differences and, consistent with this pattern, in van IJzendoorn et al. (2000), gender of child was not associated with maternal sensitivity or attachment classification per se. The strongest evidence for a hypothesis of gender similarities emerged from a review of 46 meta-analyses of the psychological and developmental research literatures. All told, those meta-analyses yielded 124 effect sizes for gender comparisons across a range of psychological domains, including cognitive, communication, social and personality, well-being, motor, and a heterogeneous variety of other categories. Effect size (Cohen's, 1988, d) was used as a metric, where a d of .20 is small, .50 medium, and .80 large. Altogether, 30% of the effect sizes fell between 0.0 and 0.10 and were interpreted as negligible, and an additional 48% fell in the range between 0.11 and 0.35 of a small difference. In sum, 78% of *reported* gender differences were small or close to 0. Domains in which gender differences proved to be small included mathematics performance, verbal skills, gregariousness and conscientiousness in personality, reward sensitivity, negative affectivity in temperament, relational aggression, tentative speech, aspects of sexuality, leadership effectiveness, self-esteem, and academic self-concept. Exceptions to gender similarities, where differences were moderate or large, included 3D mental rotation, agreeable/tender-minded personality, sensation seeking, interests in things versus people, physical aggression, and some sexual attitudes and behaviors. Therefore, considerable empirical evidence appears to support similarities between the genders. Furthermore, as Hyde (2014) pointed out, all "grand theories" of gender differences (evolutionary theory, cognitive social learning theory, sociocultural theory) can be reconstrued to sustain and explain gender similarities.

It is not the purpose of this monograph to meticulously adjudicate between these two opposing views pertaining to gender. However, for the kinds of environmental conditions we examine and the components of child well-being we consider, the newer view of gender similarity seems more fitting. The studies we report in this monograph of the SRCD analyze gender similarities and differences in an array of psychological domains across a large number of LMIC. Although we expect to find that the kinds of household conditions and parenting practices we examine will generally bear similar relations to children's development, it will be important to better define how conditions present in some LMIC contribute to gender similarities and differences, as both have implications for policy and practice.

The social contexts of many LMIC are widely believed to favor men over women (Morrison & Jütting, 2005; UNDP, 1995, 2011), as it is that gender differences and differential treatment of children by gender survive in most parts of the world, from Albania to Zimbabwe. However, the lives of girls and boys, women and men may vary substantially across LMIC; therefore, it may be inappropriate to assume that girls and boys in LMIC are treated differently. There is simply too little research on whether and how, at the family level, young girls and boys are reared in systematically similar or different ways, and what situations obtain across countries or only in select countries. This monograph of the SRCD addresses a gap in the research literature of how girls and boys are reared across LMIC. The scope of this monograph of the SRCD, in terms of the diversity of countries, peoples, and issues covered, serves to increase our understanding of how context interacts with biological predispositions to shape gender-related characteristics in children. By exploring gender in a broad range of LMIC, we can empirically assess how early similarities and differences in the treatment and experiences of girls and boys might become apparent, and whether particular country contexts moderate gender similarities and differences. Furthermore, covering a broad range of developmental topics allows us to determine whether gender similarities and differences are of comparable magnitude across different domains of development; whether, for example, girls and boys are read to similarly but disciplined differently. Such an approach depends on data from the same participants on multiple dimensions of development across multiple contexts. It also specifies direct and indirect connections between societal- and individual-level phenomena (Stewart & McDermott, 2004).

In this monograph of the SRCD, we revisit a variety of topics central to gender development in childhood and bring multinational data from the majority world of LMIC to bear on the question of gender similarities and differences.

THE BIOECOLOGICAL PERSPECTIVE ON CHILD GENDER

Children are embedded in a complex web of diverse social and physical contexts, and the relational bioecological developmental systems perspective is today the prevailing theoretical framework in developmental science (Bronfenbrenner & Morris, 2006; Lerner et al., 2015; Overton & Molenaar, 2015). The studies in this monograph of the SRCD are guided by that relational developmental systems paradigm.

Bioecological theory characterizes development as a joint function of process, person, context, and time (Bronfenbrenner & Morris, 2006). Processes refer to dynamic interactions that the developing person experiences. Characteristics and qualities of the developing person, including gender, interact with characteristics of the environment to influence the nature and structure of development. The contexts that envelop the child and shape development are conceived in terms of a hierarchically organized, interlinked set of systems, with lower-level more proximal contexts nested within higher-level more distal contexts. Each system has the potential to influence other systems. The microsystem encompasses patterns of activities, roles, and interpersonal relationships that the child experiences in face-to-face settings that are defined by specific physical and material parameters. This innermost system comprises patterns of interaction (proximal processes) between children and their immediate social milieux and physical environments. The microsystem is heterogeneous and various dimensions of the microsystem are functionally linked. Thus, the child's home environment has both social and physical components (Wachs, 2015) and the nature of proximal parent–child interactions can vary depending on characteristics of the physical microsystem, such as resources (Bradley, 2015). Distinct microsystems afford children opportunities to experience different activities that alone and in combination foster their development. Bioecological theory forces close attention on proximal processes, which Bronfenbrenner and Morris posited to be most important to development. These are the person's interactions within microsystems, including social interactions with others and engagement in particular activities with material resources in their settings. A mesosystem harbors processes and links between two or more microsystems, and the exosystem encompasses linkages between aspects of the environment the child does not directly encounter, but that influence development through lower-level micro- and mesosystems. At the outermost circle of developmental influences are overarching macrosystem patterns of beliefs, values, customs, and living conditions—culture, religion, the socioeconomic organization of society, and (most germane here) national indicators of gender equality. The macrosystem is not separate from children's more immediate environments; rather, it permeates and colors exo-, meso-, and microsystems. Understanding the meaning and effect of proximal influences on the child often requires setting them within the broader macrosystem in which they occur (Bornstein, 1995). The overarching macrosystem context can exert profound effects on how development is gendered, prescribing how girls and boys are socialized, what is considered adaptive for each gender, which tasks girls and boys are prescribed and proscribed, and what roles they likely adopt as mature women and men. Contextual expectations promote conformity to gender roles and influence how people think about themselves as gendered beings, including their general perceptions of femininity and masculinity.

In studies done in LMIC it is especially important to bear in mind that environmental conditions often interact with biological factors (some of which are connected to gender) to determine developmental course (Miller & Chen, 2013; Rendall, 2013). Many children residing in LMIC live in sparse and dangerous conditions, without the kinds of supports requisite to maintain good health or normal growth in most domains of development (Howe, Huttly, & Abramsky, 2006). Accordingly, the "impact" of particular household conditions or parenting practices may be diminished or augmented depending on key (sometimes gender based) biological conditions. Moreover, the likelihood that a particular biological factor will moderate the influence of some environmental conditions tends to be greater in the prenatal and early postnatal periods (Chen, Matthews, & Boyce, 2002).

The meaning of gender in a society is often communicated through the macrosystem (e.g., existing power and economic differentials between women and men) that in turn influence the microsystems children directly experience at home, in school, and around their neighborhood (Leaper, 2002). Thus, parents typically adopt dominant and prevailing contextual prescriptions for their girls and boys. Generally, social structure and culture—especially opportunities for women's power in the social world and male mobility—are linked to the amplification or suppression of gender differences in parenthood in different societies (Low, 1989). Countries vary greatly in whether and how they promote gender equality, and a national "culture" re gender may have repercussions for gender similarities or differences at the individual, family, and national levels. Child rearing strategies reflect adaptations by parents (and other caregivers) meant to help prepare children for success in their specific developmental context. They also reflect current demands pertaining to daily living and level of access to social and material resources. Therefore, the types of socialization practices directed toward girls and boys, and the use of girls and boys for various daily tasks, often mirror existing opportunity structures for women and men in their community. Roughly speaking, how children are treated in a society tends to correlate with divisions of labor according to gender (Best & Williams, 1997; Hewlett, 1991; Low, 1989; Rendall, 2013; Whiting, 1986). In Chile, for example, contextual standards of women as caregivers and men as providers operate early in the primary socialization contexts of families and schools (Schkolnik, 2004). The rights of adult women and men often differ in LMIC, and, therefore, young girls in these countries may be treated poorly compared to boys. That said, as indicated earlier, there is still little systematic research on how, at the family level, young girls and boys are actually treated across the developing world. In this monograph of the SRCD we assess whether girls and boys experience similar and differential treatment in a large sample of under-researched countries and a broad range of developmental domains. The studies in this monograph of the SRCD bridge near proximal contexts in which children find themselves with distal context indicators that are thought to influence children in equally compelling, if less immediately manifest, ways.

TOPICS OF GENDER RESEARCH

The chapters in this monograph of the SRCD explore how certain microsystem experiences reflect certain macrosystem variations across a large number of LMIC. These chapters attempt to provide a snapshot of how experiences and outcomes are similar and different for girls and boys in the context of key country-level sociodemographic factors. In attempting to shed new light on the statuses of girls and boys in a large variety of contemporary underresearched LMIC, we adopt a Human Rights based approach, in particular Child Rights. The Convention on the Rights of the Child (CRC; Limber & Flekkoy, 1995) is a comprehensive and legally binding articulation upholding children's rights to survival, development, protection, and participation (United Nations General Assembly, 1989). Children have inherent rights to life, survival, and development (Article 6). Both health and psychosocial well-being of the child constitute prerequisites to realizing human potential (Engle et al., 2007). In other words, all children have rights to high-standard health care and nutrition, to nurturing and stimulating caregiving, to protection from abuse and neglect (including psychological and physical violence), and to environments that support their thriving. Rooted in the Rights framework, chapters in this monograph of the SRCD examine all-important experiences and tasks in girlhood and boyhood, including physical growth and survival, experiences of caregiving, exposure to abuse, and labor participation in large numbers of families in a significant number of LMIC.

GENDER RESEARCH AND INTERNATIONAL DEVELOPMENTAL SCIENCE: PAST, PRESENT, AND FUTURE

As children develop in widely varying contexts internationally, those contexts can be expected to dramatically influence children's development (Bornstein, 2010; Packer & Cole, 2015). In consequence, studies of development in context are requisite to encompass the full scope of child development.

The main aim of this monograph of the SRCD is to examine proximal microsystem contexts and influences on growth and mortality, caregiving, discipline and violence, and labor in young girls and boys in a large number of macrosystem LMIC. To achieve this aim, we drew on the Multiple Indicator Cluster Survey (MICS), a nationally representative and internationally comparable household survey (Bornstein et al., 2012; UNICEF, 2006). The MICS is implemented periodically in approximately 50 LMIC and provides a unique source of information with which to examine protective and risk factors for child health, education, development, and well-being in different regions of the developing world.

Three kinds of empirical psychological and developmental research about gender have been identified (Stewart & McDermott, 2004). The most prevalent kind of study embraces a comparative gender similarities/differences approach and represents the one we are concerned with in this monograph of the SRCD. Most of this kind of gender studies investigate ways in which girls and boys or women and men resemble or differ from one another. This orientation considers average differences in characteristics between the genders and when, how, and why they might arise. Hypotheses proposed to account for similarities/differences range from biology to socialization to social roles to social situations. A second kind of research concerns within-gender variability, and a third kind examines gender-linked power relations that structure social institutions and interactions (people are located within social structures that capture power relations implied by those structures). The studies in this monograph of the SRCD are more about gendered parenting, experiences, and environments in childhood and less about gender development or identity. In selecting topics to study, we attempted to identify a broad set of issues that would provide insights into processes associated with child gender although also being representative of contemporary interests and future directions in the field.

Research on gender similarities and differences is important for several reasons. First, stereotypes about psychological gender differences abound, influencing people's beliefs and behaviors, and so it is important to evaluate their validity. Second, descriptions of treatment across gender lines are important because they inform theoretical approaches to understanding gender. Third, psychological gender differences are often invoked in relation to important policy questions, and so it is crucial to have accurate scientific information available to evaluate policy needs, recommendations, and justifications.

Despite consensus about the significance of early childhood and gender, and what each portends for development in the balance of the life span, the developmental literature is hampered by several context-related limitations that constrain our more complete understanding of child gender development. A narrow participant database in research is one. There is a surprising dearth of population-based multinational data from LMIC on the conditions of girls and boys and diverse (possibly gender-related) experiences. Most of what is currently known about children and gender still comes from studies of children in the minority developed world (Best, 2010; Bornstein, 2010; Tomlinson et al., 2015), of primarily middle-class, European or North American samples without considering how sociocultural factors provide the lenses through which implications about gender at large are seen. It has been estimated that, roughly speaking, 90% of the literature in developmental science emanates from regions of the world that account for less than 10% of the world's population (Kieling & Rohde, 2012; Population Reference Bureau, 2013; Tomlinson et al., 2015). In some fields, the gap may be even greater (e.g., Mari et al., 2010). Much of what is known about children and gender in the majority world of LMIC still comes from studies of small samples in single locales (such as those we cited earlier). Thus, critics wisely reject broad generalizations about girls and boys derived from contextually restricted findings (Arnett, 2008; Bornstein, 1980, 1991, 2010; Henrich, Heine, & Norenzayan, 2010; Klasen & Crombag, 2013). This general concern may be particularly relevant when applied to LMIC, as many are undergoing rapid political and economic change (Rendall, 2013; United Nations Development Programme, 2013). As a corollary, the societies typically included in developmental research are usually similar in many ways: in them, families normally adhere to the same basic nuclear organization, and parents play the same fundamental roles and share many of the same primary goals for their children. Therefore, much less is appreciated scientifically than is commonly acknowledged about girls and boys more generally or the influences of broader ecological contexts on girls and boys specifically. This restriction of range is equally limiting in terms of understanding idiosyncrasies of gender in girls and boys as it is humbling to generalizations and identifying putative universals about them. A more encompassing and valid approach to sampling would yield a more comprehensive perspective on psychological and developmental processes and is critical for testing the limits of generalization of psychological phenomena. Studies that employ a wider contextual lens also promise more penetrating insights into similarities and differences in how girls and boys think, feel, and behave as they do. Such lessons illuminate how expansive or circumscribed are the presumed universals of gender as well as how girls' and boys' experiences in specific different settings shape specific expressions of their behavior.

Therefore, population-based multinational data from LMIC are indispensable to identify the statuses, treatment, and conditions of girls and boys in the majority world of LMIC as well as how gender more generally intersects with different domains of development. Furthermore, having aggregate information would improve our comparative understanding of children and gender and help to ensure equality of opportunity for girls and boys globally. Multinational data promise to leverage better-informed national and global policies for early child development with respect to gender. In brief, population-based multinational data are crucial for monitoring the situations of girls and boys worldwide and to flesh out the database in human development. Because we use data collected under the auspices of the United Nations, our detailed analyses of LMIC data may also help inform decisions directly relevant to achieving some UN Sustainable Development Goals. In particular, the United Nations named gender equality as a specific goal of the Sustainable Development Agenda in 2015 (United Nations General Assembly, 2015).

Gender is a perennially popular subject, and innumerable studies of child gender populate the contemporary biological, behavioral, and social science literatures. Surprisingly, however, only a few (now older) large-scale, cross-national comparative studies have previously focused on gender. Barry, Bacon, and Child (1957) assessed socialization practices in more than 100 societies and found, generally, girls were reared to be nurturant, responsible, and obedient, whereas boys were reared to achieve and to be independent and self-reliant. However, Hendrix and Johnson (1985) later reanalyzed the Barry et al.'s data and deduced no evidence of a general gender differentiation in socialization; for both female and male socialization factors, self-reliance and independence had strong positive loadings, and nurturance loaded negatively. The Six Cultures study (Edwards & Whiting, 1974; Minturn & Lambert, 1964; Whiting, 1963; Whiting & Edwards, 1973) and its sequel, Children of Different Worlds (Whiting & Edwards, 1988), presented another, if smaller scale, cross-national data gathering effort that reported on child gender. Gender differences in aggression, nurturance, responsibility, and help- and attention-seeking were examined. Few gender differences were found in some locales (Kenya, the Philippines, or the United States) where girls and boys alike cared for younger siblings and performed household chores. In contrast, child gender differences were found in others (India, Mexico, and Japan) where girls and boys were treated dissimilarly, girls assuming more responsibility for siblings and household tasks. Williams and Best (1982/1990) still later focused on gender stereotypes in children in 25 countries. They unearthed a general developmental pattern of stereotype acquisition beginning prior to age 5, accelerating during the early school years, and achieving completion during adolescence. Stereotype scores were high or relatively high in some countries (Pakistan, New Zealand, and England) and low in others (Brazil, Taiwan, Germany, and France). Finally, Lytton and Romney (1991) examined differential parental socialization of girls and boys and considered especially the interaction between parent gender and child gender by investigating whether and how mothers and fathers distinguish between daughters and sons in mostly North American but also some Western non-North American societies. The only clear effect to emerge from their survey of over 150 studies was for parents' disparate encouragement of children's gender-typed activities. What is clearly lacking across this brief history of studies, and the gap we attempt to fill in this monograph of the SRCD, is a more contemporary broader multidomain assessment of similarities and differences in the lives of young girls and boys in nationally representative samples of a large number of low- and middle-income countries across the developing world. Again, these gaps are especially important to fill in light of the major structural and labor market adjustments that are occurring in many developing countries (Rendall, 2013).

This monograph of the SRCD therefore focuses on documenting international variation in physical, mental, emotional, and social experiences of young girls and boys in a substantial number of families across many LMIC in the majority world (Figure 1) using 21st-century data. The LMIC reported about in this monograph of the SRCD vary widely in terms of history and ideology, beliefs and values, social and economic situations, as well as other sociodemographic factors thought to influence gender in girls and boys. However, these countries all constitute LMI nations (UNICEF, 2006) defined with reference to the World Bank's (2014) system of classification of economies based on gross national incomes per capita, quality of life (life expectancy, literacy rates), and economic diversification (labor force, consumption). More than 650 million children under 5 years of age are estimated to live in LMIC (UNICEF, 2014).

LMIC generally have low standards of living, but conditions within and across them still vary. For example, on an index (0–5) of household material resources (electricity, radio, telephone, television, and transportation), some LMIC average over 4 resources, whereas others average fewer than 1 (Bradley & Putnick, 2012). Children living in poor households may be directly affected by inadequate resources (e.g., they do not have safe drinking water or get enough to eat) or indirectly through family interactions (e.g., poverty undermines how parents interact with their children; Engle & Black, 2008;

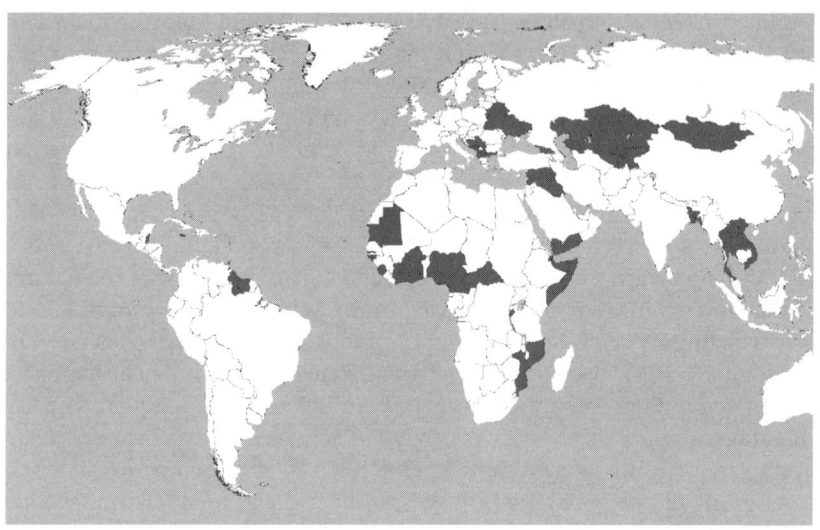

FIGURE 1.—MISC3 countries included in this monograph of the SRCD.

McLoyd, Aikens, & Burton, 2006). Given limited resources, parents decide how to allocate those resources to children and what roles to assign children within the family. In some countries, parents may favor girls or boys because one or the other is perceived to have a greater need. For example, if boys are more likely to attend school than girls, parents may be more likely to read to sons than daughters or to spend time naming and counting with them. Similarly, boys may be allocated more food if they require the stamina to work the family farm, but they may be disciplined more harshly if their misbehavior is seen as a threat to future family success (Quinn, 2005). Limited financial, material, and social resources may drive parents to engage in more gender-based differential treatment, with allocations of resources and assignments to tasks reflecting gender (Edmonds, 2006).

In brief, multinational developmental inquiry, conducted within a sensitive contextual relational systems framework, provides the medium to explore and distinguish uniformity and diversity vis-à-vis child gender. Most established relations between country-level factors and gender in children have been based on European and North American samples from the minority developed world. Our understanding of child gender is, therefore, circumscribed by the existing body of research, and it is unclear if and whether gender effects that obtain in the minority world apply to the majority world.

THIS MONOGRAPH OF THE SRCD

This introductory chapter has described the conceptual framework of the monograph in terms of gender theory and gender differences and similarities, the bioecological perspective on child gender, and past and present gender research and international developmental science. The next chapter describes the nature of the MICS microsystems survey, country-level gender equity and economic well-being macrosystem indicators used in association with the MICS, and the general analytic plan of substantive chapters in this monograph. The chapters that follow then describe situations of girls and boys with successive foci on child growth and mortality in Chapter III (Bradley & Putnick, 2016), caregiving by mothers and fathers in Chapter IV (Bornstein & Putnick, 2016), discipline and violence in Chapter V (Deater-Deckard & Lansford, 2016), and child labor in Chapter VI (Putnick & Bornstein, 2016). These reports employ a data set of approximately 2,000,000 respondents in 412,000 families in 41 LMIC. The common questions addressed in these chapters are, How do girls and boys in underresearched LMIC in the majority world vary with respect to central indicators of child growth and mortality, parental caregiving, discipline and violence, and child labor? and How do key indicators of national gender equity and economic development relate to child gender in each of these substantive areas of child development? The monograph concludes, revisiting gender theory, with a summary discussion of the main findings, interpretations of those findings, thoughts on their main methodological and substantive strengths and limitations, and finally policy implications.

According to bioecological theory (Bronfenbrenner & Morris, 2006), human lives carry the imprint of their social worlds. Girls and boys are biologically similar as well as different, and children around the world can expect to live qualitatively similar and different lives, based in part on their gender. Biological similarities and differences between the genders are exaggerated or attenuated by the forces of contextual socialization. Gender equity is a universal development goal in its own right (that is recognized in the Convention on the Elimination of All Forms of Discrimination against Women, which has been ratified by a majority of LMIC; Abu-Ghaida & Klasen, 2004). Understanding gender empirically across LMIC is prerequisite to establishing gender equality which, in turn, is prerequisite to achieving many vital Millennium Development and Sustainable Development Goals, including eliminating poverty, reducing infant mortality, achieving quality universal education, and promoting socioeconomic growth (Abu-Ghaida & Klasen, 2004 United Nations, 2005; United Nations General Assembly, 2015).

II. GENDER IN LOW- AND MIDDLE-INCOME COUNTRIES: GENERAL METHODS

Marc H. Bornstein, Diane L. Putnick, Robert H. Bradley, Kirby Deater-Deckard, Jennifer E. Lansford, and Yumiko Ota

> This article is part of the issue "Gender in Low- and Middle-Income Countries," Bornstein, Putnick, Lansford, Deater-Deckard, and Bradley (Issue Authors). For a full listing of articles in this issue, see: http://onlinelibrary.wiley.com/doi/10.1111/mono.v81.1/issuetoc.

…we will strengthen our national statistical capacity to collect, analyse and disaggregate data, including by sex, age and other relevant factors that may lead to disparities, and support a wide range of child-focused research. – Follow-up actions and assessment, A World Fit for Children

General Assembly resolution S-27/2, 10 May 2002.

THE MICS3

The 1990 World Summit for Children adopted the World Declaration on the Survival, Protection, and Development of Children and its Plan of Action, and their governments pledged to monitor progress toward achieving those goals. To aid in this effort, UNICEF developed the Multiple Indicator Cluster Survey (MICS), a nationally representative and internationally comparable household survey. With the MICS, low- and middle-income countries (LMIC) in different regions of the world were equipped to monitor and evaluate

---

Corresponding author: Dr. Marc H. Bornstein, Child and Family Research, *Eunice Kennedy Shriver* National Institute of Child Health and Human Development, Suite 8030 6705 Rockledge Drive, Bethesda, MD 20892-7971; email: Marc_H_Bornstein@nih.gov.
DOI: 10.1111/mono.12224
© 2015 The Society for Research in Child Development, Inc.

TABLE 1
COUNTRIES PARTICIPATING IN MICS3 AND SAMPLE SIZE OF EACH COUNTRY

Country	Number of Households	Country	Number of Households
Albania[a]	5,150	Mauritania[a]	10,361
Algeria	29,476	Mongolia[a]	6,220
Bangladesh[a]	62,463	Montenegro[a]	2,258
Belarus[a]	6,707	Mozambique[a]	13,995
Belize[a]	1,832	Myanmar	29,238
Bosnia and Herzegovina[a]	5,549	Nigeria[a]	26,735
Burkina Faso[a]	5,523	Palestinians in Lebanon	6,200
Burundi[a]	8,200	Palestinians in Syria	8,000
Cameroon[a]	9,667	Sao Tome and Principe	5,646
Central African Republic[a]	11,723	Serbia[a]	8,730
Côte d'Ivoire[a]	7,600	Sierra Leone[a]	7,078
Cuba	8,466	Somalia[a]	5,969
Djibouti[a]	4,888	Suriname[a]	5,746
Gambia[a]	6,071	Syrian Arab Republic[a]	19,019
Georgia[a]	12,010	Tajikistan[a]	6,684
Ghana[a]	5,939	Thailand[a]	40,511
Guinea-Bissau[a]	5,305	Togo[a]	6,492
Guyana[a]	5,008	Trinidad and Tobago[a]	5,557
Iraq[a]	17,873	Tunisia	9,580
Jamaica[a]	4,767	Turkmenistan	NA
Kazakhstan[a]	14,564	Ukraine[a]	5,243
Kenya	NA	Uzbekistan[a]	10,198
Kyrgyzstan[a]	5,179	Vanuatu[a]	2,632
Laos[a]	5,894	Vietnam[a]	8,355
Macedonia[a]	4,701	Yemen[a]	3,586
Malawi	31,200	Zimbabwe	12,500

Note. NA, neither data nor report are available for the country.
[a]Country is included in this monograph.

progress of children and women (UNICEF, 2006). The MICS supports evidence-based policy formulation, assesses trends, and measures disparities, and it has become a principal tool to assess achievement of the Millennium Declaration and the Millennium Development Goals (MDGs) and the World Fit for Children (WFFC) Declaration and Plan of Action (UNICEF, 2007a).

The MICS3 was carried out in 50 countries between 2005 and 2010. All chapters in this monograph use data from the MICS3. Table 1 shows the countries that participated in the MICS3 and the number of households sampled in each country.

Content

The MICS3 has three questionnaires: a household questionnaire, a questionnaire for individual women (15–49 years old), and a questionnaire for children under five (available at: http://www.childinfo.org/mics3_questionnaire.html). Each questionnaire is composed of core, additional, and optional modules, which are sets of standardized questions grouped by topics (see Bornstein et al., 2012). The basic criteria for inclusion of MICS3 indicators were their relevance to MDG, WFFC, and UNICEF goals, international agreement on indicators, previous testing, feasibility of collecting data, and proven quality.

In total, the three MICS3 questionnaires contain 42 modules, 21 of which are core, 8 are additional, and 13 are optional. Countries were recommended to use all (relevant) core modules, whereas additional modules focus on issues that may be applicable only to certain countries, and optional modules were included if a country expressed particular interest in a topic. The MICS covers a large array of issues, and its flexibility allows countries to adapt the survey to their particular situations and needs, but the MICS keeps comparability across countries through standardized questions and administration. Strict criteria for any customization of questionnaires at the country level were established; the general rule was not to change comparability of international indicators.

In this monograph, we use the MICS3 modules related to anthropometry (child growth), child mortality, child development (caregiving), discipline, and child labor to shed light on central issues related to child gender across the developing world. Although 50 LMIC conducted the MICS3, for analyses in this monograph, we used 41 countries (some countries had not released their data to the public at the time of our analysis, and some countries did not include modules that contain data pertinent to our main interests). The 41 LMIC we include represent 12 countries in central and eastern Europe, 6 countries in eastern Asia and the Pacific, 14 countries in sub-Saharan Africa, 4 countries in the Middle East and northern Africa, and 5 countries in Latin America and the Caribbean. The total number of families approximated 2,000,000 people in over 400,000 households, but each chapter uses a subsample based on inclusion criteria for the topic of interest (e.g., families with children under 5 who completed a particular subset of questions). Data on child gender were collected in the Household Questionnaire and were coded 0 for boy, 1 for girl.

Because fewer than 1% of questionnaires were answered by a male respondent, we included only those households where the child's principal female caregiver responded to the MICS3 questionnaire. Respondents identified the people who serve in the role of the child's mother and father. In a great majority of cases, the mother and father are the child's biological parents. However, female caregivers who were not the child's biological mother chose whether to answer the "mother" questions about themselves or about another mother figure. Presumably, mothers might include some adoptive mothers, stepmothers, aunts, grandmothers, and foster mothers, just as fathers could include some adoptive fathers, stepfathers, uncles, grandfathers, and foster fathers. Hence, when we refer to "mothers" and "fathers," we mean the people who serve in the social role of parent, regardless of their biological ties to the child (Leon, 2007).

Sampling

Each country designed and selected a probability sample, national in coverage, and field implemented the MICS with minimum deviation from an overall standard design. A three-stage sample frame was used: In the first stage, primary sampling units (PSUs) were defined, if possible, as census enumeration areas, and they were selected with systematic probability proportionate to size (pps); the second stage was the selection of segments (clusters); and the third stage was the selection of the particular households within each segment that were to be interviewed in the survey. To foster sample implementation, implicit stratification was followed. When this form of geographic stratification is used together with pps sampling, the sample proportionately distributes into each of a nation's administrative subdivisions as well as its urban and rural sectors. Depending on the country, the design was likely to vary with respect to the number of PSUs, the number of segments or clusters per PSU, and the number of households per segment, and, hence, the overall sample size. The MICS Manual (UNICEF, 2006) tables calculated sample sizes to be used by the country if the table values fit the country situation. The number of PSUs tended to range from 250 to 350, the cluster sizes (the number of households to be interviewed in each segment) ranged from 10 to 30, and the overall sample sizes ranged from 2,500 to 14,000 households. Existing samples could be used only if they were valid probability samples (e.g., a Demographic and Health Survey or a labor force survey). Because there were many families with more than one child in the target age range (e.g., under 5, 5–14), and we did not want to add within-family variance to already complex designs, we randomly selected a child from each family with more than one child in the specified age range.

Implementation

Each country followed the same stages of implementing the MICS3: making logistical arrangements, preparing the questionnaire and training materials, training fieldworkers, collecting and preparing the equipment, carrying out pilot studies, setting up data processing (computers, staff), and considering and solving ethical issues. Field teams (interviewers and supervisors) were recruited and trained in interview techniques, contents of the questionnaires, field procedures, and use of equipment. All data were entered twice into standard databases with internal consistency checks. After cleaning data files and checking data quality, countries prepared technical reports and data were centrally archived.

A MICS global team oversaw preparation of the survey tools and instruments, training of country teams, follow-up of country performance, quality of data, and approved final reports. To minimize survey biases and ensure data reliability, the same team standardized implementation procedures and prepared technical documents and programs to be used across participating MICS3 countries. Prior to implementation, UNICEF organized workshops in each region to review critical steps, such as survey design and preparation, data processing, data analysis and report writing, and data archiving and dissemination. At any time, governments could seek consultation from UNICEF. Global MICS3 evaluations confirmed that the tools, technical assistance, and data were of high quality (UNICEF, 2006).

GENDER EQUALITY INDICES

Because national gender equality can be measured in various ways, in the substantive chapters that follow MICS3, data are related to two national indicators of gender equality, each composed of different indicators. The Gender Relative Status Index (GRS; Beneria & Permanyer, 2010; Permanyer, 2010) is a measure of the extent to which one gender is favored over the other in a country in life expectancy, adult literacy rate, gross enrollment in school, and estimated earned income. Because MICS3 data were collected between 2005 and 2010, we used data from the 2008 Gender-Related Development Index (GDI; UNDP, 2008) to compute the GRS. GRS values <1 indicate that women are disadvantaged compared to men, and GRS values >1 indicate that men are disadvantaged compared to women. In the 35 countries for which data were available, all countries scored below 1 indicating that women were disadvantaged compared to men; hence, a higher score indicated greater gender equality. GRS scores were available for 36 of the 41 countries in our database (Table 2) and had adequate variance (range = .540–.929).

The Gender Inequality Index (GII; Gaye, Klugman, Kovacevic, Twigg, & Zambrano, 2010; UNDP, 2011) was developed by the United Nations in 2010 and revised in 2011 to measure women's disadvantages in areas of reproductive health (maternal mortality, adolescent fertility), empowerment

TABLE 2
Gender Equality and Human Development Indices by Country

HDI Rank	Country	GRS	GII	HDI
High HDI				
57	Trinidad and Tobago	.771	.331	.833
64	Montenegro	.804	–	.822
65	Serbia	.814	–	.821
67	Belarus	.916	–	.817
68	Macedonia	.782	.151	.808
69	Albania	.825	.271	.807
71	Kazakhstan	.929	.334	.807
75	Bosnia and Herzegovina	–	–	.802
Medium HDI				
81	Thailand	.876	.382	.786
82	Ukraine	.883	.335	.786
87	Jamaica	.863	.450	.771
88	Belize	–	.493	.771
89	Suriname	.752	–	.770
93	Georgia	–	.418	.763
105	Syrian Arab Republic	.665	.474	.736
110	Guyana	.781	.511	.725
112	Mongolia	.869	.410	.720
114	Vietnam	.865	.305	.718
119	Uzbekistan	.846	–	.701
122	Kyrgyzstan	.857	.370	.694
123	Vanuatu	.859	–	.686
124	Tajikistan	.818	.347	.684
133	Laos	.737	.513	.608
138	Yemen	.540	.769	.567
140	Mauritania	.747	.605	.557
142	Ghana	.810	.598	.533
147	Bangladesh	.718	.550	.524
150	Cameroon	.693	.639	.514
151	Djibouti	.698	–	.513
Low HDI				
154	Nigeria	.641	–	.499
159	Togo	.639	.602	.479
160	Gambia	.733	.610	.471
166	Côte d'Ivoire	.568	.655	.431
171	Guinea-Bissau	.684	–	.383
172	Burundi	.827	.478	.382
173	Burkina Faso	.716	.596	.372
175	Mozambique	.749	.602	.366
178	Central African Republic	.672	.669	.352
179	Sierra Leone	.621	.662	.329
HDI N/A				
N/A	Iraq	–	.579	–
N/A	Somalia	–	–	–

Note. GRS scores were computed based on data extracted from UNDP (2008) (Table 4). GII scores are excerpted and reproduced from UNDP (2011) (Table 4). HDI scores are excerpted and reproduced from UNDP (2008) (Table 2). N/A, not available because of missing data. –, data were not available.

(female seats in parliament, difference in male and female school enrollment), and the labor market (difference in male and female labor participation). The GII ranges from 0, which indicates that women and men fare equally, to 1, which indicates that women fare as poorly as possible in all measured dimensions. The GII can be interpreted as the percentage loss to potential human development due to gender inequality in the three dimensions. The 2011 values for the GII ranged from .049 for Sweden to .769 for Yemen. GII scores were available for 30 of the 41 countries in our database (Table 2) and had adequate variance (range = .151–.769).

THE HUMAN DEVELOPMENT INDEX

In the substantive chapters that follow, MICS3 data are organized by and also related to the Human Development Index (HDI; UNDP, 2008). The HDI was developed by the United Nations to measure the social and economic status of a country. The HDI has three major components: life expectancy (in years), education (composed of the adult literacy rate and the percentage of school-aged children enrolled in primary, secondary, and tertiary school), and gross domestic product (GDP; in purchasing power parity [PPP] in U.S. dollars). The HDI offers a proxy for the level of support that is generally available to promote human development in poor nations. As such, it connects to many physical and social aspects of the family and home environment with known relations to child well-being. Moreover, the HDI is rooted in a development paradigm that focuses on human growth and the role of contexts and environments to support the development of human potential. The focus of our analyses is on building capabilities and potential in young girls and boys. Given its underlying ethos and aims, we selected the HDI as a macrolevel indicator that mirrors a focus on economic and social development of a nation (Azariadis & Drazen, 1990; Lucas, 1988 Mankiw, Romer, & Weil, 1992; Nelson & Phelps, 1966).

The HDI ranges from 0.00 to 1.00, and countries with an HDI of 0.80–1.00 are considered high, .50–.79 medium, and .00–.49 low. This tripartite division is used to organize LMIC in the following substantive chapters (Table 2). (The HDI was not available for Iraq and Somalia because of missing GDP data.) Because the MICS3 data were collected between 2005 and 2010, we used the 2008 HDI (UNDP, 2008), which is based on 2006 data. This version of the HDI was calculated for 179 countries and territories. Our sample does not represent the 56 highest ranking countries on the HDI because this monograph addresses gender in LMIC. The sample of countries in this monograph adequately represents the rest of the range on the HDI. The 41 countries represent 11% (8 of the 75) high-HDI countries, 27% (21 of the 78) medium-HDI countries, 38% (10 of the 26) low-HDI countries, and 13% (2 of the 15) of countries for which the HDI could not be calculated.

As might be expected, the three national measures of gender equality and human development are related. The correlation between the GII and GRS was $r(25) = -.75$, $p < .001$, in our sample of countries, indicating overlap, but still nearly 44% of their variance was unshared. Also, countries with lower gender equality tended to have lower overall human development, $r(34) = .65$, $p < .001$, for GRS-HDI, and $r(27) = -.79$, $p < .001$, for GII-HDI.

MAIN AIMS, ANALYTIC PLANS, AND HYPOTHESES

The main aims of substantive chapters in this monograph are to describe the situations of multiple domains of early development in young girls and boys across the developing world and to relate them to national measures of gender equity and sociodemographic well-being. To do so, we address two common questions analyzing how developing (and previously underresearched) countries vary with respect to indicators of child growth and mortality in Chapter III (Bradley & Putnick, 2016), caregiving in Chapter IV (Bornstein & Putnick, 2016), discipline and violence in Chapter V (Deater-Deckard & Lansford, 2016), and child labor in Chapter VI (Putnick & Bornstein, 2016), and how key indicators of national gender equity (GRS and GII) and sociodemographic development (HDI) relate to each of these substantive areas of human development. Our underlying assumption is that multiple domains of development may differ by child gender, as emphasized in the Convention on the Rights of the Child, and we hypothesize that countries also vary in the situations of each domain.

To investigate the first question, we employed an analysis of mean differences between girls and boys (and mothers and fathers, if available). The statistical procedure used varies by chapter due to variations in the design and dependent variables, but in all analyses, we include country and child gender as factors and model the interaction between them. In general, we were not interested in main effects of country because these studies were designed to investigate gender differences. However, it was ideal to include country in the models to account for the sometimes vast differences in dependent variables across countries and to investigate interactions between child gender and country. In all models, we also include covariates that are appropriate to the particular dependent variables.

To investigate the second question, we collected the gender effect sizes from models for each country and correlated them with country-level indicators of the nations' gender equity and economy (GRS, GII, and HDI). Correlating the country-level indicators with effect sizes tells us, for example, if girls are at a greater disadvantage compared to boys in lower-HDI countries or countries with greater gender inequality. We did not employ covariates for these country-level correlations because the model effect sizes were already adjusted for family-level covariates.

We used the HDI to organize the 41 LMIC because we hypothesized that the extent of social and economic development of a country helps to explain some differences among countries in the situations of girls and boys. The gender-related effect sizes for each dependent variable were aggregated at the country level and correlated with the country GRS, GII, and HDI. We believe that macrolevel variables like the GRS, GII, and HDI likely antecede microlevel variables such as are tallied by the MICS3. However, in these chapters, we calculate correlations, and so we eschew language that indicates causation and restrict ourselves to the language of associations.

For all tests, we report the significance level and a measure of effect size (when available). Sample sizes are so large that many small effects are statistically significant. In this light, focus on the effect sizes is more meaningful than focus on significances. For continuous dependent variables, we report partial eta squared (η_p^2) from models and Cohen's (1988) d, and for dichotomous-dependent variables, we report odds ratios (ORs). We include Cohen's d because (unlike partial η_p^2) it is a directional measure of effect size that reflects gender differences. We use Cohen's (1988) benchmarks for small (.01), medium (.06), and large (.14) eta-squareds and small (.20), medium (.50), and large (.80) ds, which can be interpreted in terms of standard deviations from the mean (e.g., a d of 1.5 indicates that the mean for girls was 1.5 standard deviations above the mean for boys). For dichotomous-dependent variables, we report ORs, which can be interpreted in terms of their odds of occurrence (e.g., an OR of 3.5 means that the odds of girls engaging in the target behavior is 3.5 times the odds of boys engaging in the target behavior, and an OR of .50 means that the odds of girls engaging in the target behavior is half the odds of boys engaging in the target behavior). ORs are only available for main effects of gender and individual country contrasts (i.e., an individual country's deviation from the overall effect, which is not the focus of this monograph). Because there are 41 countries, ORs are not computed for overall effects of country or country by gender interactions.

III. THE ROLE OF PHYSICAL CAPITAL ASSETS IN YOUNG GIRLS' AND BOYS' MORTALITY AND GROWTH IN LOW- AND MIDDLE-INCOME COUNTRIES

Robert H. Bradley and Diane L. Putnick

> This article is part of the issue "Gender in Low- and Middle-Income Countries," Bornstein, Putnick, Lansford, Deater-Deckard, and Bradley (Issue Authors). For a full listing of articles in this issue, see: http://onlinelibrary.wiley.com/doi/10.1111/mono.v81.1/issuetoc.

States Parties recognize the right of every child to a standard of living adequate for the child's physical, mental, spiritual, moral and social development.

–Article 27.1, Convention on the Rights of the Child
General Assembly resolution 44/25, 20 November 1989.

Although the obesity epidemic is raging throughout the developed world, concerns about growth deficiencies and mortality remain paramount in countries where poverty is endemic. This is the reason why two primary Millennium Development Goals (MDGs) established by the United Nations pertain to reduction of undernutrition and child mortality (United Nations, 2000). One analysis indicates that 167,000,000 children in low- and middle-income countries (LMIC) are stunted; and even though prevalence rates of stunting decreased from about 40% in 1990 to about 27% in 2010, projections suggest that about 22% of children in developing countries will likely be stunted in 2020 (de Onis, Blossner, & Borghi, 2012). Poor nutrition and

---

Corresponding author: Robert H. Bradley, T. Denny Sanford School of Social and Family Dynamics, Arizona State University, 951 S. Cady Mall, Tempe, AZ 85287; email: robert.bradley@asu.edu
DOI: 10.1111/mono.12225
© 2015 The Society for Research in Child Development, Inc.

unsanitary conditions are presumed to be the major causes of child growth problems, such as wasting and stunting; but links between household- and community-level conditions and children's health remain incompletely characterized. Some research indicates that children's health reflects the general level of resources present in the country, community, and household and the specific sets of resources available to women (De Silva & Harpham, 2007; Else Quest & Grabe, 2012; United Nations Development Programme, 2010). A detailed analysis of information from Demographic and Health Surveys conducted throughout Africa led Sahn and Stifel (2000) to conclude that understanding the effects of economic and social policy changes at the country level requires knowledge of household-level wealth or assets. Overall housing quality and access to productive household assets are associated with children's nutritional status, a key contributor to child growth and health (Chowa, Ansog, & Masa, 2010). Ownership of durable assets, such as appliances and automobiles, increases the likelihood that families can access other resources; most importantly for the present study are assets that benefit children's health (e.g., food, medicine, health care services; De Silva & Harpham, 2007). The World Bank (2000) recognized the importance of physical capital assets (good housing, appliances, modes of transportation) as a means of making decisions and taking actions that are productive toward various ends for oneself, one's family, and one's community. There is general support for the idea that having better quality housing and greater access to durable goods improves health, but the findings are inconsistent as regards how particular assets or their accumulation are implicated in particular health outcomes for particular groups of individuals; this uncertain situation is partly owing to variations in community conditions and cultural values (Herrin, Amaral, & Balihuta, 2013).

In this study, we document similarities and differences between girls and boys in growth (height-for-age and stunting, weight-for-age and underweight, and weight-for-height and wasting) and mortality in 40 LMIC. We also assess associations between physical environmental factors connected with home life and patterns of growth and mortality for young girls and boys. In societies where household facilities and access to material resources are generally low, even small differences in resource availability may loom large in determining parents' decisions pertaining to health care and nutrition thereby affecting children's growth trajectories and their chances of survival (Boyle et al., 2006; Darmon & Drewnowski, 2008; De Silva & Harpham, 2007; Wachs, 2008).

INDICATORS OF CHILD GROWTH AND MORTALITY

According to the World Health Organization (WHO, 1997), low height-for-age or stunting most often reflect prolonged undernutrition. Low weight-for-age and underweight may also reflect poor nutrition and chronic illness, but children who score low on this indicator could either be stunted and of appropriate weight-for-stature, or taller and underweight, making interpretation a challenge. Low weight-for-height, or wasting, is generally indicative of acute recent weight loss, due either to starvation or serious illness.

Only three of nine UN regions appear to be on track to meet the MDGs pertaining to undernutrition (United Nations, 2011b); and even in regions generally on track to meet MDGs (e.g., Latin America and the Caribbean) only 6 of 13 countries are on track as regards stunting (Lutter, Chaparro, & Muñoz, 2010). Similarly, although there has been progress in pursuit of low mortality, the goal has been met in only three of nine UN regions (United Nations, 2011a). In the 60 countries with the highest rates of childhood mortality, only 7 are on track to meet the 2015 targets for child mortality (Lawn, Costello, Mwansambo, & Osrin, 2007).

GENDER DIFFERENCES IN CHILD GROWTH AND MORTALITY

Demographic and Health Surveys from 35 developing countries in the late 1980s and early 1990s revealed that girls were less likely to be stunted and wasted than boys (Hill & Upchurch, 1995). Girls showed better growth than boys in Ethiopia (Medhin et al., 2010), Nigeria (Luke et al., 2007), Pakistan (Mahmood & Mahmood, 1995), and 10 countries in Sub-Saharan Africa (Wamani, Åstrøm, Peterson, Tumwine, & Tylleskär, 2007). That said, there was little gender difference in stunting or in height-for-age in Bangladesh (Moestue et al., 2004).

Overall mortality rates of girls in 35 developing countries were also lower than those for boys (Hill & Upchurch, 1995). In a report on gender differences in under-5 mortality, the United Nations Department of Economic and Social Affairs, Population Division (2011) concluded that in most developing countries (excluding China and India), girls have the advantage over boys. However, trends in 21 countries worldwide, especially in Sub-Saharan Africa and Eastern and Southern Asia, indicate that girls are still at greater risk for childhood mortality than boys. According to Pande (2003), gender discrimination in these countries, especially India and South and East Asia, contributes to disproportionate mortality in young girls.

SOURCES OF GENDER DIFFERENCES IN CHILD GROWTH AND MORTALITY

The greater likelihood boys will have a growth problem or die in early childhood suggests that genetic mechanisms may leave boys more susceptible

35

to ecological adversities (Dercon & Singh, 2013; United Nations, Department of Economic and Social Affairs, Population Division, 2011). Given equivalent exposure to pathogens, boys are more likely to develop diseases and are more severely affected by diseases than girls (Klein, 2007). However, the precise mechanisms responsible for boys' susceptibility are still debated. For example, a study in India showed that boys had slightly higher odds ratios of being stunted, wasted, and underweight, but part reflected girls' greater propensity for catching up after initial problems with low weight (Bisai & Mallick, 2009). The potential complexity of gender differences in conditions associated with malnutrition can be seen in a study conducted in the Philippines. Specifically, stunting was more prevalent among boys at all ages. However, wasting was more prevalent for boys during infancy, shifting to a slightly greater prevalence for girls thereafter (Ricci & Becker, 1996). In effect, children's growth appears to depend on cultural and environmental factors as well as genetic predispositions, with likely different sets of factors applying to different growth outcomes at different ages.

Some of the factors implicated in mortality also remain elusive. Overall rates of mortality, particularly after the neonatal period, have declined owing to better health care and community-level improvements in water and sanitation (Masanja et al., 2008). A differential that favors girls during the first 6 months of life remains (likely owing to genetic factors; Klein, 2007), with some evidence that cultural values can discriminate against girls after that point (e.g., quality of feeding or utilization of health care; Mahmood & Mahmood, 1995). However, findings are inconsistent, leaving unclear how gender is implicated in specific health outcomes (Nuruddin, Hadden, Petersen, & Lim, 2009).

Genes and environments interact to determine growth and health trajectories for young children, but many uncertainties remain as to their precise interplay in most health outcomes (Burgner, Jamieson, & Blackwell, 2006; Cunningham-Rundles, Moon, & McNeeley, 2008; Rushton & Elliott, 2003). In especially adverse circumstances, genetic factors that afford resilience or lead to vulnerability may play a more consequential role in health status given that individuals/parents have little discretion in addressing shortages or potentially damaging exposures. However, as conditions diminish in severity, discretionary behavior on the part of caregivers is likely to play a greater role (Rendall, 2012). In effect, gender discrimination favoring males may have somewhat greater health consequences in settings where poverty and instability are not overly severe. That said, the relation between societal level gender inequality and child health is unlikely to be straightforward. In their study of factors connected to gender differences in nutrition status, educational aspirations and perceived self-efficacy in Ethiopia, India, Vietnam and Peru, Dercon, and Singh (2013, p. 47) found "no common thread that can be used to characterize gender differences across these different countries." It appears that societal values pertaining to gender are among many cultural values that help determine parental actions regarding to children's health. Matsumoto and Fletcher (1996) looked at three cross-national differences in value orientation in addition to gender (uncertainty avoidance, individualism/collectivism, and power distance) in an effort to account for country-level differences in six diseases. They found that power distance (i.e., the degree to which society fostered conformity and obedience to authority, used autocratic decision making, and had hierarchical social structures) was more strongly associated with disease prevalence (including infant mortality) than was masculinity orientation. Furthermore, although value orientations inform individual actions, the pathway of household decision-making processes pertaining to health care has multiple steps. It moves from the perception of illness to choices about the type of care needed and the providers to use and then to expenditures of time and money to address any health needs. A study done in Nepal showed that, while gender was implicated in step one (perceptions of illness), it was not implicated in subsequent care seeking (Pokhrel & Sauerborn, 2004). To shed further light on these gender issues, we explore how various environmental conditions relate to growth and mortality differentially for girls and boys as these conditions afford different opportunities and challenges for families: housing quality (water and sanitation, household composition, and cooking and food storage) and household material resources (transportation, electricity, radio, telephone, and television). We also analyze overall wealth in the country (HDI), which conveys the broader level of resources available to a family. Conditions present in different geographic locations interact with genes to affect many aspects of child well-being, including height and weight (Davis, Haworth, Lewis, & Plomin, 2012).

THE HOME ENVIRONMENT'S RELATIONS WITH CHILD GROWTH AND MORTALITY

Inadequate food, poor hygiene practices, and poor-quality sanitation contribute to infections and growth problems in children (Grantham-McGregor et al., 2007; Hall, Hewitt, Tuffrey, & de Silva, 2008). In developing countries children who grow up in wealthier households are at lower risk for mortality and stunted growth than children who grow up in households with few assets (Chowa et al., 2010). Because factors contributing to growth problems in early childhood tend to persist and because of collateral damage to other biologic systems, growth retardation in early childhood often augurs difficulties in cognitive processing and school achievement (Berkman, Lescano, Gilman, Lopez, & Black, 2002; Cheung, 2006; Martorell, Rivera, Kaplowitz, & Pollitt, 1992).

Sanitation Facilities

Poor hygiene and sanitation contribute to diarrhea and growth problems for children (Hong, Banta, & Betancourt, 2006; Podewils, Mintz, Nataro, & Parashar, 2004; Ricci & Becker, 1996). There is a higher incidence of intestinal parasites in children who share toilets or use toilets that lack connection to a city sewer system (Ludwig, Fernando, Firmino, & Joao Tadeu, 1999; Mahfouz, El-Morshedy, Fargaly, & Khalil, 1997). Fecal-oral spread of bacterial pathogens, resulting from lack of access to appropriate toilets, contributes to diarrheal illness. Inadequate facilities to deal with waste increase risk for childhood illness and mortality in poor countries (Agha, 2000; Podewils et al., 2004).

Food Storage and Refrigeration

Contamination resulting from poor food storage facilities is a major problem for health and growth in children (Hong et al., 2006). Contamination of foods used to wean children from the breast is a leading cause of diarrhea and malnutrition (Motarjemi, Käferstein, Moy, & Quevedo, 1993). Because young children can hold limited quantities of food in their stomachs, they often need several small meals a day to obtain the necessary nutrients. When homes contain inadequate facilities for food storage, food is often left out for later consumption, increasing the likelihood of food contamination (Bartlett, 2005).

Provisions for Water

WHO estimates that water contaminants account for 4% of all deaths and 6% of all disease burden for young children. When water does not come into the house, storage of water becomes a major issue as regards contamination. Young children may dip their hands into water or drop water scoops on the floor, which then become a source of disease that can lead to growth retardation and even death (Abou-Ali, 2003; Halpenny, Koski, Valdes, & Scott, 2012; Lindskog & Lundqvist, 1998; Ouattara, N'Guéssean, Yapi, & N'Goran, 2010). A study done in Malawi showed that diarrhea in children could be significantly reduced by measures as simple as an improved bucket for carrying water (Roberts et al., 2001). Having piped water can reduce wasting and stunting (e.g., in the Philippines; Ricci & Becker, 1996). Child survival rates have improved in Latin America and the Caribbean as sanitation and access to clean water have improved along with greater access to health services (Mitra & Rodriguez-Fernandez, 2010).

Cooking Facilities

An open stove with no chimney in the household increases indoor pollutants that can pose health risks (Awasthi, Glick, & Fletcher, 1996; Collins,

Sithole, & Martin, 1990). In poor nations, acute respiratory illness associated with exposure to indoor air pollution is a leading cause of death among young children (Gauderman et al., 2004). Having a stove that used wood for fuel is associated with stunting among children in the Philippines and in Bangladesh (Hong et al., 2006; Ricci & Becker, 1996).

Quality of Housing and Access to Durable Goods

Having access to physical and social assets at home is critical for health maintenance and survival of family members. Under general conditions of economic hardship, having such access can be particularly important as it enables adults in the household to avoid disease (Obrist et al., 2007). In developing countries, gaining access to electricity helps reduce mortality (Wagstaff, Bustreo, Bryce, Claeson, & the WHO-World Bank Child Health and Poverty Working Group, 2004; Wang, 2003). Child survival seems especially sensitive to improvements in material conditions present in the home; albeit, details on how particular components of home conditions are implicated in child health remain unclear and may vary from region to region (Chalasani, 2010; Marmot, 2005). A high percentage of homes in developing countries are small, poorly constructed, and lack basic amenities (Aribigbola, 2008; Fiadzo, 2004). Such conditions increase the likelihood of contracting diseases, sustaining a serious injury, stunting, and death among young children (Gielen, Wilson, Faden, Wissow, & Harvilchuck, 1995; Leventhal & Newman, 2010), with variations both within and across countries.

There has been an increasing effort to look at relations between household quality and children's well-being in a more holistic fashion. Researchers have composed household wealth indices that include indicators of specific durable assets (e.g., appliances, automobiles, electricity, telephones, disposable drinking water, bathing facilities, bicycles) and types of construction materials used for dwellings (e.g., type of flooring, material used for roofing, materials used for the walls). For parents living in developing countries there are often many challenges in gaining access to household and community assets, constraining their capacities to promote health and cope with disease (De Silva & Harpham, 2007; Obrist et al., 2007). Studies done across Asia, Africa, Latin America, and the Pacific Islands reveal relations between these household wealth indices and a diversity of health markers, including receipt of immunizations and vitamins, growth, and survival (Aerts, Drachler, & Giugliani, 2004; Boyle et al, 2006; Choi, Bishai, & Hill, 2005; De Silva & Harpham, 2007; Larrea & Freire, 2002; Larrea & Kawachi, 2005; Xie & Dow, 2005). Some studies indicate gender differences, usually favoring girls (Wamani et al., 2007). Some studies indicate that household wealth predicts child health net of factors such as country level GDP and maternal education (Boyle et al., 2006); but cultural and geographic factors play into the equation as well (Matsumoto & Fletcher, 1996; Pascual, Bouma, & Dobson, 2002).

This Study

This study attempts to increase understanding about child growth and mortality in LMIC. Using data from 40 LMIC, we compare girls and boys on seven indicators of growth and mortality. We also explore how environmental conditions relate to growth and mortality with a focus on gender and country-level resource differences in these patterns. Finally, we explore how gender differences in growth and mortality relate to international indicators of gender equality and sociodemographic development.

METHOD

Participants

Forty of the 41 LMIC from which we had data asked questions about child growth and/or child mortality. Child growth data were available from 139,614 children under age 5 in 34 LMIC, and child mortality data were available from 226,798 women between the ages of 15 and 49 who had ever given birth (henceforth called mothers) in an overlapping but different set of 34 LMIC. Characteristics of the samples are presented in Table 3.

Procedures

We used the Multiple Indicator Cluster Survey (MICS3), the Human Development Index (HDI; UNDP, 2008), the Gender Relative Status Index (GRS; Beneria & Permanyer, 2010; Permanyer, 2010), and the Gender Inequality Index (GII; UNDP, 2011); additional information about the MICS3 and country-level indices are available in Chapter II.

Growth Data

As part of the MICS administration, trained administrators weighed and measured every child under 5 who was present in the home using standard equipment and a common WHO protocol provided by UNICEF (2012). Using the resulting weight and height data, we adapted and implemented the World Health Organization's (WHO, 2011) Child Growth Standards SPSS macro for the MICS data. This macro uses standard data files to calculate z-scores for height-for-age, weight-for-age, and weight-for-height, based on the WHO (2006; WHO & UNICEF, 2009) Child Growth Standards. We then used

TABLE 3
Descriptive Statistics for the Child Growth and Child Mortality Samples

	Child growth sample								Child mortality sample							
		Child age (months)		Mother education[a]		# Children under 5				Mother age (years)		Mother education[a]		# Children born alive	
Country	n	M	SD	M	SD	M	SD	n	M	SD	M	SD	M	SD
Albania	948	32.16	17.33	2.43	.57	1.15	.39	3,237	36.96	7.53	2.45	.54	2.48	1.15
Belarus	2,812	30.58	16.50	2.28	.45	1.08	.29	4,872	33.51	8.40	2.24	.43	1.73	0.85
Belize	593	30.02	17.38	1.38	.72	1.34	.56	1,145	33.60	8.42	1.41	.73	3.67	2.55
Bosnia and Herzegovina	2,711	31.22	16.38	1.76	.61	1.18	.40	—	—	—	—	—	—	—
Burkina Faso	4,168	27.08	15.94	0.17	.47	1.27	.47	5,637	32.33	8.46	0.18	.50	4.53	2.72
Burundi	—	—	—	—	—	—	—	5,819	32.57	8.24	0.80	.54	4.43	2.75
Cameroon	4,490	27.67	16.48	1.05	.78	1.42	.59	—	—	—	—	—	—	—
Central African Republic	6,706	26.95	16.90	0.68	.70	1.41	.59	9,039	29.90	8.77	0.68	.70	3.98	2.82
Côte d'Ivoire	6,604	27.26	16.64	0.47	.69	1.30	.52	—	—	—	—	—	—	—
Djibouti	1,549	29.63	15.73	0.52	.78	1.45	.64	2,620	34.09	7.36	0.45	.75	4.00	2.55
Gambia	4,909	25.62	15.94	0.51	.77	1.33	.52	6,774	30.97	8.03	0.52	.79	4.06	2.61
Georgia	1,684	30.13	17.26	2.18	.73	1.21	.42	6,395	36.21	8.08	2.02	.75	2.16	0.94
Ghana	2,661	28.86	16.75	0.86	.90	1.30	.52	4,038	33.52	8.30	0.92	.91	3.89	2.37
Guinea-Bissau	4,532	27.21	16.22	0.40	.66	1.29	.51	5,979	30.49	8.53	0.47	.72	4.02	2.68
Guyana	1,839	30.21	17.21	1.73	.60	1.36	.56	3,583	33.68	8.63	1.74	.58	3.39	2.24
Iraq	10,594	28.09	17.01	1.11	.72	1.55	.69	14,546	32.87	8.21	1.10	.74	4.29	2.73
Jamaica	—	—	—	—	—	—	—	2,542	34.56	8.52	2.08	.43	2.83	1.80
Kazakhstan	3,543	28.87	16.81	2.24	.45	1.25	.48	9,595	36.26	8.05	2.23	.43	2.43	1.36
Kyrgyzstan	2,358	29.93	17.60	2.22	.43	1.27	.48	4,478	34.62	8.28	2.20	.42	2.86	1.58
Laos	3,044	28.51	16.62	0.80	.71	1.36	.55	—	—	—	—	—	—	—
Macedonia	3,230	33.04	16.02	1.27	.75	1.41	.56	5,195	32.78	8.39	1.23	.73	2.51	1.30

(Continued)

TABLE 3. (Continued)

Country	Child growth sample							Child mortality sample						
	n	Child age (months)		Mother education[a]		# Children under 5		n	Mother age (years)		Mother education[a]		# Children born alive	
		M	SD	M	SD	M	SD		M	SD	M	SD	M	SD
Mauritania	5,983	26.91	16.08	0.82	.67	1.45	.61	8,033	32.30	8.64	0.83	.67	4.45	2.84
Mongolia	3,053	28.32	17.05	2.19	.60	1.16	.39	5,576	33.77	7.97	2.21	.59	2.76	1.71
Montenegro	817	31.97	17.15	1.93	.65	1.30	.55	—	—	—	—	—	—	—
Mozambique	8,246	27.81	16.76	0.84	.63	1.39	.56	11,288	30.69	8.66	0.86	.64	3.75	2.49
Nigeria	12,292	27.59	16.14	0.75	.91	1.35	.56	16,472	31.75	8.01	0.79	.93	4.17	2.53
Serbia	2,898	30.09	16.89	1.65	.82	1.30	.54	—	—	—	—	—	—	—
Sierra Leone	4,258	28.59	16.45	0.32	.67	1.23	.46	6,365	30.90	7.77	0.37	.73	4.44	2.82
Somalia	3,889	28.69	17.14	0.41	.56	1.62	.71	4,581	30.69	8.07	0.43	.58	4.45	2.84
Suriname	1,750	30.80	17.18	1.49	.79	1.29	.52	3,537	34.66	8.28	1.57	.73	2.97	1.98
Syrian Arab Republic	7,562	28.85	15.83	1.32	.79	1.46	.62	12,899	33.86	7.96	1.29	.83	4.27	2.53
Tajikistan	3,139	29.92	17.01	2.05	.37	1.36	.55	6,058	34.58	8.01	2.06	.37	3.82	2.12
Thailand	8,419	29.41	17.05	1.58	.79	1.12	.34	24,018	36.77	7.79	1.50	.77	2.02	1.03
Togo	3,169	27.39	16.32	0.61	.74	1.29	.49	4,549	32.36	8.10	0.62	.74	3.92	2.52
Trinidad and Tobago	—	—	—	—	—	—	—	2,608	36.51	8.30	1.81	.56	2.51	1.54
Ukraine	—	—	—	—	—	—	—	4,863	33.08	8.74	2.31	.68	1.62	0.85
Uzbekistan	3,881	29.05	16.93	2.09	.29	1.28	.49	8,897	34.51	8.12	2.11	.32	3.01	1.57
Vanuatu	1,283	27.91	16.68	1.29	.65	1.27	.50	1,969	32.45	8.08	1.28	.64	3.21	1.91
Vietnam	—	—	—	—	—	—	—	6,283	35.99	8.04	1.60	.72	2.62	1.46
Yemen	—	—	—	—	—	—	—	3,308	32.16	8.56	0.44	.71	5.20	3.27
Total	139,614	28.44	16.66	1.11	.93	1.34	.56	226,798	33.44	8.45	1.28	.94	3.43	2.39

Note. —, Data not collected.
[a]Education is rated as 0 = none or preschool, 1 = primary school, nonstandard curriculum, religious school, 2 = secondary, vocational, tertiary school, and 3 = higher education.

predefined cut-off values of 2 *SD* below the mean to identify children who were stunted (<−2.00 on height-for-age), underweight (<−2.00 on weight-for-age), and wasting (<−2.00 on weight-for-height). As a basis for comparison, the percentages of children who are stunted, underweight, and wasting in a particular country can be compared with 2.3%, which is the expected percentage of children below −2 *SD* in a normal population (i.e., based on the standardization sample of typically developing, singleton children in the United States, Oman, Norway, Brazil, and affluent neighborhoods of Ghana and India with no known environmental growth constraints; WHO, 1997, p. 50).

Child Mortality Data

Each woman aged 15–49 in a household was asked if she had ever given birth to a live baby, even if the newborn had only lived for a few minutes. If the woman answered yes, she was then asked a series of questions designed to ascertain the total number of live births of girls and boys and the total number of girls and boys who were born alive but later died. From these questions, for each woman who had given birth we calculated the percentage of girls and boys born alive who subsequently died.

Home Environment Data

The home environment questions pertaining to quality of housing and material resources were taken from the water and sanitation and household characteristics modules of the MICS3 Household Questionnaire.

Quality of Housing Indicators

Following the WHO and UNICEF's (2008) drinking water ladder, we coded drinking water into three categories: unimproved (1; unprotected springs or wells, tanker-trucks or carts with a small tank/drum, surface water, or bottled water), improved (2; public taps or standpipes, tube wells or boreholes, protected wells or springs, or rainwater collection), and piped (3; piped directly to the household dwelling, plot, or yard). Following the sanitation ladder recommended by WHO and UNICEF (2008), we coded toilet facilities into four categories: open defecation (1; no facilities or toileting in the bush or field), unimproved (2; pit latrines without a slab or platform, hanging latrines, and bucket latrines), shared improved (3), and unshared improved (4). Improved facilities included flush or pour-flush latrines, ventilated improved pit (VIP) latrines, pit latrines with slabs, and composting toilets. The main material of the dwelling floor was recoded into the three existing superordinate categories of natural (1), rudimentary (2), and finished (3) flooring. Cooking was recoded to indicate whether household cooking was done on an open fire or stove (0) or in a closed stove (1).

Household Materials Indicators

Nine household items (radio, TV, mobile telephone, non-mobile telephone, refrigerator, motorcycle or scooter, animal-drawn cart, car or truck, and boat with motor) were coded as absent (0), present (1). Mobile and non-mobile telephone were recoded into a single item to indicate the absence (0) or presence (1) of either type of telephone in the household. Finally, the four items about household transportation—motorcycle or scooter, animal-drawn cart, car or truck, and boat with a motor—were recoded into a single item to indicate the absence (0) or presence (1) of any kind of transportation not powered by humans.

Quality of Housing and Household Materials Summary Indices

Following Bradley and Putnick (2012), we organized the quality of housing and household materials into summary indices. Summary scores were computed for each index, allowing one item to be missing and prorating the total based on the remaining items. We consider these aggregates to be indices and not scales because they are conceptually related as indicators of child development, but they are not necessarily statistically related (see Bradley, 2004; Streiner, 2003). The Quality of Housing Index was computed as the standardized average of drinking water, toilet facilities, household flooring, cooking, and refrigeration. Higher scores on these five items indicated a healthier and safer home environment for children under 5. The Household Materials Index was computed as the sum of the presence of a radio, television, telephone, nonhuman-powered transportation, and electricity in the household. Higher scores on these five items indicated the availability of a broader range of experiences for children under 5.

Analytic Plan

First, we explored whether girls and boys differed on height-for-age, stunting, weight-for-age, underweight, weight-for-height, wasting, and mortality. For child growth z-scores, we performed child gender by country analyses of variance (ANOVAs); for stunting, underweight, and wasting, child gender by country binary logistic regressions; and for child mortality, child gender by country repeated-measures analyses of variance (RM-ANOVAs) with child gender as a within-subjects factor. If the interaction between child gender and country was significant, we reanalyzed the child gender models within country. Next, we performed explanatory models designed to assess whether quality of housing and household materials were associated with growth and mortality and whether they interacted with gender.

In the explanatory models, we used maternal education as a covariate. Maternal education was associated with child growth z-scores, $rs(129,282–134,720) = .16–.30$, $ps < .001$, and child mortality for girls and boys, $rs(226,512) = -.19$, $ps < .001$. There were also large differences in education across countries, $F(33, 139,401) = 3,173.37$, $p < .001$, $\eta_p^2 = .429$, for the child growth sample, and $F(33, 226,572) = 5,886.02$, $p < .001$, $\eta_p^2 = .462$, for the child mortality sample, and controlling for maternal education has the advantage of accounting for across-country differences as well as within-country differences.

To assess whether the country's overall level of human development was associated with the gender differences we found in growth and mortality, the effect sizes for child gender for each country were correlated with the country's HDI and its constituent indicators. The effect sizes we used were Cohen's (1988) d for z-scores and mortality and odds ratios (OR) for stunting, underweight, and wasting status, based on the child gender by country models.

Finally, to determine whether country-level gender equality was associated with markers of child growth and mortality net of HDI, we computed partial correlations between two country-level indices of gender equality (GRS and GII) and gender differences in each child outcome, controlling for HDI.

RESULTS

Overall, findings indicated that boys were disadvantaged relative to girls in growth and mortality, especially in lower-HDI countries. Quality of housing and material resources were generally related to growth and mortality for both genders, and there were only small differences in the relative relations of quality of housing and material resources with growth and mortality in girls and boys.

Growth and Mortality by Gender and Country

Height-for-Age and Stunting

The Gender by Country interaction for height-for-age was significant, $F(33, 131,398) = 1.81$, $p < .01$, $\eta_p^2 = .000$, as were the main effects for gender, $F(1, 131,398) = 110.83$, $p < .001$, $\eta_p^2 = .001$, and country, $F(33, 131,398) = 298.88$, $p < .001$, $\eta_p^2 = .070$. To decompose the interaction of gender and country, we computed the ANOVA by gender within countries. Boys had lower height-for-age z-scores than girls in 9 of 16 medium-HDI countries, 8 of 9 low-HDI countries, and both HDI-N/A countries, but girls and boys did not differ in any of the 7 High-HDI countries. Effect sizes were all small.

The gender by country interaction for stunting was nonsignificant, Wald $\chi^2(33) = 40.27$, ns. Main effects of gender, Wald $\chi^2(1) = 189.57$, $p < .001$, OR = .84, and country, Wald $\chi^2(33) = 7614.11$, $p < .001$, were significant. Across all countries, higher percentages of boys than girls were stunted. Despite the nonsignificant interaction between gender and country, we computed logistic regressions within country to parallel the analyses for height-for-age. Higher percentages of boys than girls were stunted in 1 of the 7 high-HDI countries (Bosnia & Herzegovina), 10 of the 16 medium-HDI countries, 7 of the 9 low-HDI countries, and 1 of the 2 HDI-N/A countries (Iraq), and girls and boys did not differ in the other 15 countries (see Supplemental Table S3.1).

Weight-for-Age and Underweight

The gender by country interaction for weight-for-age was significant, $F(33, 134{,}821) = 4.18$, $p < .001$, $\eta_p^2 = .001$, as were the main effects for gender, $F(1, 134{,}821) = 55.69$, $p < .001$, $\eta_p^2 = .000$, and country, $F(33, 134{,}821) = 724.87$, $p < .001$, $\eta_p^2 = .151$. To decompose the interaction of gender and country, we computed the ANOVA by gender within countries. Boys had lower weight-for-age z-scores than girls in 7 of 16 medium-HDI countries, 8 of 9 low-HDI countries, and 1 of the 2 HDI-N/A countries (Somalia), but girls and boys did not differ in any of the 7 high-HDI countries. Effect sizes were all small.

The gender by country interaction for underweight was nonsignificant, Wald $\chi^2(33) = 36.93$, ns. Main effects of gender, Wald $\chi^2(1) = 164.65$, $p < .001$, OR = .82, and country, Wald $\chi^2(33) = 8633.50$, $p < .001$, were significant. Higher percentages of boys than girls were underweight. Despite the nonsignificant interaction between Gender and Country, we computed regressions within country to parallel the analyses for weight-for-age. Higher percentages of boys than girls were underweight in 1 of the 7 high-HDI countries (Serbia), 7 of the 16 medium-HDI countries, 6 of the 9 low-HDI countries, and 1 of the 2 HDI-N/A countries (Somalia; see Supplemental Table S3.2).

Weight-for-Height and Wasting

The gender by country interaction for weight-for-height was significant, $F(33, 129{,}374) = 1.56$, $p < .05$, $\eta_p^2 = .001$, as was the main effect of country, $F(33, 129{,}374) = 349.23$, $p < .001$, $\eta_p^2 = .082$, but not gender, $F(1, 129{,}374) = .46$, ns, $\eta_p^2 = .000$. To decompose the interaction of gender and country, we computed the ANOVA by gender within countries. Boys had lower weight-for-height z-scores than girls in two countries (Laos and Somalia), girls had lower weight-for-height than boys in three countries (Thailand, Mongolia, and Iraq), and girls and boys did not differ in the other 29 countries. Effect sizes were all small.

The gender by country interaction for wasting was nonsignificant, Wald $\chi^2(33) = 42.57$, ns. Main effects of gender, Wald $\chi^2(1) = 51.23$, $p < .001$, OR = .87, and country, Wald $\chi^2(33) = 3845.62$, $p < .001$, were significant. Across all countries, higher percentages of boys than girls were wasting. Despite the nonsignificant interaction between gender and country, we computed logistic regressions within country to parallel the analyses for weight-for-height. Higher percentages of boys than girls were wasting in 1 of the 7 high-HDI countries (Serbia), 3 of the 16 medium-HDI countries (Laos, Mauritania, and the Syrian Arab Republic), 4 of the 9 low-HDI countries (Burkina Faso, Côte d'Ivoire, Mozambique, and Sierra Leone), 1 of the 2 HDI-N/A countries (Somalia), and girls and boys did not differ in the other 25 countries (see Supplemental Table S3.3).

Mortality

The gender by country interaction for child mortality was significant, $F(33, 226{,}672) = 5.38$, $p < .001$, $\eta_p^2 = .001$, as were the main effects for gender, $F(1, 226{,}672) = 402.26$, $p < .001$, $\eta_p^2 = .002$, and country, $F(33, 226{,}672) = 936.36$, $p < .001$, $\eta_p^2 = .120$. To decompose the interaction of gender and country, we computed the RM-ANOVA by gender within countries. Higher percentages of boys than girls had died in all 5 high-HDI countries, 14 of 18 medium-HDI countries, all 9 low-HDI countries, and both HDI-N/A countries. The percentages of girls and boys who had died did not differ in Belize, Vanuatu, Yemen, and Djibouti. Effect sizes were all small (see Supplemental Table S3.4).

Explanatory Models

We next explored whether quality of housing and household material resources were associated with child growth and mortality; and we explored interactions of gender with housing quality and household material resources to determine whether they might help to explain any observed gender differences in growth and mortality controlling for maternal education. Finally, we included interactions with country in case there was a country-specific effect.

Quality of housing

The three-way interactions for country, gender, and housing quality were nonsignificant for all dependent variables: height-for-age, $F(33, 129{,}565) = 1.01$, ns, $\eta_p^2 = .000$, stunting, Wald $\chi^2(33) = 25.30$, ns, weight-for-age, $F(33, 132{,}943) = 1.24$, ns, $\eta_p^2 = .000$, underweight, Wald $\chi^2(33) = 44.82$, ns, weight-for-height, $F(33, 127{,}562) = .94$, ns, $\eta_p^2 = .000$, wasting, Wald $\chi^2(33) = 19.86$, ns, and child mortality, $F(32, 221{,}341) = .80$, ns, $\eta_p^2 = .000$.

Country by housing quality interactions were significant for all outcomes: height-for-age, $F(33, 129{,}565) = 10.40$, $p < .001$, $\eta_p^2 = .003$, stunting, Wald

$\chi^2(33) = 345.15$, $p < .001$, weight-for-age, $F(33, 132{,}943) = 13.57$, $p < .001$, $\eta_p^2 = .003$, underweight, Wald $\chi^2(33) = 229.57$, $p < .001$, weight-for-height, $F(33, 127{,}562) = 9.55$, $p < .001$, $\eta_p^2 = .002$, wasting, Wald $\chi^2(33) = 117.98$, $p < .001$, and child mortality, $F(32, 221{,}341) = 27.23$, $p < .001$, $\eta_p^2 = .004$.

Better housing quality was associated with taller height-for-age in 6 of 7 high-HDI countries ($\eta_p^2 = .003$–$.017$), 14 of 16 medium-HDI countries ($\eta_p^2 = .003$–$.022$), 8 of 9 low-HDI countries ($\eta_p^2 = .003$–$.036$), and both HDI-N/A countries ($\eta_p^2 = .001$–$.046$), but the effects were not significant in the other 4 countries (Albania, Georgia, Vanuatu, and Guinea-Bissau). Similarly, better housing quality was associated with a lower probability of stunting in 6 of 7 high-HDI countries (OR = .11–.65), 14 of 16 medium-HDI countries (OR = .49–.78), all 9 low-HDI countries (OR = .44–.85), and both HDI-N/A countries (OR = .34–.81), but relations were not significant in the remaining 3 countries (Albania, Georgia, and Vanuatu; see Supplemental Table S3.5).

Better housing quality was associated with greater weight-for-age in 5 of 7 high-HDI countries ($\eta_p^2 = .002$–$.013$), 15 of 16 medium-HDI countries ($\eta_p^2 = .001$–$.042$), all 9 low-HDI countries ($\eta_p^2 = .001$–$.045$), and both HDI-N/A countries ($\eta_p^2 = .002$–$.060$), and was unrelated in the remaining 3 countries (Albania, Bosnia and Herzegovina, and Vanuatu). Better housing quality was associated with a lower probability of being underweight in 1 of 7 high-HDI countries (OR = .23), 8 of 16 medium-HDI countries (OR = .50–.70), 8 of 9 low-HDI countries (OR = .36–.81), and both HDI-N/A countries (OR = .32–.79; see Supplemental Table S3.6).

Results were less consistent for weight-for-height and wasting. Better housing quality was significantly associated with lower weight-for-height in 2 of 7 high-HDI countries (Belarus and Bosnia and Herzegovina; $\eta_p^2 = .002$–$.009$), greater weight-for-height in 1 of 7 high-HDI countries (Macendonia; $\eta_p^2 = .002$), 6 of 16 medium-HDI countries ($\eta_p^2 = .002$–$.031$), 5 of 9 low-HDI countries ($\eta_p^2 = .001$–$.011$), and both HDI-N/A countries ($\eta_p^2 = .001$–$.013$), and was unrelated in the remaining 18 countries. Better quality of housing was significantly associated with a higher probability of wasting in 1 of 16 medium-HDI countries (Vanuatu; OR = 1.78), a lower probability of wasting in 4 of 16 medium-HDI countries (OR = .63–.75), 5 of 9 low-HDI countries (OR = .48–.72), both HDI-N/A countries (OR = .63–.85), and was unrelated in the remaining 22 countries (including all high-HDI countries; see Supplemental Table S3.7). Finally, better housing quality was associated with lower mortality in 1 of 5 high-HDI countries, 9 of 15 medium-HDI countries, all 9 low-HDI countries, and 1 of 2 HDI-N/A countries (see Supplemental Table S3.8).

Housing quality did not significantly interact with gender for height-for-age, $F(1, 129{,}565) = 1.83$, ns, $\eta_p^2 = .000$, stunting, Wald $\chi^2(1) = .24$, ns,

OR = 1.01, weight-for-age, $F(1, 132,943) = 2.18$, ns, $\eta_p^2 = .000$, underweight, Wald $\chi^2(1) = .08$, ns, OR = 1.01, or child mortality, $F(1, 221,341) = .16$, ns, $\eta_p^2 = .000$. However, the interaction between housing quality and gender was significant for weight-for-height, $F(1, 127,562) = 6.01$, $p < .05$, $\eta_p^2 = .000$, and wasting, Wald $\chi^2(1) = 5.99$, $p < .05$, OR = 1.07. Follow-up tests indicated that better quality of housing was associated with greater weight-for-height in boys, $F(1, 65,152) = 21.66$, $p < .001$, $\eta_p^2 = .000$, but not girls, $F(1, 62,409) = 3.07$, ns, $\eta_p^2 = .000$ (although with tiny effect sizes in both groups). Similarly, the effect of quality of housing on wasting was slightly stronger for boys, Wald $\chi^2(1) = 79.99$, $p < .001$, OR = .76, than for girls, Wald $\chi^2(1) = 32.78$, $p < .001$, OR = .83, but for both girls and boys having better housing quality was still significantly associated with a lower probability of wasting.

Overall, quality of housing was associated with better growth and less mortality, but results varied by country. Housing quality was related to height-for-age and stunting in most countries, was more often related to weight-for-age, underweight, and mortality in low- and medium-HDI countries than high-HDI countries, and was less consistently related to weight-for-height and wasting by HDI. Quality of housing had slightly stronger relations with the weight-for-height and wasting status of boys than girls across countries, but there were no gender differences in relations between housing quality and mortality or the other growth problems.

Household material resources

The three-way interactions for country, gender, and material resources were nonsignificant for height-for-age, $F(32, 130,190) = .91$, ns, $\eta_p^2 = .000$, stunting, Wald $\chi^2(32) = 35.06$, ns, weight-for-height, $F(32, 128,169) = 1.01$, ns, $\eta_p^2 = .000$, underweight, Wald $\chi^2(32) = 40.69$, ns, wasting, Wald $\chi^2(32) = 30.53$, ns, and child mortality, $F(31, 220,597) = 1.19$, ns, $\eta_p^2 = .000$. The three-way interaction was significant for weight-for-age, $F(32, 133,594) = 1.49$, $p < .05$, $\eta_p^2 = .000$. Follow-up tests indicated that the interaction between gender and material resources was significant for Cameroon, $F(1, 4,310) = 7.99$, $p < .01$, $\eta_p^2 = .002$, Kyrgyzstan, $F(1, 2,289) = 4.82$, $p < .05$, $\eta_p^2 = .002$, and Nigeria, $F(1, 11,944) = 6.36$, $p < .05$, $\eta_p^2 = .001$, only. In Cameroon, having more material resources was associated with greater weight-for-age for both girls, $F(1, 2,180) = 27.86$, $p < .001$, $\eta_p^2 = .013$, and boys, $F(1, 2,129) = 77.68$, $p < .001$, $\eta_p^2 = .035$. In Kyrgyzstan, having more material resources was associated with greater weight-for-age for boys, $F(1, 1,183) = 8.09$, $p < .01$, $\eta_p^2 = .007$, but not girls, $F(1, 1,105) = .45$, ns, $\eta_p^2 = .000$. In Nigeria, material resources was not associated with weight-for-age for girls, $F(1, 5,874) = .81$, ns, $\eta_p^2 = .000$, or boys, $F(1, 6,069) = 3.36$, ns, $\eta_p^2 = .001$.

Significant country by household materials interactions emerged for all outcomes: height-for-age, $F(32, 130,190) = 7.93$, $p < .001$, $\eta_p^2 = .002$, stunting,

Wald $\chi^2(32) = 260.08$, $p < .001$, weight-for-age, $F(32, 133{,}594) = 13.11$, $p < .001$, $\eta_p^2 = .003$, underweight, Wald $\chi^2(32) = 182.14$, $p < .001$, weight-for-height, $F(32, 128{,}169) = 9.07$, $p < .001$, $\eta_p^2 = .002$, wasting, Wald $\chi^2(32) = 106.81$, $p < .001$, and mortality, $F(31, 220{,}597) = 24.01$, $p < .001$, $\eta_p^2 = .003$.

Having more material resources was associated with taller height-for-age in all 6 high-HDI countries ($\eta_p^2 = .007-.017$), 14 of 16 medium-HDI countries ($\eta_p^2 = .005-.038$), 8 of 9 low-HDI countries ($\eta_p^2 = .002-.030$), and both HDI-N/A countries ($\eta_p^2 = .002-.014$), and was unrelated in the Syrian Arab Republic, Kyrgyzstan, and Nigeria. Having more material resources was associated with a lower probability of stunting in 5 of 6 high-HDI countries (OR = .58–.83), 13 of 16 medium-HDI countries (OR = .64–.86), all 9 low-HDI countries (OR = .75–.95), and both HDI-N/A countries (OR = .78–.91), and was unrelated in Montenegro, the Syrian Arab Republic, Kyrgyzstan, and Vanuatu (see Supplemental Table S3.9).

Having more material resources was associated with greater weight-for-age in 5 of 6 high-HDI countries ($\eta_p^2 = .002-.013$), 13 of 16 medium-HDI countries ($\eta_p^2 = .002-.052$), 8 of 9 low-HDI countries ($\eta_p^2 = .001-.021$), both HDI-N/A countries ($\eta_p^2 = .001-.024$), and was unrelated in Montenegro, Suriname, Georgia, Kyrgyzstan, and Nigeria. Having more material resources was associated with a lower probability of being underweight in 2 of 6 high-HDI countries (OR = .53–.65), 10 of 16 medium-HDI countries (OR = .77–.89), all 9 low-HDI countries (OR = .72–.94), 1 of the 2 HDI-N/A countries (OR = .74), and was unrelated in the remaining 11 countries (see Supplemental Table S3.10).

Having more material resources was associated with greater weight-for-height in 1 of 6 high-HDI countries (Macedonia; $\eta_p^2 = .002$), 6 of 16 medium-HDI countries ($\eta_p^2 = .002-.017$), 5 of 9 low-HDI countries ($\eta_p^2 = .001-.010$), and 1 of the 2 HDI-N/A countries (Somalia; $\eta_p^2 = .011$), and was unrelated in the remaining 20 countries. Having more material resources was associated with a higher probability of wasting in 1 medium-HDI country (Guyana; OR = 1.19), a lower probability of wasting in 3 medium-HDI countries (Syrian Arab Republic, Mauritania, and Cameroon; OR = .85–.91), 3 low-HDI countries (Burkina Faso, Mozambique, and Togo; OR = .81–.92), 1 of the 2 HDI-N/A countries (Somalia; OR = .84), and was unrelated in 25 countries (see Supplemental Table S3.11). Finally, for mortality, having more material resources was associated with lower mortality in 2 of 6 high-HDI countries, 10 of 16 medium-HDI countries, 8 of 9 low-HDI countries, neither of the HDI-N/A countries, and was unrelated to mortality in 12 countries (see Supplemental Table S3.8).

Material resources did not significantly interact with gender for height-for-age, $F(1, 130{,}190) = .04$, ns, $\eta_p^2 = .000$, stunting, Wald $\chi^2(1) = .58$, ns, OR = 1.01, weight-for-age, $F(1, 133{,}594) = .65$, ns, $\eta_p^2 = .000$, underweight,

Wald $\chi^2(1) = .78$, ns, OR = 1.01, weight-for-height, $F(1, 128169) = 1.94$, ns, $\eta_p^2 = .000$, or child mortality, $F(1, 220{,}597) = .07$, ns, $\eta_p^2 = .000$. The interaction between child gender and material resources was significant for wasting, Wald $\chi^2(1) = 5.43$, $p < .05$, OR = 1.03. Follow-up tests by gender indicated that the effect of material resources on wasting was slightly stronger for boys, Wald $\chi^2(1) = 49.80$, $p < .001$, OR = .92, than girls, Wald $\chi^2(1) = 17.36$, $p < .001$, OR = .95, but for both girls and boys having more material resources was still associated with a lower probability of wasting.

Overall, having more material resources in the house was associated with better growth and reduced mortality, but the strength and significance of the effects varied by country. Material resources were almost uniformly related to height-for-age and stunting, were more related to weight-for-age, underweight, and mortality in low- and medium-HDI countries than high-HDI countries, and were less consistently related to weight-for-height and wasting by HDI. Material resources had a slightly stronger relation with weight-for-age in boys than girls in Cameroon and Kyrgyzstan and with the wasting status of boys than girls across countries.

Relations Between Gender Effect Sizes and the HDI

Table 4 displays correlations between effect sizes for the gender difference in growth and mortality (Cohen's d or ORs) and the country HDI and its constituent indices. A positive correlation means that as HDI increases, the difference between boys and girls increasingly favors boys. In other words, in low-HDI countries boys are at a disadvantage compared to girls; but in high-HDI countries, the gap between girls and boys is smaller, or even reverses. Large positive correlations emerged for the effect sizes for all z-scores with the HDI and all of its indices. However, the effect sizes for stunting, underweight, wasting, and mortality were unrelated to the HDI, life expectancy index, and GDP index. Effect sizes for stunting and underweight were modestly related to the education index and literacy, and the effect size for stunting was also modestly related to schooling. As an example, Figure 2 displays the scatterplot of gender effect size (Cohen's d) for weight-for-age by HDI. Effect sizes <0 indicate that boys had lower weight-for-age than girls, and effect sizes >0 indicate that girls had lower weight-for-age than boys. Boys were at a disadvantage compared to girls in all low-HDI countries (<.50), and some medium-HDI countries (.51–.70). Although we only show one figure, there were two visible groupings of countries for all three z-scores (height-for-age, weight-for-age, and weight-for-height): (1) low-medium-HDI countries where boys are at a disadvantage and (2) medium-high-HDI countries where boys are at less of a disadvantage, or even gain the advantage over girls (see Figure 2).

TABLE 4
CORRELATIONS BETWEEN THE HDI AND ITS CONSTITUENT INDICES, GRS, AND GII WITH EFFECT SIZES FOR GENDER DIFFERENCES IN GROWTH AND MORTALITY

	Height-for-age	Stunting	Weight-for-age	Underweight	Weight-for-height	Wasting	Mortality
HDI	.64***	.32	.70***	.10	.73***	.30	−.11
Life Expectancy Index	.52**	.18	.65***	.12	.66***	.28	−.19
Education Index	.61***	.37*	.63***	.06	.70***	.35*	.06
Literacy	.58***	.35*	.57***	−.01	.69***	.41*	.03
Schooling	.61***	.38*	.70***	.22	.66***	.17	.12
GDP Index	.63***	.29	.67***	.09	.68***	.22	−.19
GRS[a]	.35	.12	.50**	.34	.36	−.10	.23
GII[a]	−.13	−.12	.14	−.00	−.19	−.68***	−.05

Note. N = 32–34 countries for the HDI and indicators. The HDI and GDP Index were not available for Iraq or Somalia, and the Education Index and its components were not available for Somalia. N = 29–30 for GRS and N = 23–26 for GII.
[a]Controlling for HDI.
*$p \leq .05$.
**$p \leq .01$.
***$p \leq .001$.

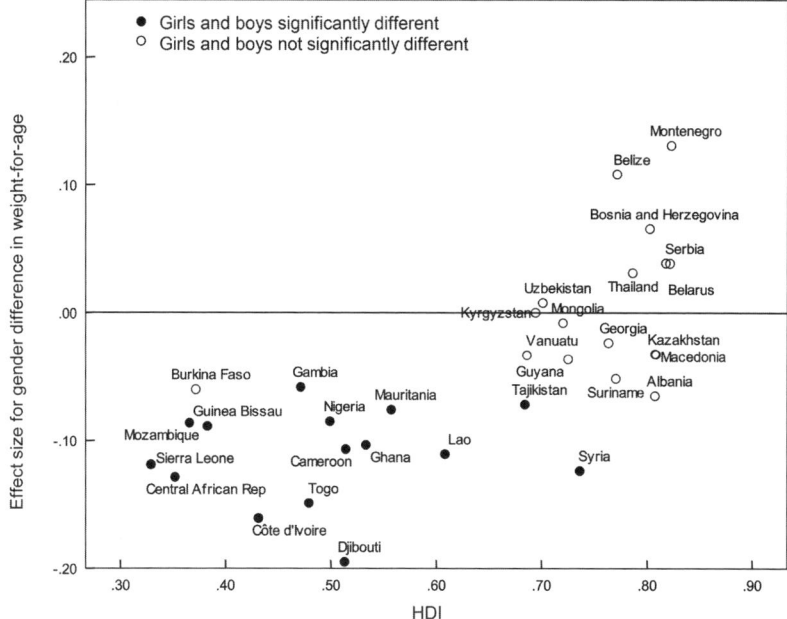

FIGURE 2.—Scatterplot between the HDI and the effect size for gender difference in weight-for-age.

Relations Between Gender Equality Indices and Gender Differences in Markers of Child Health

As shown in Table 3, GRS was a significant predictor for only one child outcome (weight-for-age) controlling for HDI ($r = .50$, $p < .01$), indicating that in countries with better national gender equality boys were at less of a disadvantage compared to girls on weight-for-age. Likewise, GII was a significant predictor for only one child outcome (wasting) controlling for HDI ($r = -.68$, $p < .01$), indicating that in countries with better national gender quality (low score) boys were at less of a disadvantage compared to girls.

DISCUSSION

Malnutrition and exposure to various pathogens present serious risks to children growing up in poverty. Consequently, it is important to further delineate how specific resources at home and in the broader community contribute to growth difficulties and mortality in young children. Our results show that family level physical capital assets, in the form of household quality and material resources, are differentially associated with some indicators of growth in girls and boys; but relations differed by country and all gender effects were quite small. Across all countries, weight-for-height and wasting were more strongly related to housing quality for boys. Wasting was also more strongly related to material resources for boys than girls. Gender disparities, favoring girls, were most prevalent in countries where socioeconomic capital is scarce, consistent with the idea that genes that promote resilience may play a relatively larger role in adverse environments. As countries are able to improve infrastructure pertaining to water, sanitation, and health care, severe malnutrition and childhood mortality subside, at which point gender differences attenuate (Pelletier, 1994). However, when resources in a country remain low, growth problems and mortality for both girls and boys continue to be prevalent, consistent with the broader literature on malnutrition and disease exposure (Cuningham-Rundles et al., 2008). In general, the disparate pattern of findings for child gender across countries appears to attest to the value of considering the resources available at household, community, and societal levels when trying to determine influences on children's health status (Sahn & Stifel, 2000). Results from this study also indicate that country-level gender equality may be a minor factor in determining the likelihood young children will present with growth problems, albeit significant results emerged for only two of the seven health indicators we examined once the overall socioeconomic level of the country was controlled.

Micronutrient deficiencies coincident with frequent diarrhea can lead to malabsorption and significant weight loss for young children. The combination of poor nutrition and diarrhea can become a vicious cycle leading to serious growth problems, even death (Podewils et al., 2004). Genetic differences between girls and boys generally result in fewer serious growth problems and lower rates of mortality for girls (Klein, 2007). Our findings confirm that stunting is more prevalent in boys than girls who live in the countries sampled in the MICS. In just more than half of the countries sampled, girls fared better than boys (albeit, all effect sizes were small). In the remainder of the countries there was no difference. Notably, gender differences for height-for-age and stunting were nonsignificant in almost all high-HDI countries.

Our findings pertaining to weight-for-age were similar to our findings pertaining to height-for-age. That is not surprising in that being underweight also tends to reflect multiplicative effects of poor nutrition and poor health circumstances over time (Ricci & Becker, 1996). There was a higher prevalence of low weight-for-age among boys in 16 countries (again, the effect sizes were small). Technically the interaction between gender and country was nonsignificant, but greater percentages of boys were underweight in 15 LMIC. Like the results of height-for-age and stunting, gender differences for weight-for-age and underweight were nonsignificant in almost all high-HDI countries.

The basic genetic advantage present for girls tends to be less protective with respect to health conditions such as weight-for-height that reflect transient circumstances and parents' discretionary behaviors (Hill & Upchurch, 1995). Thus, it was not surprising to find fewer gender differences in weight-for-height. Relatedly, even though there was a significant overall difference in wasting, favoring girls, the gender difference was only observed in 9 countries. GII predicted the likelihood of wasting net of HDI, showing that boys were at less of a disadvantage relative to girls in countries with better national gender equality. Had we separated children by age, we may have found that gender differences pertaining to wasting favoring girls only obtained for infants because early infancy is the most vulnerable period of development.

The United Nations, Department of Economic and Social Affairs (2011) reported a very complex pattern pertaining to gender differences in mortality for children under age 5. Girls from 122 countries showed a slight advantage over boys in rates of mortality. However, there was little gender variation in India and China, where there remain strong preferences for male offspring, and there is evidence for differential treatment surrounding childhood illnesses (Hesketh & Xing, 2006). In large measure, our findings are consistent with that report. Specifically, we observed a main effect of gender (favoring girls) as well as a gender by country interaction. In our study, boys died at higher rates than girls in 30 countries. However, consistent with prior studies, the effect sizes were small. In overview, research on child mortality suggests that there is interplay between various genetic factors and multiple environmental conditions, including cultural values (both those connected with gender equality and those that treat other social and emotional issues). The interplay becomes more complicated given that there have been rapid changes in both policy and infrastructure in many LMIC. In Tanzania, for example, rapid improvements in the health system between 2000 and 2004 resulted in a reduction of mortality in infancy from 141/1,000 to 83/1,000 (Masanja et al., 2008). These shifts, sometimes complemented by changes in the education infrastructure (especially for women), can change the pathway of household decision making pertaining to nutrition and health care dramatically such that all children are given better health care (Pokhrel & Sauerborn, 2004).

When we looked at overall housing quality (including construction materials and facilities therein), we found fairly consistent effects on height-for-age and stunting, weight-for-age and overweight, and mortality, but the relations were inconsistent for weight-for-height and wasting. The effects of housing quality on weight-for-height and wasting were a little stronger for boys than girls. The observed modest impacts on growth and mortality may reflect generally improved access to clean water and sanitation facilities as well as improved maternal literacy and access to certain forms of health care. Thus, even though poor housing construction can increase the likelihood of respiratory problems and poor household facilities can increase the likelihood of infections leading to diarrhea (Wagstaff et al., 2004), improvements in these areas may have reduced the likelihood of mortality and the most consequential types of growth problems in many countries (Mitra & Rodriguez-Fernandez, 2010; Nuruddin et al., 2009).

Our findings pertaining to material resources parallel those observed for household quality. Having more material resources in the home was related to better height-for-age and stunting, weight-for-age and underweight, and less mortality in most countries. The pattern for weight-for-height was consistent, with positive associations between material resources and weight-for-height in 13 countries, but the pattern was less consistent for wasting, with a positive association in 1 county, negative associations in 7 countries, and no relations in 25 countries. Material resources showed slightly stronger relations with weight-for-age in boys than girls in Cameroon and Kyrgyzstan, and material resources were more strongly related to the wasting status of boys across countries. The fact that owning goods, such as TVs, radios, telephones, and automobiles, showed varying relations to growth problems and mortality in our study comports with other research. Past studies have implicated household assets as a major contributor to growth, injury, and mortality (Howe et al., 2006; Ricci & Becker, 1996), but in a study conducted in Uganda, a household assets index that included both quality of housing and material resources available did not predict stunting once maternal education was included in the model (Wamani, Tylleskär, Åstrøm, Tumine, & Peterson, 2004). Bakeera et al. (2009) conducted another study in Uganda that would seem to bear on how having material resources influence utilization of health care and ultimately health status. Specifically, they conducted a series of focus groups, using the health access livelihood framework as a guide. Individual material resources and the availability of public resources were critical to decisions about using health care, but social resources sometimes compensated for lack of individual resources (e.g., others provided information, financial help, transportation, and the like). In effect, although household assets continue to matter, their role may vary as a consequence of other resources available to the household—a particularly difficult interplay to track in an era of improvements in health and education policies and infrastructure in many developing countries.

Our study reveals that gender differences favoring girls in certain critical markers of child well-being are more pronounced in countries low in wealth per capita. A review of studies conducted in Sub-Saharan Africa revealed a similar pattern (Svedberg, 1990), as did a study of older children in Ethiopia (Dercon & Singh, 2013). In low-HDI countries, boys were more likely to show low height- and weight-for-age and low weight-for-height. The same pattern emerged for GDP, the life expectancy index, and the education index. The education index was also related to wasting and stunting. In general, such findings are consistent with the idea that severe shortages of resources and chronic exposure to potentially damaging conditions leave parents with little discretion as regards treatment of their offspring; thus, giving more precedence to genetic factors that increase resilience or vulnerability. Figure 2 reveals two distinct groupings of countries. The lower- to middle-HDI group (HDI < .65) all scored below 0, indicating a disadvantage for boys. However, because all but one country in this lower-scoring group were African, it may be that geography rather than HDI is the relevant factor, given that geographic conditions appear to play a consequential role in many aspects of child well-being (Davis et al., 2012). Different climatic conditions are associated with different geographic regions; and it is well known that climate is a major contributor to infectious diseases (Dunn, Davies, Harris, & Gavin, 2010). More specifically, individual infectious agents (protozoa, bacteria, viruses, etc.) tend to concentrate in regions with particular climatic conditions because their host organisms can only thrive in those conditions (Patz et al., 2004). Tropical areas, such as are present in much of Africa, are dense with pathogens that lead to the types of infections implicated in poor growth and mortality (Dunn et al., 2010). High levels of pathogens, in combination with low HDI, may make it very difficult for parents to cope with disease generally (their own or their children's). This combination of conditions may reduce the influence of gender-based values on children's health status, such as our limited findings pertaining to GRS and GII suggest. That possibility granted, given that we had no detailed information on the social and physical conditions present in particular geographic locales, it would be useful to conduct additional studies that included more detailed information about community and household conditions and levels of exposure to key pathogens to determine particular conditions relevant to specific growth and health problems. It is likely that some of these conditions will be targeted as part of the newly released Sustainable Development Goals (SDGs; United Nations General Assembly, 2015).

Limitations

This study has limitations that raise additional questions about gender in LMIC. Some general and specific limitations associated with the MICS are addressed in Chapter VII. We were limited by not having more information on the assets available to families at country, community, and household levels and by not having more detailed information on gender equity at multiple levels as well (Else-Quest & Grabe, 2012; Sahn & Stifel, 2000). In general, we were limited by the items contained in MICS3. The environment questions were all close ended and specific. The mortality questions did not include information about the circumstances surrounding child death, the date of birth, date of death, or age of the child who died. Consequently, we do not know how many of the children who died were under 5. We only know that a woman in the household aged 15–49 lost the child. This limitation acknowledged, MICS3 data were collected in large numbers in 40 countries using a standard protocol that allowed us to make critical cross-country comparisons that are almost completely lacking in the literature.

Conclusions and Implications

Improvements in infrastructure and access to health care over the past two decades have decreased the likelihood children will die or suffer growth deficiencies. These movements toward fulfillment of the UN MDGs have advantaged both girls and boys. However, the improvements have not been uniform within or across countries. To some extent those improvements have shifted what matters as regards community resources, parenting practices, and household accoutrements; but certain factors (e.g., genetic predispositions favoring girls, cultural values favoring boys, social and physical conditions in the surrounding area that may favor boys in some cases and girls in others) continue to play a role in who will survive and who will grow normally. Whether one has access to supportive social networks also matters—an issue of significance given rapid urbanization in some areas, together with immigration and forced evacuations connected with war. Our findings suggest that achievement of MDGs pertaining to child health and equity requires continued efforts to modernize community infrastructure and health services and to increase economic well-being. That said, to provide the kind of precise information health officials and policymakers need to further improve life prospects for children, our findings need to be placed in broader context. It is well known that poor people and poor houses tend to cluster. It is also well known that diseases tend to cluster (Ouattara et al., 2010). Montgomery and Hewitt (2004), using data from 73 Demographic and Health Surveys, found that, when the quality of the neighborhood was included in a model that also included housing quality, neighborhood cluster predicted height-for-age in 22 samples, whereas housing quality was a significant predictor in 45. However, ratios varied depending on geography. In effect, the quality of a child's living conditions matters, but (consistent with ecological theories of development) how much it matters varies depending on other aspects of the child's ecology.

Not to be forgotten is the need to educate both adults and children. As Wachs (2008 see also Gakidou, Cowling, Lozano, & Murray, 2010) aptly noted, having parents (especially mothers) who are better educated contributes to the likelihood that children will be better nourished, gain greater access to needed health care, and have better access to educational opportunities. Better-educated parents are likely to make more productive decisions at each step along the pathway of choices leading to child health promotion (Pokhrel & Sauerborn, 2004).

SUPPORTING INFORMATION

Additional supporting information may be found in the online version of this article at the publisher's website.

IV. MOTHERS' AND FATHERS' PARENTING PRACTICES WITH THEIR DAUGHTERS AND SONS IN LOW- AND MIDDLE-INCOME COUNTRIES

Marc H. Bornstein and Diane L. Putnick

This article is part of the issue "Gender in Low- and Middle-Income Countries," Bornstein, Putnick, Lansford, Deater-Deckard, and Bradley (Issue Authors). For a full listing of articles in this issue, see: http://onlinelibrary.wiley.com/doi/10.1111/mono.v81.1/issuetoc.

States Parties shall use their best efforts to ensure recognition of the principle that both parents have common responsibilities for the upbringing and development of the child. Parents or, as the case may be, legal guardians, have the primary responsibility for the upbringing and development of the child. The best interests of the child will be their basic concern.

–Article 18.1, Convention on the Rights of the Child
General Assembly resolution 44/25, 20 November 1989.

PARENTAL CAREGIVING

Although parenting is an adult stage of development, parenting is also a job whose primary object of attention and action is the child. Beyond their children's survival, parents are fundamentally invested in their children's

---

Corresponding author: Marc H. Bornstein, Child and Family Research, *Eunice Kennedy Shriver* National Institute of Child Health and Human Development, 6705 Rockledge Drive, Suite 8030, Bethesda, MD 20892. email: Marc_H_Bornstein@nih.gov
DOI: 10.1111/mono.12226
© 2015 The Society for Research in Child Development, Inc.

education and socialization. Healthy human children do not and cannot grow up without competent and engaging caregivers, as in early life children first learn how to express and read basic human emotions, forge their first social bonds, and first make sense of the physical world. Normally, parents lead young children through these developmental firsts. Thus, mothers' and fathers' cognitions and practices contribute in important ways to the course and outcome of child development (Bornstein, 2002, 2015; Collins, Maccoby, Steinberg, Hetherington, & Bornstein, 2001). Moreover, parents (among others) socialize and educate children in ways that, appropriate to their stage of childhood, prepare children to adapt to the life roles and contexts they will occupy as they grow.

Caregiving blends intuition and tuition. Parents sometimes act on their intuitions about caregiving. For example, almost everywhere parents speak to their newborns even though they know that babies cannot yet understand language. However, parents also acquire knowledge of what it means to parent, and generational, social, and media images of caregiving, children, and family life play significant roles in helping parents formulate their caregiving cognitions and guide their caregiving practices (Bornstein & Lansford, 2010). All societies prescribe certain expected characteristics of their members and proscribe certain others (Harkness & Super, 2002). Some prescriptions and proscriptions are essentially universal, such as the requirement for parents to nurture and protect their offspring. Others vary across societies: For example, parents in some societies play with their children and see children as interactive partners, whereas parents in other societies think that adult play with young children falls outside their purview (Bornstein, 2007). Thus, parents from different places vary in their caregiving, and caregiving from very early in life varies in terms of opinions about the significance of different specific competencies for children's successful adjustment, the ages expected for children to reach developmental milestones, when and how to care for children, and so forth (Bornstein, 2010). Indeed, socially constructed beliefs are so powerful that parents sometimes act on them more than on what their senses tell them about their own children (Ochs, 1988), and national origins shape parental expectations and interactions with children (Goodnow, Cashmore, Cotton, & Knight, 1984).

How does caregiving vary across low- and middle-income countries (LMIC)? How do mothers and fathers caregive with their daughters and sons? The present study addresses these questions using items from the Multiple Indicator Cluster Survey (MICS3), a nationally representative and internationally comparable household survey of LMIC (UNICEF, 2006). The MICS3 asks about parents' taking children to accompany them outside the home, playing with children, singing songs, naming, counting, and drawing, telling stories, and reading with young children.

PARENTAL CAREGIVING X GENDER

Gender shapes parent–child relationships in multiple ways. Parenting influences and is influenced by parent gender and by child gender.

Mothers and Fathers

Traditionally, mothers have been cast as caregivers and home managers embedded in the family, whereas fathers are seen as more powerful and separated from the family (Bird, 1997; Goldman & Goldman, 1983; Weisner, Garnier, & Loucky, 1994). Thus, mothers and fathers have different relationships with their children (Barnard & Solchany, 2002; Parke, 2002; Pleck, 2012) beginning with initial childcare. In nearly 100% of mammalian species, including human beings, females take responsibility for early childcare, whereas males have little direct investment in offspring (Clutton-Brock, 1989, 1991). Analyzing data from 186 societies worldwide, Weisner and Gallimore (1977) found that in the vast majority, mothers (and female adult relatives and female children) served as the primary caregivers of infants and young children. In high-income countries (HIC), women's and men's roles have undergone a major transformation. Women work more outside the home, and men are more involved with childcare. However, egalitarian parenting is still not the norm, and parents with egalitarian attitudes still treat their girls and boys differently (Gelman, Taylor, & Nguyen, 2004). Even in the United States, where fathers may provide more care to their infants and young children, fathers still do considerably less baby tending than mothers (Pleck, 2012). Observations of parental care in preindustrial traditional societies, such as the !Kung San (Botswana), where social customs center on equality among group members, reveal the same pattern found in modern and Western nations (Flinn, 1992; Griffin & Griffin, 1992; West & Konner, 1976). In another hunter-gatherer society, the Aka (Central African Republic), fathers provide more direct care to their children than do fathers in any other society that has been studied (Hewlett, 1988, 1992). Nevertheless, during the course of the day, "the father would on average hold his infant for a total of 57 minutes while the mother would hold the infant 490 minutes" (Hewlett, 1988, p. 268).

These differences cannot be attributed to a general inability of males to care for young children. When fathers interact with infants and children, they show many of the same child-centered characteristics as mothers (e.g., they switch to child-directed speech), and fathers can provide competent routine care (Parke, 2002; Pleck, 2012). These gender differences cannot be attributed to father absence either (because fathers tend to be away hunting or working outside of the home). When both parents are present, for example, U.S. American mothers still spontaneously engage their infants and provide routine care more frequently than do fathers (Belsky, Gilstrap, &

Rovine, 1984; even if these differences may have narrowed somewhat at least for some men; see Pleck, 2012).

Evolutionary psychology attributes these consistent differences in mothering and fathering principally to maternal internal gestation and obligatory postpartum suckling (Clutton-Brock, 1989). Gender differences in the relative costs and benefits of producing versus maintaining offspring are argued to play a key part in understanding the evolution of gender differences not only in reproductive strategies but also in parental investment (Trivers, 1972). The gender with the lower potential rate of reproduction invests more in parenting efforts (Clutton-Brock & Vincent, 1991; Trivers, 1972).

In overview, in almost all mammalian species and in human beings in all regions of the world, across a wide diversity of activities and ideologies, studies indicate more maternal than paternal obligatory caregiving of young children. We do not know, however, if the same division of labor holds for discretionary parenting activities, such as playing and reading. We know that mothers tend to hold more implicit gender stereotypes and are less concerned with gender role conformity and fathers more explicit gender stereotypes and are more concerned with gender role conformity (Endendijk et al., 2013; Leaper, 2002). We do not know what divisions of labor in these respects are common across LMIC. And we do not know how that labor is divided between girls and boys.

Daughters and Sons

Parents are widely believed to construe and to interact with children differently by child gender. Classic "Baby X" studies (where the gender of the infant is not known to study participants) in the United States have shown that unidentified infants are judged more frequently to be male and that parents conceive of and behave toward infants differently depending on whether they think they are interacting with a girl or a boy (Seavey, Katz, & Zalk, 1975; Sidorowicz & Lunney, 1980). Even before birth, after finding out their child's gender via ultrasound, parents begin to describe their girls and boys differently (Sweeney & Bradbard, 1989). After birth, adults rate newborn girls softer, more finely featured, and "beautiful, pretty, and cute" more frequently than newborn boys, even when the infants do not differ in weight, length, or Apgar score (Rubin, Provenzano, & Luria, 1974). Parents then purchase gender-stereotyped toys for their children prior to when children could express gender-typed toy preferences themselves (Pomerleau, Bolduc, Malcuit, & Cossette, 1990), and later parents encourage gender-typed play (Eisenberg, Wolchik, Hernandez, & Pasternack, 1985; Fisher-Thompson, 1993; Robinson & Morris, 1986). Thus, gender differences encourage different parental expectations and behaviors (girls talked to and boys touched: Lewis, 1972; Seavey et al., 1975), and adults' gender labeling of children relates to how development is organized (Money & Erhart, 1965; Seavy et al., 1975).

Indeed, parents' cognitions and practices communicate to children about gender in many convergent ways. Parents socialize, model, and scaffold gender, they reinforce gendered beliefs and behaviors, and they also organize children's activities and environments within and outside the family in relation to gender. One direct avenue of influence flows through parents' differential treatment of daughters and sons. For example, parents hold different cognitions, beliefs, and expectations for their girls and boys. Mothers underestimate their toddler girls' motor skills and overestimate those of their boys, even when objective tests show no gender differences in children's motor performance (Mondschein, Adolph, & Tamis-LeMonda, 2000). Another type of differential treatment occurs through parenting practices. Mothers teach daughters how to cook a meal, fathers teach sons how to build a fence. Parents also model different roles. To the extent that mothers and fathers are important and powerful figures in children's lives, often to be emulated or feared, they shape children's impressions of what it means to be a woman or a man simply by acting like a woman or a man (Bussey & Bandura, 1999). Mothers and fathers tend too to scaffold girls' and boys' participation in different activities in anticipation of adult gender role differences (Goodnow, 1988; Leaper, 2000a, 2000b). Parents also reinforce children's conformity to expected or desired gender norms, as when adults compliment a girl when she tends to a younger sibling and a boy for his building skills, and children's tendencies to engage in different behaviors often reflect rewards or injunctions associated with their outcomes. For example, gender-differentiated patterns of parent reinforcement in the domain of emotions may contribute to girls learning to express versus boys learning to mute their emotions (Eisenberg, Cumberland, & Spinrad, 1998). Finally, parents treat daughters and sons differently through the types of opportunities they provide or promote (Bussey & Bandura, 1999; Lytton & Romney, 1991). For example, parents tend to assign household chores along gender stereotyped lines (Antill, Goodnow, Russell, & Cotton, 1996). Access to certain settings gives children chances to develop corresponding conceptions of themselves and to engage in particular activities as well as to receive encouragement for repeating those activities (Lott & Maluso, 1993). For example, feminine-stereotyped toys tend to induce caregiving behaviors (e.g., feeding a doll), whereas masculine-stereotyped toys tend to generate instrumental behaviors (e.g., building a fence; Martin & Dinella, 2002). Parents further influence gender in their children by tending to place girls and boys in gender-distinctive contexts (e.g., rooms with gender-stereotyped furnishings; Pomerleau et al., 1990). To the extent that gender-differentiated situations are customary in their lives, children's gender-related knowledge, expectations, abilities, and activities are likely to be refined. Effecting these kinds of controls over children's opportunity structures also means that parents do not need to differentially socialize, model, scaffold, or reinforce gendered beliefs or behaviors in their children because contexts alone may elicit or establish desired gendered outcomes in children.

Mothers and Fathers, Daughters and Sons

Insofar as parent and child gender exert powerful and pervasive influences on relationships within the family, it follows that individual parent–child dyad combinations might display distinct gendered dynamics. Considering gender alone reveals four parent–child dyad types: mother–son, mother–daughter, father–son, and father–daughter (Collins & Russell, 1991; Cowan, Cowan, & Kerig, 1993; Starrels, 1994). However, reviewing the literature, Russell and Saebel (1997) could find only one study (Noller & Callan, 1990) that clearly showed that the four dyads differ from each other. In actuality, mothers are involved in the caregiving of sons and daughters, whereas fathers tend to be more involved with sons (Rohner & Rohner, 1982) and promote sex-typed activities more than mothers (Lytton & Romney, 1991). Fathers are more likely to hold children to stereotypical norms than mothers, and fathers encourage and reinforce gender stereotypes (Chaplin et al., 2005), including rewarding girls' negative emotions and punishing boys' negative emotions (Garside & Klimes-Dougan, 2002). Therefore, mothers and fathers vary in the ways they explicitly socialize children based on their child's gender (Brody, 2000; Chaplin et al., 2005; Garside & Klimes-Dougan, 2002; Zahn-Waxler, 2000).

In summary, parenthood and childhood are both gendered. Parents differ in their parent investment strategies by their own gender, and they parent their children differently relative to their child's gender. The result is a fourfold taxonomy of possibly gender-distinctive intrafamilial relationships. Overall, differences in how mothers and fathers caregive to girls and boys might vary as a function of parent gender, child gender, domain of caregiving, and place.

PARENTAL CAREGIVING X GENDER X CONTEXT

Many factors influence caregiving, child development, and parent–child relationships. In the prevailing bioecological model of human development (Bronfenbrenner & Morris, 2006), these spheres of influence range from the distal macrosystem to the proximal microsystem. Factors that define a society, such as its economy, political structure, traditions, and laws, constitute the macrosystem of caregiving and child development.

Mothers and fathers follow many macrosystem customs in differentially rearing daughters and sons. Every context is characterized (and distinguished from others) by thoroughgoing, deep-seated, and consistent themes that inculcate what one needs to know, to feel, and to behave as a well-functioning participant in that context. Gender is one major domain of this thematicity (the repetition of the same cultural idea across mechanisms and in diverse circumstances). Context, therefore, has profound effects on gender-related beliefs and behaviors, prescribing how children are socialized and by whom, which behaviors are considered adaptive and which maladaptive, which tasks children are taught, and what roles as mature women and men they will adopt (Best & Williams, 1997; Whiting & Edwards, 1988). Caregiving reflects adaptations by parents meant to help prepare children for success in their specific societal context.

Context shapes gendered caregiving and gender in children pervasively and does so in both subtle and overt ways. For this reason, we studied mothering and fathering of daughters and sons in 39 distinct societal contexts. Those contexts consisted of LMIC across the developing world.

COUNTRY-LEVEL GENDER EQUITY AND ECONOMIC FACTORS AND CAREGIVING

Countries vary greatly in whether and how they promote gender equality. For example, in nations where it is normative for women to be less educated and work outside the home less than men, parents may perpetuate these patterns by promoting cognitive tasks (e.g., reading, learning numbers) less with girls than boys. Another way national gender inequality may "trickle down" is that limiting the education of a mother can have a profound impact on her parenting and her children. Gakidou, Cowling, Lozano, and Murray (2010) estimated that over half of the reduction in child mortality from 1970 to 2009 could be attributable to gains in maternal education across the same period. Less educated mothers are less likely to understand their child's capabilities (Ertem et al., 2007) and parent in an effective manor (Valenzula, 1997).

Challenging even in optimal circumstances, successful caregiving is rendered even more difficult when family, societal, and national resources are inadequate (Edin & Lein, 1997). The stresses on poor parents stemming from the day-to-day struggles to find resources, and the stresses of trying to cope with living in deteriorated dangerous circumstances, undermine effective caregiving (McLoyd, Aikens, & Burton, 2006). Compared to middle-SES parents, low-SES parents (even in developed countries) are less likely to provide children with stimulating learning experiences, such as reading (Feitelson & Goldstein, 1986) or appropriate play materials in the home (Gottfried, 1984). Lower-SES mothers converse less with their children, and in systematically less sophisticated ways, than middle-SES mothers do with their children (Hart & Risley, 1995; Hoff, Laursen, & Tardif, 2002).

To explore country-level correlates of mothers' and fathers' caregiving of girls and boys, we evaluated relations of gender differences in six common caregiving practices with national indicators of gender equality and economic development.

THIS STUDY

With these several considerations in mind, the present study documents mothers' and fathers' caregiving of daughters and sons in more than 170,000 families with children under 5 years of age in 39 LMIC around the world. We build on a previous study of country differences in mothers' cognitive and socioemotional caregiving in 28 LMIC (Bornstein & Putnick, 2012) by exploring the differences between mothers' and fathers' caregiving of their daughters and sons in 39 LMIC. This work was guided by two main questions. First, what are the prevalences of six caregiving practices in mothers and fathers of girls and boys in each country, and how do mothers and fathers and girls and boys compare on each? Second, how are gender differences in these caregiving practice related to country-level indicators of the nations' gender equity and economy?

METHODS

Participants

This study evaluates mothers' and fathers' caregiving to daughters and sons in 171,456 families in 39 LMIC (Table 5). Across countries, the average number of children under 5 in the family was 1.32 ($SD = .54$, range = 1–8). The target children averaged 28.79 months of age ($SD = 16.72$, range = 0–59), and 48.9% were girls. Girls and boys were similar in age, $M = 28.74$, $SD = 16.72$, for girls and $M = 28.84$, $SD = 16.72$, for boys, $t(171,448) = -1.26$, ns. Questions were usually answered by the child's biological mother (94.8%). Of the 5.2% of questionnaires that were completed by another female mother figure, 94.2% of families had no biological mother living in the household. Mothers averaged 29.66 years ($SD = 8.40$, range = 15–95), and the highest level of education they had completed was none or preschool for 32.4%, primary school/nonstandard curriculum/religious school for 30.3%, secondary/vocational/tertiary school for 31.9%, and higher for 5.4%. Mothers of girls were slightly but not meaningfully older ($M = 29.72$, $SD = 8.47$) and less educated ($M = 1.10$, $SD = .92$) than mothers of boys ($M = 29.60$,

TABLE 5
Sample Descriptive Statistics

Country	n	Child Age M	Child Age SD	Mother Education[a] M	Mother Education[a] SD	Number of Children Under 5 M	Number of Children Under 5 SD
High HDI							
Trinidad and Tobago	918	30.24	17.04	1.91	.53	1.20	.45
Montenegro	814	32.31	16.95	1.93	.65	1.30	.55
Serbia	2,868	29.84	17.06	1.66	.82	1.31	.54
Belarus	2,810	30.52	16.52	2.28	.45	1.09	.29
Macedonia	3,225	33.39	16.01	1.27	.75	1.41	.56
Albania	944	32.22	17.53	2.43	.57	1.15	.39
Kazakhstan	3,536	28.68	16.83	2.24	.45	1.25	.48
Bosnia and Herzegovina	2,704	31.04	16.35	1.76	.61	1.18	.40
Medium HDI							
Thailand	8,312	29.29	17.12	1.58	.79	1.12	.34
Jamaica	1,168	30.05	16.89	2.08	.44	1.20	.46
Belize	585	30.12	17.29	1.37	.72	1.35	.56
Suriname	1,732	30.97	17.04	1.49	.79	1.29	.52
Georgia	1,683	30.17	17.21	2.18	.73	1.21	.42
Syrian Arab Republic	7,553	28.92	15.95	1.32	.79	1.46	.62
Guyana	1,812	30.52	17.03	1.73	.60	1.36	.56
Mongolia	3,040	28.20	17.09	2.19	.60	1.16	.39
Vietnam	2,302	29.89	16.86	1.54	.78	1.15	.39
Uzbekistan	3,876	28.95	16.91	2.09	.29	1.29	.49
Kyrgyzstan	2,353	30.17	17.53	2.22	.43	1.27	.49
Vanuatu	1,278	28.08	16.56	1.29	.65	1.27	.50
Tajikistan	3,136	29.50	17.02	2.05	.37	1.36	.55
Laos	3,020	28.46	16.73	.80	.71	1.36	.55
Yemen	2,409	27.48	16.78	.47	.72	1.56	.67
Mauritania	5,889	26.96	15.88	.82	.66	1.45	.61
Ghana	2,624	28.80	16.71	.85	.90	1.31	.52
Bangladesh	26,206	31.07	16.85	1.03	.87	1.20	.43
Cameroon	4,450	27.37	16.41	1.05	.78	1.42	.59
Djibouti	1,547	29.95	15.77	.52	.78	1.45	.64
Low HDI							
Nigeria	12,220	27.50	16.15	.75	.91	1.35	.56
Togo	3,151	27.42	16.36	.61	.74	1.29	.49
Gambia	4,886	25.52	16.01	.51	.77	1.33	.52
Côte d'Ivoire	6,541	27.16	16.61	.46	.69	1.30	.52
Guinea-Bissau	4,485	26.96	16.14	.40	.66	1.29	.51
Burkina Faso	4,160	27.12	15.98	.17	.47	1.27	.47
Mozambique	8,148	27.62	16.78	.83	.63	1.39	.56
Central African Republic	6,565	26.47	16.76	.67	.69	1.42	.60
Sierra Leone	4,066	28.27	16.35	.31	.66	1.23	.46

(*Continued*)

TABLE 5. (*Continued*)

Country	n	Child Age		Mother Education[a]		Number of Children Under 5	
		M	SD	M	SD	M	SD
HDI N/A							
Iraq	10,587	28.01	16.98	1.11	.72	1.55	.69
Somalia	3,853	28.36	17.11	.41	.56	1.63	.71
TOTAL	171,456	28.79	16.72	1.10	.92	1.32	.54

Note. [a]*Mother education is rated as* 0 = *none or preschool,* 1 = *primary school, nonstandard curriculum, religious school,* 2 = *secondary, vocational, tertiary school, and* 3 = *higher education.*

$SD = 8.33$, and $M = 1.11$, $SD = .92$, respectively), ts(170,523.19 and 171,278) = 3.00 and −3.28, ps < .01 and .001, respectively.

Procedures

We use the Multiple Indicator Cluster Survey (MICS3), the Gender Relative Status Index (GRS; Beneria & Permanyer, 2010; Permanyer, 2010), the Gender Inequality Index (GII; UNDP, 2011), and the Human Development Index (HDI; UNDP, 2008). Additional information about the MICS3, GRS, GII, and HDI is available in Chapter II (Bornstein et al., 2016).

This study included only the responses from female caregivers about the caregiving mothers and fathers did with their children in the past 3 days. Six MICS3 items for each parent were each coded as 0 = mother/father did not take outside/play/sing songs/name, count, draw/tell stories/read books with the child, 1 = mother/father took outside/played/sang songs/named, counted, drew/told stories/read books with the child.

Analytic Plan

To assess how mothers and fathers compare on 6 caregiving practices, first, we explored whether mothers' and fathers' caregiving was correlated across countries. Next, to determine whether mothers and fathers parent their girls and boys similarly across countries, the 6 caregiving items were explored with binomial generalized estimating equations (GEE) with logit link functions. Parent gender (mother–father) was treated as a within-subjects factor to account for shared family variance, and child gender and country were treated as between-subjects factors. We modeled main effects and all two- and three-way interactions between and among parent gender, child gender, and country. Because country had 39 levels and the models were complex, the GEE models would not converge when country was included as a factor (Allison, 2008). Consequently, we split the file by country and computed parent gender by child gender models within countries. Finally, to assess how each caregiving practice in mothers and fathers of girls and boys related to country-level indicators of nations' gender equity and economy, the effect sizes for parent gender and child gender for each country (odds ratios) were correlated with the country's Gender Relative Status Index and Gender Inequality Index (with and without controlling for the country's Human Development Index) and with the Human Development Index.

For all analyses except correlations with the country-level gender indices, we used child age, number of children under 5 in the family, and maternal education as covariates. Parents were slightly more likely to take older than younger children outside, $r(342,524) = .04$, $p < .001$, name, count, or draw with them, $r(342,278) = .12$, $p < .001$, tell stories, $r(342,253) = .17$, $p < .001$, and read to them, $r(341,980) = .20$, $p < .001$. However, parents were slightly less likely to play with, $r(342,588) = -.02$, $p < .001$, and sing songs to, $r(342,384) = -.01$, $p < .001$, older than younger children. Parents with more children under 5 were slightly less likely to engage in all caregiving practices, $rs(341,980–342,588) = -.03$ to $-.07$, $ps < .001$. Finally, parents from families where mothers had higher education were more likely to engage in all caregiving practices, $rs(341,650–342,248) = .12–.29$, $ps < .001$. There were large differences in maternal education across countries, $F(38, 171,246) = 2,710.48$, $p < .001$, $\eta^2 = .376$, and controlling for maternal education accounts for across-country as well as within-country differences.

RESULTS

Overall, we found that within families, mother and father caregiving practices were correlated in most countries. Furthermore, there were robust, consistent differences by parent gender with mothers generally more likely than fathers to engage in caregiving practices, and there were only small, inconsistent differences in caregiving activities by child gender.

Mother–Father Agreement

Taking children outside for mothers and fathers was positively correlated overall ($\phi = .23$, $p < .001$) and in 32 of 39 countries ($\phi = .02–.48$, $ps < .001$), negatively correlated in Laos, Macedonia, Tajikistan, and Uzbekistan ($\phi = -.06$ to $-.10$, $ps < .001$), and unrelated in Albania, Georgia, and Kazakhstan (Supplemental Table S4.1). Play for mothers and fathers was positively correlated overall ($\phi = .35$, $p < .001$) and in 37 of 39 countries

($\phi = .06–.47$, $ps < .05–.001$) but unrelated in Laos and Tajikistan (Supplemental Table S4.2). Singing for mothers and fathers was positively correlated overall ($\phi = .25$, $p < .001$) and in 34 of 39 countries ($\phi = .07–.39$, $ps < .001$), negatively correlated in Laos and Tajikistan ($\phi = -.06$ to $-.11$, $ps < .01–.001$), and unrelated in Albania, Georgia, and Uzbekistan (Supplemental Table S4.3). Naming, counting, and drawing for mothers and fathers were positively correlated overall ($\phi = .33$, $p < .001$) and in 37 of 39 countries ($\phi = .08–.48$, ps $< .001$), negatively correlated in Laos ($\phi = -.14$, $p < .001$), and unrelated in Albania (Supplemental Table S4.4). Storytelling for mothers and fathers was positively correlated overall ($\phi = .28$, $p < .001$) and in 34 of 39 countries ($\phi = .04–.59$, $ps < .05–.001$), negatively correlated in Georgia, Laos, and Tajikistan ($\phi = -.07$ to $-.09$, $ps < .001$), and unrelated in Albania and Uzbekistan (Supplemental Table S4.5). Finally, reading for mothers and fathers was positively correlated overall ($\phi = .35$, $p < .001$) and in 37 of 39 countries ($\phi = .06–.51$, $ps < .001$), and negatively correlated in Laos and Tajikistan ($\phi = -.06$ to $-.07$, $ps < .01–.001$; Supplemental Table S4.6).

Group Differences by Parent and Child Gender

Take Outside

Overall, 59% of mothers and 30% of fathers reportedly took their children outside the yard, compound, or enclosure in the past 3 days (Figure 3; see Supplemental Table S4.1). More mothers than fathers reportedly took their child outside in 36 countries, more fathers than mothers in 1 country (Guinea-Bissau), and mothers and fathers did not differ

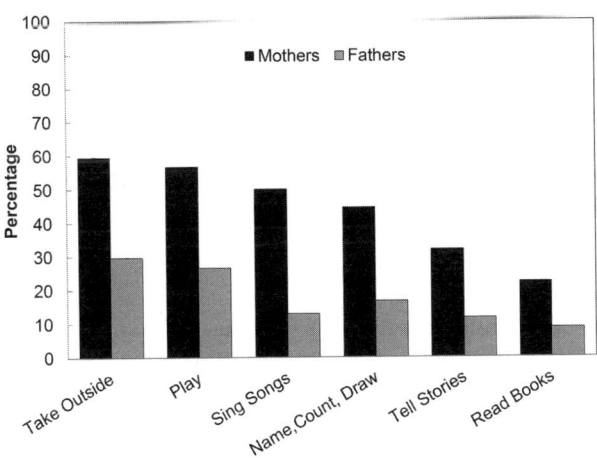

FIGURE 3.—Percentages of mothers and fathers who had engaged in each caregiving practice in the past 3 days. Standard errors were all $<.13$.

in 2 countries (Djibouti and Iraq; but see the interaction for Iraq). Parents reportedly took more boys than girls outside in 15 countries, and parents of girls and boys did not differ in the other 24 countries. Finally, there were significant parent gender by child gender interactions in 14 countries. Post hoc tests indicated that more fathers of boys took their child outside than fathers of girls in Bangladesh, Bosnia and Herzegovina, Burkina Faso, Central African Republic, Côte d'Ivoire, Iraq, Nigeria, Somalia, and Syria. More mothers of girls took their child outside than mothers of boys in Iraq, Nigeria, and Yemen, and more mothers of boys took their child outside than mothers of girls in Guinea-Bissau.

Play

Overall, 57% of mothers and 27% of fathers reportedly played with their children in the past 3 days (Figure 3; see Supplemental Table S4.2). More mothers than fathers reportedly played with their children in all 39 countries. Furthermore, parents reportedly played with more boys than girls in 7 countries (Bangladesh, Bosnia and Herzegovina, Burkina Faso, Côte d'Ivoire, Iraq, Serbia, and Thailand), and there were no differences by child gender in the other 32 countries. Finally, there were parent gender by child gender interactions for Iraq and Thailand. Post hoc tests indicated that more fathers of boys reportedly played than fathers of girls in Iraq and Thailand, but similar proportions of mothers of boys and girls played with their children in both countries.

Sing Songs

Overall, 50% of mothers and 13% of fathers reportedly sang songs to their children in the past 3 days (Figure 3; see Supplemental Table S4.3). More mothers than fathers reportedly sang songs in 38 of 39 countries; parents did not reportedly differ in Laos. Parents sang to more girls than boys in Macedonia, and to more boys than girls in Thailand. Finally, there were parent gender by child gender interactions in Bosnia and Herzegovina, Iraq, and Thailand. More fathers of boys reportedly sang than fathers of girls in Thailand, but mothers and fathers in Bosnia and Herzegovina and Iraq reportedly sang to approximately equal proportions of girls and boys (despite the significant interactions).

Name, Count, Draw

Overall, 44% of mothers and 17% of fathers reportedly named, counted, and drew with their child in the past 3 days (Figure 3; see Supplemental Table S4.4). More mothers than fathers reportedly had named, counted, and drawn in all 39 countries. There were also main effects of gender in 5 countries, with more parents reportedly naming, counting, and drawing with boys than girls in Bosnia and Herzegovina, Côte d'Ivoire, Ghana, Iraq, and Thailand. Finally, there were significant parent gender by child gender interactions in the same 5 countries, indicating that the main effects of gender were driven by fathers' interactions because more fathers of boys reportedly named, counted, and drew than fathers of girls, but mothers of girls and boys did not differ.

Tell Stories

Overall, 32% of mothers and 12% of fathers reportedly told their child stories in the past 3 days (Figure 3; see Supplemental Table S4.5). More mothers than fathers reportedly told their children stories in 37 of 39 countries, more fathers told stories than mothers in Guinea-Bissau, and mothers and fathers did not differ in Laos. There was a main effect of gender in Iraq, with stories being told more to boys than girls. There were also parent gender by child gender interactions for Guyana, Iraq, and Mozambique. Mothers reported that more mothers of girls told stories than mothers of boys in Guyana, more fathers of boys told stories than fathers of girls in Iraq, and there were no differences between mother and father storytelling to girls and boys in Mozambique.

Read Books

Overall, 22% of mothers and 9% of fathers reportedly read to their child in the past 3 days (Figure 3; see Supplemental Table S4.6). More mothers than fathers reportedly read to their child in 32 of 39 countries, and the percentages of mothers and fathers who read to their children in the past 3 days did not differ in the other 7 countries (2 of 20 medium-HDI countries and 5 of 10 low-HDI countries). In Iraq, there was a significant interaction between parent and child gender and a main effect of gender. In Sierra Leone and Thailand, there were also main effects of child gender. For all 3 countries with child gender effects, mothers reported that more boys had been read to than girls. In Iraq, mothers reported that more fathers of boys had read to their child than fathers of girls, but mothers of boys and girls did not differ.

Relations With National Indexes of Gender Equality and Economy

To assess whether differences between mothers' and fathers' caregiving with girls and boys reflected national gender or economic well-being disparities, we computed correlations of the effect sizes for parent and child gender derived from the models above for each country with national level GRS, GII, and HDI scores (Table 6). For parent gender, a larger effect size indicated that more mothers reportedly practiced that caregiving than fathers and a smaller effect size that fathers and mothers were more equal (or, rarely, slightly more fathers practiced that caregiving than mothers). For child gender, a larger effect size indicated that more parents reportedly practiced

TABLE 6

CORRELATIONS OF PARENT AND CHILD GENDER EFFECT SIZES WITH COUNTRY-LEVEL GENDER EQUALITY AND ECONOMIC DEVELOPMENT

	GRS	GII	HDI
Parent gender			
Take outside	.01	.30	−.05
Play	−.12	.19	−.07
Sing songs	.17	−.36	.19
Name, count, draw	.22	−.58***/−.49**,a	.40*
Tell stories	.33*/−.08	−.47*/−.06	.53**
Read	.58***/.18	−.64***/−.15	.70***
Child gender			
Take outside	.24	−.29	.35*
Play	−.13	−.06	.08
Sing songs	.06	−.21	.20
Name, count, draw	.21	−.48**/−.34	.37*
Tell stories	−.15	−.15	−.10
Read	.18	−.47*/−.11	.50**

Note. GRS, Gender Relative Status Index; GII, Gender Inequality Index; HDI, Human Development Index. Correlations after the slash control for the Human Development Index.
[a]For this analysis, Macedonia emerged as an influential outlier. When Macedonia was removed, the raw correlation between naming, counting, and drawing and GII was $r(25) = -.43$, $p < .05$, and the partial correlation controlling for HDI was $r(24) = -.25$, ns. * $p < .05$. ** $p < .01$. *** $p < .001$.

that caregiving with girls than boys, and a smaller effect size that more parents reportedly practiced that caregiving with boys than girls.

Neither the GRS, GII, nor HDI related to taking the child outside, playing, or singing songs by parent or child gender, with the exception of the child gender effect size for taking the child outside with the HDI. Countries in which more mothers practiced caregiving than fathers on naming, counting, and drawing, storytelling, and reading had higher gender equality on the GRS and/or the GII and human development on the HDI. For child gender, countries in which more parents of boys reportedly practiced caregiving than parents of girls on naming, counting, and drawing, and reading had higher gender inequality on the GII. However, countries with lower gender equality tended to have lower overall human development, and in the countries with lower gender equality, both mothers and fathers tended to caregive less with their children (e.g., fewer than 10% of mothers and fathers in low-HDI countries had read to their child) and, therefore, the difference between mothers and fathers was smaller. To remove the variance in the gender indices associated with overall economic level of the country, we controlled the GRS and GII correlations (first 2 columns of Table 6) for the HDI, and all effects attenuated to nonsignificance except for mother-father naming, counting, and drawing with the GII (but see Table 6 note).

DISCUSSION

Parents are responsible for developmentally important caregiving as children under 5 have limited agency. We studied six caregiving practices in mothers and fathers of girls and boys in over 170,000 families in 39 under-researched LMIC.

Mother and Father Caregiving of Girls and Boys in LMIC

Parents' practices are directed to meet the biological and physical needs as well as socioemotional and cognitive requirements of children. The six caregiving practices we studied are prominent, active, and enriching parental responsibilities that vary globally. In most countries, more mothers than fathers reportedly engaged in the six caregiving activities. The few significant differences in the parenting of young girls and boys were very small. There was some evidence of differential treatment of girls and boys by mothers and fathers (i.e., an interaction between parent and child gender), but these effects tended to be small. Overall, taking a child outside the home was the most prevalent form of caregiving, followed by playing, singing, naming, telling stories, and finally reading books.

In most mammalian species, females engage in more childcare, such as carrying the infant and foraging for food. In fact, actual male parenting is observed in less than 5% of mammal species (Moller, 2003). Anthropological evidence indicates that mothers are the primary caregivers of children in the vast majority of cultures. Despite dramatic increases in maternal labor force participation, mothers invest more hours in parenting, and they continue to outpace fathers. Although married fathers make greater investments in parenting, their investment, relative to mothers', has not increased since the 1990s. One study found that 55% of fathers and 64% of mothers reported that mothers were mainly responsible for basic childcare (Clutton-Brock, 1991; see also Coltrane, 1996).

The scattered and small differences in the treatment of young girls and boys were somewhat surprising. In these LMIC, there is often evidence that adult women have fewer opportunities and rights than men. Perhaps, in this young age group, girls and boys are reared similarly but differential treatment begins later in life. The few gender differences might also be an indication that this cohort of parents has shifted their ideologies to include similar treatment for their female and male children. Perhaps gender gaps will narrow even further as this cohort of children ages.

Country-Level Gender Equality and Economic Factors and Caregiving

What accounts for country-level differences in gendered caregiving in LMIC? To begin to address this question, we explored the GRS, GII, and HDI.

Gender differences in parenting were largely unrelated to national measures of gender equality but were sometimes related to a national measure of socioeconomic development. Country-level HDI related to gender differences in naming, counting, and drawing, storytelling, and reading. Notably, Halle et al. (2009) identified significant disparities in cognitive development as early as 9 months of age in a nationally representative U.S. sample based on low-income and low-maternal education.

Limitations

This study has limitations that raise additional questions about caregiving and gender in LMIC. Some general and specific limitations associated with the MICS are addressed in Chapter VII (Bornstein, Putnick, Bradley, Deater-Deckard, & Lansford, 2016). In addition, here we compare mothers' reports about themselves with their reports of their perceptions of their husbands/children's fathers. Reports on fathers must be understood in this light.

The MICS uses a limited number of specific and presumably universal (etic) items to quantify caregiving. This limitation has two consequences. First, it is useful to simply tally the different ways mothers and fathers stimulate their girls and boys, but their sum does not represent the broader dimension of parenting or even stimulation. The MICS items are important and helpful indicators, but they are nowhere near representative of the full range of caregiving practices. Second, caregivers in different countries may engage in other country-specific (emic) forms of caregiving that adequately substitute for specific MICS items. For example, among the Bengali of northern India, a mother peeling an orange for her child is a high expression of socioemotional caring (Rohner, 1994). Moreover, next to quantitative aspects of caregiving, qualitative aspects matter a great deal. In addition to considering the form and level of caregiving, it is critical to consider the content and timing of caregiving with respect to children's ongoing activities and development.

Conclusions and Implications

Caregiving varies among mothers and fathers and in small degree daughters and sons in LMIC. Caregiving has benefits as well as costs for offspring. Positive caregiving in terms of socialization and education promotes children's social and cognitive competencies and improves success in managing their lives. However, compromised caregiving jeopardizes optimal child development, especially among parents who lack the resources, knowledge, investment, or competencies to rear their young so as to augment individual and common good (Bugental & Grusec, 2006). Stereotypes can be powerful.

Caregiving matters. Consider book reading, a caregiving practice that was engaged in at a fairly low frequency. Of course, in these LMIC caregiving is often distributed socially, and so many caregivers (other than mothers and fathers) may be reading to children. In this sense (and in others), the MICS data set may underestimate actual caregiving experience of children. Moreover, as pointed out later, who reads with the child and the quality of their interactions may well outstrip quantity. Governments and NGOs alike inspire parents to read to children and expose them to books from early in life as early reading exposure provides a foundation for subsequent educational achievement in the school years. Shared book reading stimulates children's interest and provides opportunities for parents to create an interactive learning environment with their child. The frequency with which adults read to children in English or Spanish and the frequency of maternal labeling questions (e.g., What do you call this little animal?) while reading books together correlate positively with children's vocabulary in both languages (Quiroz, Snow, & Zhao, 2010). In HIC as well as LMIC, long-term benefits from high-quality early intervention programs to improve parenting in these domains include better health outcomes for children, higher verbal and mathematics achievement, greater success at school, improved employment and earnings, less welfare dependency, and lower crime rates (Adair, 1999; Deaton, 2001; UNESCO, 2005). Throughout the world, mothers and fathers are the first and primary individuals entrusted with caring for girls and boys and the central task of rearing children to become competent members of their society. Child survival is achieved through parental protection and provision, but child thriving is attained through caregiving that involves inculcating interpersonal competencies through socialization and sharing information through education. Mothers and fathers who engage their daughters and sons in caregiving activities also gain access to their children's emotional competence, social style, and learning potential, and they learn about their children's proclivities, capabilities, and limits. Such knowledge can lead to more appropriate and beneficial child interactions with the salutary result of enhanced child development and well-being.

SUPPORTING INFORMATION

Additional supporting information may be found in the online version of this article at the publisher's web-site

V. DAUGHTERS' AND SONS' EXPOSURE TO CHILDREARING DISCIPLINE AND VIOLENCE IN LOW- AND MIDDLE-INCOME COUNTRIES

Kirby Deater-Deckard and Jennifer E. Lansford

> This article is part of the issue "Gender in Low- and Middle-Income Countries," Bornstein, Putnick, Lansford, Deater-Deckard, and Bradley (Issue Authors). For a full listing of articles in this issue, see: http://onlinelibrary.wiley.com/doi/10.1111/mono.v81.1/issuetoc.

States Parties shall take all appropriate legislative, administrative, social and educational measures to protect the child from all forms of physical or mental violence, injury or abuse, neglect or negligent treatment, maltreatment or exploitation, including sexual abuse, while in the care of parent(s), legal guardian(s), or any other person who has the care of the child.

–Article 19. 1, Convention on the Rights of the Child
General Assembly resolution 44/25, 20 November 1989.

In early childhood, there is tremendous variation between families in the kinds and levels of discipline and aggressive or violent behaviors shown toward children by parents. Caregivers endorse a wide variety of beliefs regarding the appropriateness and utility of various forms of rewarding, punishing, and reasoning that they do with children in their efforts to redirect misbehavior and socialize more acceptable behavior. But does child gender influence the kinds and levels of nonviolent and aggressive or violent behaviors directed toward young children (2–4 year olds) by parents in low- and middle-income countries (LMIC)? And does the answer depend on national differences in indices of

---

Corresponding author: Kirby Deater-Deckard, Department of Psychological and Brain Sciences, University of Massachusetts, 441 Tobin Hall, Amherst, MA 01003. email: kdeaterdeck@umass.edu
DOI: 10.1111/mono.12227
© 2015 The Society for Research in Child Development, Inc.

gender equality and healthy human development? We sought to answer these questions using data from the UNICEF Multiple Indicator Cluster Survey (MICS3; UNICEF, 2009) data set.

NATIONAL AND CULTURAL VARIATION IN DISCIPLINE

There is remarkable variability within and between cultural groups and countries in attitudes and practices of child discipline and socialization (Bornstein & Lansford, 2010; Garcia-Coll & Magnuson, 1999; Mistry, Chaudhuri, & Diez, 2003). There is a wide array of punitive and harsh practices, as well as nonpunitive practices, that vary in prevalence and frequency across cultures. These include various forms of name calling, isolation, removal of potential rewards, reasoning, and physical punishment (Ember & Ember, 2005; Fung, 1999; Gershoff et al., 2010; Kim & Hong, 2007; Whiting & Whiting, 1975). At the same time, child attributes play a role in eliciting particular forms of discipline, with more aggressive or violent caregiver behaviors directed toward children who show higher levels of behaviors that are difficult to redirect or manage and that are emotionally aversive to caregivers (e.g., noncompliance, aggression, hyperactivity, impulsivity; Deater-Deckard, 2004).

Most of the research and policy work has focused on harsh practices. In 1989, the Convention on the Rights of the Child (CRC) was adopted by the United Nations (UN) General Assembly, and ratified by every country except the United States and Somalia. The CRC sets out international standards that must be met to protect children from abuse and exploitation, including in their homes, with the goal of eventually ending "adult justification of violence against children, whether accepted as 'tradition' or disguised as 'discipline'" (Pinheiro, 2006, p. 5). Physical and psychological violence toward children is defined by the UN as a violation of children's rights based on the CRC. As ratifying countries have examined their policies and laws, more than 100 have banned corporal punishment in schools, with 43 of these also banning it in all settings including homes (Durrant, 2008; endcorporalpunishment.org).

The current study is based on the United Nations Children's Fund (UNICEF) MICS3 survey (see Bornstein et al., 2016). It is an expanded analysis of Lansford and Deater-Deckard (2012), in which we examined four categories of caregiver responses to child behavior based on UN definitions, including nonviolent discipline, psychological aggression, physical violence, and severe physical violence. In the 2012 paper, we analyzed data from 24 LMIC that had complete MICS3 data at that time. We reported national differences in a variety of caregiver responses that were associated with between-country differences in human development indicators (e.g., maternal education), a pattern consistent with other international cross-cultural studies (Gershoff et al., 2010; Lansford et al., 2005).

GENDER DIFFERENCES IN DISCIPLINE

Over the past century, social science theories have attempted to address the question of whether males and females are qualitatively and quantitatively distinct in their psychological attributes, and whether these differences are socialized by parents (Shields, 1975). Prominent among theories of socialization are purported social learning mechanisms involving modeling and reinforcement of gender stereotypical behavior by parents of both genders, with caregiver motivation rooted in concern for bringing up the child in ways that make her or him a typical and healthy member of the broader culture and society (Bussey & Bandura, 1999). In a broader context, this reinforcement of "gender typical" behavior can be viewed as arising from and commensurate with biological and cultural co-evolution to yield survival advantages arising from sexual dimorphism in physical and psychological characteristics (Buss & Schmitt, 1993; Low, 1989). In contrast, among theories that emphasize gender similarities, the focus is on empirical evidence showing that variation within each gender group dwarfs between-group variance and does not indicate qualitatively different developmental and psychological processes for males and females for most attributes (Hyde, 2005; Jacklin, 1989).

What remains largely unknown is whether there are child gender differences in the patterns of caregiver responses to child misbehavior across a wide variety of countries and cultural groups. The goal of the current study is to address this gap. Do parents treat their young daughters and sons differently when it comes to discipline, punishment, and redirecting their behavior? Lytton and Romney's (1991) widely cited meta-analysis on studies of many aspects of parent–child interaction and relationship quality found little evidence for child gender differences in parental discipline practices or other aspects of childrearing, with a few exceptions. They reported a small effect of harsher forms of discipline for boys compared to girls, but they found this only in a handful of studies in non-North American Western nations.

Lytton and Romney (1991) reviewed research in the postwar decades through the 1980s, during a time of rapid shifts in gender roles in families and workplaces in Western and many non-Western nations (Mason & Jensen, 1995) that continue to play out today. Have studies conducted since then in Western samples shown different patterns of results since Lytton and Romney's (1991) meta-analysis? In short, the answer is no. In the subsequent studies, nearly all of which were conducted in the United States, different teams of researchers using different approaches to sampling and measurement have published results that converge on a very consistent pattern that basically replicates the Lytton and Romney meta-analysis finding. There is a very small gender difference that is sometimes statistically significant and sometimes not, depending on statistical power of the study. Statistical significance aside, the small gender difference effect size indicates that boys receive slightly higher levels of discipline, punishment, and harsh and violent caregiving responses compared to girls (Barkin, Scheindlin, Ip, Richardson, & Finch, 2007; Jansen et al., 2012; Lansford et al., 2010; MacKenzie, Nickklas, Brooks-Gunn, & Waldfogel, 2011; Regalado, Sareen, Inkelas, Wissow, & Halfon, 2004; Starrels, 1994; Straus & Stewart, 1999). MacKenzie et al. (2011) suggested that that differences in discipline and violent responses to girls versus boys might reflect different expectations regarding the behavior of girls and boys or differences in norms and attitudes regarding disciplining girls and boys. In addition, children who are difficult and engage in problem behaviors elicit more discipline from their parents than do children who are well behaved (Larzelere, 2000; Lytton, 1990). To the extent that boys engage in more problem behaviors than do girls (e.g., Archer, 2004), parents may be more likely to discipline and aggress against sons than daughters.

Although a very clear and consistent pattern has emerged in data for Western (primarily United States) families in high-income countries (HIC), relatively little is known in regard to other nations and particularly those in LMIC. There is widespread preference for sons over daughters in many cultures, especially those in LMIC in which sons are viewed as more critical to the family's socioeconomic resources in the future and girls are viewed as more critical to the family's social support in the future (Raley & Bianchi, 2006). There may be systematic differences in the degree of differential treatment of girls and boys as a function of prevailing cultural values regarding the relative equality of girls and boys. Yet to our knowledge, there has been no systematic analysis of the question regarding child gender differences that has spanned a variety of nations with representative samples. One possible exception is our prior study of 7–9 year olds, in which we examined caregiver nonviolent and violent caregiving behaviors in nine countries including China, Colombia, Italy, Jordan, Kenya, Philippines, Sweden, Thailand, and the United States. The analysis focused on two harsh caregiving scores that captured moderate and severe treatment. There were few significant gender differences, but the pattern of modest effect sizes indicated that boys were receiving slightly higher levels of harsher responses (Lansford et al., 2010).

However, the Lansford et al. (2010) study's sampling of countries and families did not include children in a large number and variety of LMIC. This highlights a long-standing point of concern in the literature, noted by Lytton and Romney (1991). Virtually none of the published research has investigated families in non-Western and LMIC. A second major concern, also noted by

Lytton and Romney, is that sample sizes have tended to be small, and there have been no large survey studies that have addressed whether there is a child gender difference across a wide range of LMIC. Little has changed in the literature in this regard since 1991. We have attempted to address both of these gaps in the current study.

THIS STUDY

Our main question was, Does child gender "matter" when it comes to the kinds and levels of nonviolent and aggressive or violent behaviors reported by caregivers of young children (2–4 year olds) in LMIC? Our secondary question was, Does the answer to the main question depend on internationally varying broader indices of gender equality and human healthy development? There is a well-established finding based on U.S. and other Western country samples that caregivers with less education and fewer socioeconomic resources place a higher value on child compliance and obedience, and more frequently use punitive forms of punishment (Deater-Deckard & Dodge, 1997; Peterson & Hann, 1999). Furthermore, in multiple countries, direct and indirect measures of resources (e.g., safe water and sanitation, healthcare), stress, and health have been shown to be correlated with each other, with overall levels of parental education and income, and potentially also related to children's exposure to harsh and violent treatment or abuse (Annerbäck, Svedin, & Gustafsson, 2010; Crouch & Behl, 2001; Lansford & Deater-Deckard, 2012). To examine relevant dimensions of country-level variation, in the current study, we examined three broad indicators of the degree to which one gender receives more resources and is favored over another in a country (Gender Relative Status index [GRS] and the Gender Inequality Index [GII]) and the overall level of resources and health in a country (Human Development Index [HDI]). These are described in more detail in Bornstein et al. (2016) and below.

It also is important to consider child age. There is considerable evidence, again based primarily on data from families in Western nations, that caregiver discipline and other parenting behaviors vary as a function of child age. These studies suggest that harsh forms of punishment increase then decrease over early childhood and peak at 3–4 years of age with severe forms of physical mistreatment persisting over middle childhood (Straus & Stewart, 1999), whereas verbalized reasoning increases steadily over early childhood as children become fluent speakers and begin to understand explanations for behaving in certain ways (Collins, Madsen, & Susman-Stillman, 2002). Because of these age-related variations in typical caregiver discipline practices, and because of the salience of discipline practices for behavioral management in early childhood, we constrained the age range from 2 to

4 years by including only families who had a target child in that range. We statistically controlled child age in the analyses by including this variable as a covariate.

METHODS

Participants

The sample included 37,132 mothers of 2.00- to 4.99-year-old children who had complete data in regard to maternal education level, child age, and child gender. Of these, 35,994 had data for discipline responses. Of the 41 countries with completed data sets at the time of analysis, 32 implemented the MICS3 discipline questionnaire, which was administered to mothers of children aged 2–14 years. Samples sizes varied across countries. The nine countries that did not administer the discipline questionnaire were Bangladesh, Burundi, Mauritania, Mozambique, Nigeria, Somalia, Thailand, Uzbekistan, and Vanuatu. Mongolia administered only some of the discipline questionnaire items and so was excluded from analyses involving those scores. As described above, we focused our analyses only on 2–4 year olds. Overall, children were 2.96 years old on average ($SD = .80$), and 49% were girls (gender coded as $0 = $ girl, $1 = $ boy). Among mothers, 25.4% had no formal education, 25.8% had a primary school education, 39.0% had a secondary school education, and 9.7% had more than a secondary school education. Child gender, age, and maternal education were independent (as described in Results and Table 7).

TABLE 7
Statistical Associations (R or Φ) Among Child Gender, Child Age, Mother Education Level, and Caregiver Responses

	1.	2.	3.	4.	5.	6.	7.
1. Child gender	–						
2. Child age	.00	–					
3. Mother education	.01**	.02***	–				
4. Nonviolence	−.03***	−.02***	.15***	–			
5. Psychological aggression	.03***	.05***	−.15***	−.73***	–		
6. Physical violence	.03***	.05***	−.14***	−.68***	.51***	–	
7. Severe violence	.02***	.04***	−.14***	−.22***	.25***	.28***	–
8. Need for physical punishment	.02***	.00	−.18***	−.22***	.24***	.27***	.21***

Note. Associations estimated as Pearson or point-biserial correlations for continuous–continuous and binary-continuous variable associations, and as phi coefficients for binary–binary variable associations. Two-tailed p-values,
**$p < .01$,
***$p < .001$.

Procedures and Measures

We used the MICS3, the GRS (Beneria & Permanyer, 2010; Permanyer, 2010), the GII (UNDP, 2011), and the HDI. Details about the MICS3, GRS, GII, and HDI are available in Bornstein et al. (2016).

Mothers completed the MICS3 household questionnaire. The discipline questions were an optional module included in the MICS3 household questionnaire. During the interview, the mother was told, "All adults use certain ways to teach children the right behavior or to address a behavior problem. I will read various methods that are used and I want you to tell me if you or anyone else in your household has used this method with (name of child) in the past month." The 11 responses included the following: (1) Explained why something (the behavior) was wrong; (2) gave the child something else to do; (3) took away privileges, forbade something, or did not allow the child to leave the house; (4) shouted, yelled at, or screamed at the child; (5) called the child dumb, lazy, or another name like that; (6) spanked, hit, or slapped the child on the bottom with a bare hand; (7) hit or slapped the child on the hand, arm, or leg; (8) shook the child; (9) hit the child on the bottom or elsewhere on the body with something like a belt, hairbrush, stick, or other hard object; (10) hit or slapped the child on the face, head, or ears; (11) beat the child up with an implement (hit over and over as hard as one could). Each item was coded as $0 =$ no, or $1 =$ yes; if the mother did not know or did not respond, that item was coded as missing data. These 11 items were adapted from the Parent–Child Conflict Tactics Scale (Straus, Hamby, Finkelor, Moore, & Runyan, 1998) and the WorldSAFE survey questionnaire (Sadowski, Hunter, Bangdiwala, & Munoz, 2004). A 12th item asked whether the mother believes that to bring up, raise, or educate the target child properly it is necessary to punish her or him physically; "don't know" and "no opinion" responses for this item were treated as missing data (UNICEF, 2006). Only items 1, 2, 4, 5, and 11 were asked in Mongolia.

In addition to the individual items, UNICEF (2006) established four indices based on these items to represent various behavioral responses regarding parental discipline and violence. Each index represented the presence versus absence of the relevant indicators within each index; in aggregate, the indices represented the percentage of children who experienced any of the relevant behaviors within each index's domain of response items. The nonviolence index included children whose mothers reported explaining why something was wrong, giving the child something else to do, or taking away privileges, but did not report any other responses. The psychological aggression index included yelled at the child, or called the child a name. The physical violence index included spanked with a hand, hit on the extremities, shaken, or hit with an object. Finally, the severe physical violence index included hit on the head or beat with an implement.

Analytic Plan

We first computed descriptive statistics and estimates of statistical associations between study variables for the entire sample. Second, to test whether there was a child gender difference in maternal responses, we examined statistical effects of child gender as well as country using logistic regression (child age and maternal education as covariates) in accounting for variance in each of the four response indices—nonviolence, psychological aggression, physical violence, and severe violence. Finally, we estimated correlations between between-country variance in the GII, GRS, and HDI indices and variance in (i.e., direction and magnitude of) the gender difference for each response index, represented by the odds ratio (OR) of the gender difference as estimated from the logistic regression equations. This final exploratory analysis allowed us to test whether between-country differences in GII/GRS/HDI were related to the degree of gender difference in maternal responses across the entire sample of countries.

RESULTS

As outlined in detail next, there are several major findings that emerged in the current analyses. First, there was wide variation between countries in childrearing discipline and violent behaviors that were reported by mothers. Second, reported behaviors covaried in expected ways; endorsement of harsher methods of discipline was associated with more frequent reporting of use of physical forms of punishment. Third, on average, boys received harsher treatment than girls, but the effect size was very small and was not consistent across countries.

Descriptive Statistics

Overall, the average number of endorsed behaviors was 3.73 ($SD = 2.40$), ranging from as few as 2.01 ($SD = 1.72$) in Kazakhstan to as many as 5.81 ($SD = 2.60$) in Yemen. In the whole sample, an average of 16.9% reported only nonviolent responses, 66.5% reported psychological aggression, 63.2% reported physical violence, and 17.0% reported severe violence. However, these behaviors varied widely by country, ranging from a low of 0.61% reporting severe violence in Kazakhstan to a high of 89.2% reporting psychological aggression in Yemen. Figure 4 shows the percentages of the total sample that reported that someone in the household engaged in that behavior toward the child in the last month for each gender. The overall pattern of frequency of each response, scores for the four indices (nonviolence, psychological aggression, physical violence, and severe violence), and the attitude item regarding the need for physical punishment,

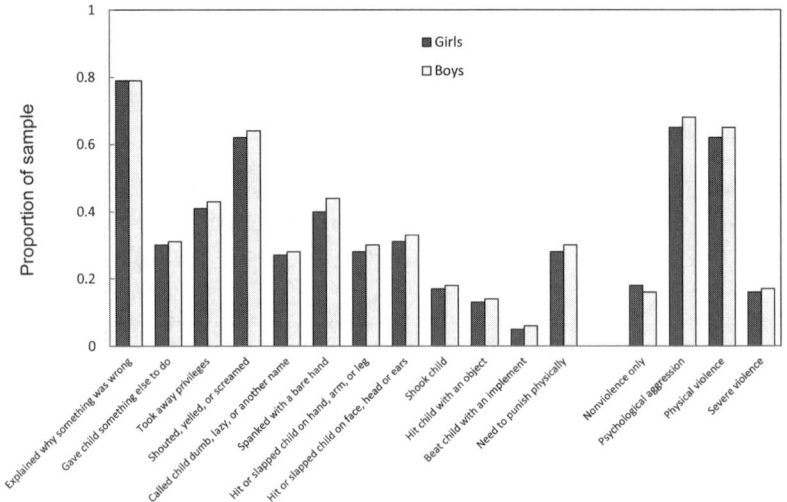

FIGURE 4.—Proportion of sample reporting that they or someone in their household had used each response with their child in the last month, by child gender. Standard errors too small to display, given very large sample size.

were very similar to that reported by Lansford and Deater-Deckard (2012), based on an earlier version of the MICS3 data set that included relevant data for 24 countries. Unique to the current monograph was the estimation of responses separately for girls and boys as shown in Figure 4. Visual inspection suggested slightly lower rates for females compared to males for most of the individual responses, scales, and the attitude item regarding need for physical punishment. Standard errors (too small to display given the sample size) ranged from 0.17% to 0.38%. The most commonly reported action was explanation (79% for mothers of girls and boys) and the least commonly reported action was to beat the child with an implement (5% for mothers of girls and 6% for mothers of boys). Nearly one-third of mothers endorsed the need for physical punishment.

We estimated the statistical associations between study variables, shown in Table 7. Depending on the nature (i.e., binary or continuous) of any two variables in question, we used the appropriate Pearson correlation, point-biserial correlation, or phi coefficient estimation method for each pair of variables. Child gender (0 = female, 1 = male) was independent of child age, and showed negligible but significant correlations with the other study variables suggesting slightly higher levels of attitudinal support and execution of harsh treatment for boys compared to girls. Older children were negligibly though significantly more likely to have mothers with more education, were less likely to experience nonviolence, and were more likely to experience psychological aggression, physical violence, and severe violence. More highly educated mothers reported more nonviolence and less aggression and violence. Finally, nonviolence was associated with less aggression and violence, and the aggression and violence indices covaried positively with each other. These associations were very similar for endorsement of the need for physical punishment compared to reports of use of severe violence.

Testing for Gender Differences

To examine child gender differences in responses, we used logistic regression and focused on the four major response indices and the endorsement of physical punishment attitude item. Each equation included as predictors: child age and maternal education (covariates), and child gender (0 = female, 1 = male), country (deviation from grand mean), and the two-way interaction between gender and country. Five models were estimated, one for each of the four response indices and a fifth for the physical punishment attitude item. Given the number of categories for the nominal country variable, none of the four models converged. Therefore, we removed country and its two-way interaction with child gender from the equation and estimated each equation again, first for the total sample then separately for each country. Descriptive statistics are shown in Tables 8 through 12.

For the total sample combined across countries, all five equations were significant, with significant effects at $p<.001$ for the covariates (maternal education and child age) and child gender in each equation. For nonviolence, $\chi^2(3) = 793.44$, $p<.001$, explaining 2.4% variance (Cox and Snell R^2) to 4.0% variance (Nagelkerke R^2); the effect size for child gender was OR = .817, $p<.001$, indicating that girls were more likely than boys to experience only nonviolence. For psychological aggression, $\chi^2(3) = 949.73$, $p<.001$, explaining 2.6% variance (Cox and Snell R^2) to 3.6% variance (Nagelkerke R^2); the effect size for child gender was OR = 1.123, $p<.001$, indicating that boys were more likely than girls to experience psychological aggression. For physical violence, $\chi^2(3) = 823.53$, $p<.001$, explaining 2.4% variance (Cox and Snell R^2) to 3.2% variance (Nagelkerke R^2); the effect size for child gender was OR = 1.168, $p<.001$, indicating that boys were more likely than girls to experience physical violence. For severe violence, $\chi^2(3) = 728.49$, $p<.001$, explaining 2.1% variance (Cox and Snell R^2) to 3.5% variance (Nagelkerke R^2); the effect size for child gender was OR = 1.112, $p<.001$, indicating that boys were more likely than girls to experience severe violence. Finally, for endorsement of the item regarding the need for physical punishment, $\chi^2(3) = 1168.91$, $p<.001$, explaining 3.3% variance (Cox and Snell R^2) to 4.7% variance (Nagelkerke R^2); the effect size for child gender was OR = 1.095, $p<.001$, indicating that mothers of boys were more likely than mothers of girls to endorse the need for physical

TABLE 8

NONVIOLENCE: DESCRIPTIVE STATISTICS AND GENDER DIFFERENCE ODDS RATIOS, BY COUNTRY AS A FUNCTION OF HUMAN DEVELOPMENT INDEX (HDI)

	Total		Girls		Boys		
	M (SD)	n	M (SD)	n	M (SD)	n	OR
High HDI							
Trinidad and Tobago	.1257 (.33189)	382	.1500 (.02531)	200	.0989 (.02219)	182	0.618
Montenegro	.3195 (.46688)	385	.3543 (.03626)	175	.2905 (.03140)	210	0.770
Serbia	.1705 (.37622)	1,302	.1778 (.01512)	641	.1634 (.01439)	661	0.941
Belarus	.1333 (.34001)	1,388	.1534 (.01398)	665	.1148 (.01186)	723	0.719*
Macedonia	.2253 (.41792)	1,518	.2349 (.01544)	745	.2160 (.01481)	773	0.892
Albania	.4848 (.50046)	361	.5000 (.03846)	170	.4712 (.03621)	191	0.911
Kazakhstan	.4054 (.49119)	1,110	.4429 (.02206)	508	.3738 (.01973)	602	0.752*
Bosnia/Herzegovina	.5867 (.49263)	1,217	.6050 (.01989)	605	.5686 (.02004)	612	0.842
Medium HDI							
Ukraine	.3700 (.48297)	1,446	.4260 (.01849)	716	.3151 (.01721)	730	0.602*
Belize	.2873 (.45375)	181	.2727 (.04775)	88	.3011 (.04783)	93	1.159
Jamaica	.0800 (.27161)	425	.0769 (.01913)	195	.0826 (.01819)	230	1.080
Suriname	.0900 (.28644)	611	.0855 (.01521)	339	.0956 (.01786)	272	1.117
Georgia	.1697 (.37565)	660	.1941 (.02272)	304	.1489 (.01889)	356	0.727
Syrian Arab Republic	.0745 (.26269)	2,576	.0731 (.00764)	1,162	.0757 (.00704)	1,414	1.030
Guyana	.1336 (.34046)	599	.1382 (.02805)	275	.1296 (.01869)	324	0.930
Mongolia	n/a		n/a		n/a		n/a
Vietnam	.0683 (.25251)	454	.0734 (.01770)	218	.0636 (.01591)	236	0.867
Kyrgyzstan	.4035 (.49102)	575	.4429 (.02927)	289	.3636 (.02849)	286	0.710*
Tajikistan	.2522 (.43453)	900	.2907 (.02117)	461	.2118 (.01952)	439	0.655*
Lao PDR	.2047 (.40373)	928	.2109 (.01904)	460	.1987 (.01847)	468	0.917
Yemen	.0462 (.21011)	714	.0459 (.01090)	370	.0465 (.01137)	344	0.980
Ghana	.0657 (.24798)	791	.0677 (.01284)	384	.0639 (.01214)	407	0.926

(*Continued*)

TABLE 8. (Continued)

	Total		Girls		Boys		OR
	M (SD)	n	M (SD)	n	M (SD)	n	
Cameroon	.0311 (.17361)	1319	.0423 (.00769)	686	.0190 (.00542)	633	0.434*
Djibouti	.2189 (.41393)	466	.2605 (.03000)	215	.1833 (.02447)	251	0.631*
Low HDI							
Togo	.0962 (.29508)	821	.0990 (.01470)	414	.0934 (.01444)	407	0.928
Gambia	.1276 (.33381)	917	.1096 (.01494)	438	.1441 (.01606)	479	1.335
Côte d'Ivoire	.0741 (.26198)	1,539	.0635 (.00907)	724	.0834 (.00969)	815	1.341
Guinea-Bissau	.2088 (.40668)	996	.2280 (.01816)	535	.1866 (.01816)	461	0.773
Burkina Faso	.0751 (.26374)	852	.0833 (.01350)	420	.0671 (.01205)	432	0.785
Central African Republic	.0911 (.28785)	2,107	.0889 (.00885)	1,035	.0933 (.00889)	1,072	1.047
Sierra Leone	.0705 (.25607)	1,135	.0737 (.01095)	570	.0673 (.01055)	565	0.928
HDI N/A							
Iraq	.1435 (.35062)	3,192	.1499 (.00906)	1,554	.1374 (.00851)	1,638	0.898

Note. n/a, not applicable. Descriptive statistics for total sample are presented in Figure 4 and in text.
*$p < .05$;
**$p < .01$.

TABLE 9
Psychological Aggression: Descriptive Statistics and Gender Difference Odds Ratios, by Country as a Function of Human Development Index (HDI)

	Total		Girls		Boys		OR
	M (SD)	n	M (SD)	n	M (SD)	n	
High HDI							
Trinidad and Tobago	.6577 (.47506)	409	.6065 (.03332)	216	.7150 (.03258)	193	1.586*
Montenegro	.5407 (.49895)	405	.5243 (.03682)	185	.5545 (.03359)	220	1.092
Serbia	.6250 (.48430)	1,400	.6230 (.01850)	687	.6269 (.01812)	713	0.991
Belarus	.7437 (.43675)	1,424	.7233 (.01713)	683	.7625 (.01564)	741	1.218
Macedonia	.5713 (.49505)	1,649	.5554 (.01735)	821	.5870 (.01712)	828	1.152
Albania	.0720 (.25874)	403	.0838 (.02010)	191	.0613 (.01652)	212	0.718
Kazakhstan	.3547 (.47857)	1,469	.3249 (.01809)	671	.3797 (.01719)	798	1.273*
Bosnia/Herzegovina	.2461 (.43088)	1,333	.2144 (.01590)	667	.2778 (.01737)	666	1.443**
Medium HDI							
Ukraine	.5186 (.49982)	1,529	.4597 (.01813)	757	.5764 (.01780)	772	1.665**
Belize	.4322 (.49663)	199	.4545 (.05030)	99	.4100 (.04943)	100	0.831
Jamaica	.7084 (.45500)	439	.6915 (.03266)	201	.7227 (.02908)	238	1.190
Suriname	.8141 (.38934)	624	.8075 (.02117)	348	.8225 (.02304)	276	1.106
Georgia	.5688 (.49555)	807	.5822 (.02607)	359	.5580 (.02349)	448	0.902
Syrian Arab Republic	.7723 (.41943)	2,837	.7548 (.01191)	1,305	.7872 (.01046)	1,532	1.214*
Guyana	.6549 (.47578)	649	.6645 (.02726)	301	.6466 (.02566)	348	0.923
Mongolia	.7217 (.44834)	1,272	.6943 (.01859)	615	.7473 (.01697)	657	1.309*
Vietnam	.8662 (.34078)	456	.8545 (.02382)	220	.8771 (.02142)	236	1.209
Kyrgyzstan	.3380 (.47338)	648	.3108 (.02571)	325	.3653 (.02683)	323	1.260
Tajikistan	.5806 (.49370)	1,042	.5627 (.02165)	526	.5988 (.02160)	516	1.162
Lao PDR	.6041 (.48927)	1,013	.6320 (.02159)	500	.5770 (.02183)	513	0.779
Yemen	.8921 (.31050)	732	.8892 (.01615)	379	.8952 (.01633)	353	1.083
Ghana	.7824 (.41289)	850	.7700 (.02073)	413	.7941 (.01937)	437	1.196

(Continued)

TABLE 9. (Continued)

	Total		Girls		Boys		OR
	M (SD)	n	M (SD)	n	M (SD)	n	
Cameroon	.8345 (.37172)	1,372	.8129 (.01463)	711	.8578 (.01360)	661	1.413*
Djibouti	.4336 (.49601)	565	.4147 (.03073)	258	.4495 (.02844)	307	1.135
Low HDI							
Togo	.7625 (.42579)	880	.7640 (.02015)	445	.7609 (.02047)	435	0.986
Gambia	.6829 (.46559)	987	.6904 (.02117)	478	.6758 (.02077)	509	0.951
Côte d'Ivoire	.8393 (.36738)	1,624	.8392 (.01324)	771	.8394 (.01258)	853	0.992
Guinea-Bissau	.5702 (.49528)	1,068	.5453 (.02080)	574	.5992 (.02207)	494	1.247
Burkina Faso	.7939 (.40470)	922	.7978 (.01896)	450	.7903 (.01876)	472	0.961
Central African Republic	.7775 (.41603)	2,238	.7783 (.01250)	1,105	.7767 (.01238)	1,133	0.998
Sierra Leone	.7795 (.41473)	1,193	.7629 (.01734)	603	.7966 (.01659)	590	1.201
HDI N/A							
Iraq	.7802 (.41419)	3,298	.7743 (.01043)	1,608	.7858 (.00998)	1,690	1.071

Note. Descriptive statistics for total sample are presented in Figure 4 and in text.
*$p < .05$;
**$p < .01$.

TABLE 10
Physical Violence: Descriptive Statistics and Gender Difference Odds Ratios, by Country as a Function of Human Development Index (HDI)

	Total		Girls		Boys		OR
	M (SD)	n	M (SD)	n	M (SD)	n	
High HDI							
Trinidad and Tobago	.7042 (.45698)	409	.6852 (.03167)	216	.7254 (.03221)	193	1.223
Montenegro	.5333 (.49950)	405	.4757 (.03682)	185	.5818 (.03333)	220	1.498*
Serbia	.6507 (.47693)	1,397	.6117 (.01863)	685	.6882 (.01737)	712	1.377**
Belarus	.6749 (.46859)	1,424	.6208 (.01858)	683	.7247 (.01642)	741	1.618*
Macedonia	.5931 (.49141)	1,649	.5700 (.01729)	821	.6159 (.01691)	828	1.205
Albania	.4516 (.49827)	403	.4293 (.03591)	191	.4717 (.03437)	212	1.158
Kazakhstan	.3009 (.45880)	1,469	.2742 (.01724)	671	.3233 (.01657)	798	1.263*
Bosnia/Herzegovina	.2784 (.44838)	1,329	.2613 (.01704)	666	.2956 (.01774)	663	1.217
Medium HDI							
Ukraine	.3780 (.48505)	1,529	.3461 (.01730)	757	.4093 (.01771)	772	1.349
Belize	.5729 (.49591)	199	.5556 (.05019)	99	.5900 (.04943)	100	1.153
Jamaica	.8398 (.36720)	437	.8250 (.02694)	200	.8523 (.02309)	237	1.248
Suriname	.7060 (.45597)	619	.6988 (.02484)	342	.7148 (.02718)	277	1.088
Georgia	.5488 (.49792)	809	.5583 (.02621)	360	.5412 (.02354)	449	0.928
Syrian Arab Republic	.7474 (.43456)	2,835	.7291 (.01232)	1,303	.7631 (.01087)	1,532	1.208*
Guyana	.7069 (.45554)	638	.6881 (.02702)	295	.7230 (.02420)	343	1.183
Mongolia	n/a		n/a		n/a		n/a
Vietnam	.7588 (.42830)	456	.7136 (.03055)	220	.8008 (.02605)	236	1.612*
Kyrgyzstan	.4496 (.49784)	645	.4143 (.02754)	321	.4846 (.02781)	324	1.338
Tajikistan	.5202 (.49983)	1,042	.5152 (.02181)	526	.5252 (.02200)	516	1.040
Lao PDR	.5405 (.49860)	1,012	.5140 (.02237)	500	.5664 (.02192)	512	1.237
Yemen	.8281 (.37755)	733	.8158 (.01991)	380	.8414 (.01947)	353	1.202
Ghana	.7291 (.44469)	849	.7251 (.02205)	411	.7329 (.02117)	438	1.065

(*Continued*)

TABLE 10. (Continued)

	Total		Girls		Boys		
	M (SD)	n	M (SD)	n	M (SD)	n	OR
Cameroon	.8078 (.39415)	1,379	.8056 (.01481)	715	.8102 (.01523)	664	1.035
Djibouti	.5664 (.49601)	565	.5620 (.03095)	258	.5700 (.02830)	307	1.014
Low HDI							
Togo	.7216 (.44847)	880	.7236 (.02122)	445	.7195 (.02156)	435	0.984
Gambia	.7188 (.44982)	985	.7149 (.02069)	477	.7224 (.01989)	508	1.057
Côte d'Ivoire	.7370 (.44038)	1,620	.7390 (.01584)	770	.7353 (.01514)	850	0.967
Guinea-Bissau	.6467 (.47823)	1,067	.6300 (.02019)	573	.6660 (.02124)	494	1.176
Burkina Faso	.5917 (.49178)	921	.5746 (.02336)	449	.6081 (.02249)	472	1.155
Central African Republic	.7294 (.44435)	2,236	.7231 (.01347)	1,105	.7356 (.01312)	1,131	1.074
Sierra Leone	.7167 (.45080)	1,193	.6965 (.01874)	603	.7373 (.01813)	590	1.196
HDI N/A							
Iraq	.6877 (.46351)	3,298	.6704 (.01173)	1,608	.7041 (.01111)	1,690	1.181*

Note. n/a, not applicable. Descriptive statistics for total sample are presented in Figure 4 and in text.
*$p < .05$;
**$p < .01$.

TABLE 11

Severe Violence: Descriptive Statistics and Gender Difference Odds Ratios, by Country as a Function of Human Development Index (HDI)

	Total	Girls	Boys	
	M (SD) n	M (SD) n	M (SD) n	OR
High HDI				
Trinidad and Tobago	.0293 (.16896) 409	.0231 (.01026) 216	.0363 (.01349) 193	1.556
Montenegro	.0591 (.23613) 406	.0541 (.01667) 185	.0633 (.01642) 221	1.154
Serbia	.0853 (.27943) 1,395	.0716 (.00987) 684	.0985 (.01118) 711	1.371
Belarus	.0119 (.10868) 1,423	.0059 (.00292) 683	.0176 (.00483) 740	2.845
Macedonia	.1511 (.35825) 1,648	.1585 (.01276) 820	.1437 (.01220) 828	0.907
Albania	.0620 (.24152) 403	.0628 (.01760) 191	.0613 (.01652) 212	0.967
Kazakhstan	.0061 (.07806) 1,469	.0060 (.00297) 671	.0063 (.00280) 798	1.050
Bosnia/Herzegovina	.0347 (.18300) 1,327	.0330 (.00693) 666	.0363 (.00728) 661	1.138
Medium HDI				
Ukraine	.0137 (.11642) 1,529	.0119 (.00394) 757	.0155 (.00446) 772	1.335
Belize	.0459 (.20984) 196	.0303 (.01732) 99	.0619 (.02459) 97	10.980
Jamaica	.0369 (.18865) 434	.0203 (.01007) 197	.0506 (.01427) 237	2.654
Suriname	.0744 (.26269) 618	.0559 (.01248) 340	.0971 (.01779) 278	1.879*
Georgia	.2339 (.42358) 808	.2201 (.02190) 359	.2450 (.02032) 449	1.138
Syrian Arab Republic	.2088 (.40656) 2,825	.2012 (.01114) 1,297	.2153 (.01052) 1,528	1.097
Guyana	.1577 (.36477) 653	.1650 (.02136) 303	.1514 (.01919) 350	0.902
Mongolia	n/a	n/a	n/a	n/a
Vietnam	.0943 (.29256) 456	.0773 (.01804) 220	.1102 (.02042) 236	1.458
Kyrgyzstan	.0266 (.16105) 639	.0221 (.00827) 317	.0311 (.00968) 322	1.413
Tajikistan	.1478 (.35506) 1,042	.1312 (.01473) 526	.1647 (.01635) 516	1.313
Lao PDR	.0809 (.27289) 1,013	.0720 (.01157) 500	.0897 (.01263) 513	1.280
Yemen	.4055 (.49132) 730	.3931 (.02512) 379	.4188 (.02637) 351	1.076
Ghana	.0638 (.24446) 847	.0730 (.01285) 411	.0550 (.01094) 436	0.753

(Continued)

TABLE 11. (Continued)

	Total	Girls	Boys	
	M (SD) n	M (SD) n	M (SD) n	OR
Cameroon	.2400 (.42722) 1,371	.2289 (.01576) 712	.2519 (.01692) 659	1.143
Djibouti	.2036 (.40301) 560	.2062 (.02529) 257	.2013 (.02307) 303	0.949
Low HDI				
Togo	.2375 (.42579) 880	.2270 (.01988) 445	.2483 (.02074) 435	1.130
Gambia	.1714 (.37705) 986	.1702 (.01724) 476	.1725 (.01675) 510	1.047
Côte d'Ivoire	.1789 (.38336) 1,599	.1908 (.01426) 760	.1618 (.01292) 839	0.843
Guinea-Bissau	.2085 (.40639) 1,065	.2049 (.01691) 571	.2126 (.01843) 494	1.051
Burkina Faso	.1630 (.36961) 920	.1473 (.01676) 448	.1780 (.01762) 472	1.259
Central African Republic	.2925 (.45501) 2,236	.2847 (.01359) 1,103	.3001 (.01362) 1,133	1.088
Sierra Leone	.2020 (.40167) 1,193	.2023 (.01637) 603	.2017 (.01653) 590	0.985
HDI N/A				
Iraq	.2768 (.44750) 3,298	.2568 (.01090) 1,608	.2969 (.01111) 1,690	1.229*

Note. n/a = not applicable. Descriptive statistics for total sample are presented in Figure 4 and in text.
*$p < .05$;
**$p < .01$.

TABLE 12
NEED TO PHYSICALLY PUNISH: DESCRIPTIVE STATISTICS AND GENDER DIFFERENCE ODDS RATIOS, BY COUNTRY AS A FUNCTION OF HUMAN DEVELOPMENT INDEX (HDI)

	Total	Girls	Boys	
	M (SD) n	M (SD) n	M (SD) n	OR
High HDI				
Trinidad and Tobago	.2739 (.44654) 387	.2475 (.03044) 202	.3027 (.03387) 185	1.316
Montenegro	.0509 (.22005) 393	.0506 (.01647) 178	.0512 (.01506) 215	1.006
Serbia	.1096 (.31253) 1,341	.0962 (.01145) 665	.1228 (.01263) 676	1.260
Belarus	.1439 (.35109) 1,397	.1377 (.01334) 668	.1495 (.01322) 729	1.088
Macedonia	.0727 (.25973) 1,513	.0530 (.00816) 755	.0923 (.01052) 758	1.864**
Albania	.0410 (.19860) 390	.0435 (.01508) 184	.0388 (.01349) 206	0.828
Kazakhstan	.0634 (.24373) 1,420	.0602 (.00935) 648	.0661 (.00895) 772	1.105
Bosnia/Herzegovina	.0682 (.25225) 1,275	.0651 (.00972) 645	.0714 (.01027) 630	1.152
Medium HDI				
Ukraine	.1156 (.31985) 1,436	.1013 (.01132) 711	.1297 (.01248) 725	1.323
Belize	.2564 (.43777) 195	.2474 (.04404) 97	.2653 (.04483) 98	10.072
Jamaica	.3356 (.47276) 432	.3232 (.03332) 198	.3462 (.031170) 234	1.126
Suriname	.1867 (.38998) 616	.1760 (.02065) 341	.2000 (.02416) 275	1.202
Georgia	.1275 (.33374) 753	.1335 (.01856) 337	.1226 (.01610) 416	0.895
Syrian Arab Republic	.9352 (.24623) 2,870	.9265 (.00718) 1,320	.9426 (.00591) 1,550	1.288
Guyana	.2722 (.44542) 643	.2776 (.02594) 299	.2674 (.02390) 344	0.952
Mongolia	.1423 (.34948) 1,230	.1313 (.01387) 594	.1526 (.01427) 636	1.216
Vietnam	.3463 (.47603) 953	.3182 (.02119) 484	.3753 (.02238) 469	1.253
Kyrgyzstan	.0574 (.23282) 627	.0351 (.01043) 313	.0796 (.01530) 314	2.442*
Tajikistan	.1092 (.31201) 971	.1165 (.01439) 498	.1015 (.01390) 473	0.855
Lao PDR	.1839 (.38761) 995	.1984 (.01805) 489	.1700 (.01671) 506	0.822
Yemen	.4372 (.49640) 709	.4622 (.02595) 370	.4100 (.02675) 339	0.763
Ghana	.4609 (.49876) 844	.4583 (.02470) 408	.4633 (.02391) 436	1.010

(*Continued*)

TABLE 12. (Continued)

	Total		Girls		Boys		OR
	M (SD)	n	M (SD)	n	M (SD)	n	
Cameroon	.4357 (.49604)	1,338	.4465 (.01891)	692	.4241 (.01946)	646	0.924
Djibouti	.3258 (.46913)	534	.2898 (.02904)	245	.3564 (.02822)	289	1.350
Low HDI							
Togo	.3099 (.46274)	855	.2841 (.02170)	433	.3365 (.02303)	422	1.286
Gambia	.3009 (.45889)	977	.3100 (.02133)	471	.2925 (.02024)	506	0.949
Côte d'Ivoire	.3768 (.48474)	1,587	.3806 (.01769)	754	.3733 (.01677)	833	0.960
Guinea-Bissau	.2215 (.41544)	1,034	.2156 (.01752)	552	.2282 (.01914)	482	1.080
Burkina Faso	.4004 (.49026)	904	.3900 (.02325)	441	.4104 (.02289)	463	1.084
Central African Republic	.2456 (.43056)	2,178	.2472 (.01316)	1,076	.2441 (.01295)	1,102	0.988
Sierra Leone	.5495 (.49775)	1,181	.5260 (.02045)	597	.5736 (.02048)	584	1.209
HDI N/A							
Iraq	.2369 (.42524)	3,183	.2358 (.01078)	1,552	.2379 (.01055)	1,631	1.023

Note. Descriptive statistics for total sample are presented in Figure 7 and in text.
*$p<.05$;
**$p<.01$.

punishment. The magnitudes of the effect sizes for child gender were very small, and statistically significant only because of the large sample size.

The equations for the four behavioral response scales and the attitude item were estimated again, separately for each country. The ORs for the child gender effect are shown in Tables 8 through 12. The OR is an effect size representing the magnitude and direction of the gender difference from the logistic regression equations. An OR < 1 indicated a higher percentage for girls compared to boys, and >1 indicated a lower percentage for girls compared to boys. The range of effect sizes indicated that the pattern of gender differences was from "no gender difference" to "harsher treatment of boys." With Mongolia excluded from three equations due to missing data, this resulted in 157 equations being estimated. As these tables show, most of the ORs were not significant, although the effect sizes (ignoring p-values) as well as the significant effects all indicated harsher treatment of boys compared to girls (i.e., OR for nonviolence was <1, and OR for harsh psychological or physical treatment was >1).

Exploring Country-Level Correlates of the Gender Difference

Although gender differences were very small, the magnitude of the difference (estimated as an OR and shown in Table 8) varied between countries, ranging from 0.60 to 1.34 for nonviolence, 0.72 to 1.44 for psychological aggression, 0.93 to 1.62 for physical violence, 0.90 to 2.85 for severe violence, and 0.76 to 2.44 for the attitude item regarding the need for punishment. In the final set of analyses, we examined whether the estimated gender difference within each country (represented by the ORs reported in Tables 8 through 12) was associated with between-country variance in HDI, GRS, and GII. For this analysis, the sample size was the number of countries rather than the number of individual participants.

We estimated correlations between the OR values on all four response scales and the HDI, GRS, and GII; the correlations are shown in Table 13. A

TABLE 13

Correlations Between OR on Four Discipline Response Scales and Human Development Index (HDI), Gender Relative Status Index (GRS), and Gender Inequality Index (GII)

	HDI	GRS	GII
Nonviolence	−.19	−.39*	.37*
Psychological aggression	.18	.28	−.24
Physical violence	.48**	.59***	−.44*
Severe violence	.40*	.44*	−.18

Note. $df = 28$ or 29. Two-tailed p-values.
*$p < .05$,
**$p < .01$,
***$p < .001$.

very consistent pattern emerged. Two or all of the HDI, GRS, and GII indices were significantly correlated with the magnitude of the OR for nonviolence, physical violence, and severe violence. The significant correlations were moderate in magnitude, ranging from ±.37 to .59. Recall that the overall pattern for the violence scales suggested no gender difference or that a higher percentage of boys than girls were exposed. Therefore, the pattern of correlations with HDI, GRS, and GII suggested that boys were more likely to be recipients of violence compared to girls in countries with higher HDI and gender equality scores. However, this should be interpreted within the broader context of the previous analyses that showed very modest gender differences within each country and overall in the sample.

DISCUSSION

Gendered patterns of behavior reflect transactions between biological and environmental influences that arise in part from the evolution of sexually dimorphic physical and psychological attributes (Buss & Schmitt, 1993). These influences include the socialization effects of mothers and fathers on daughters and sons, including reinforcement, punishment, and modeling of behavior that contributes to individual differences in behavior (Bussey & Bandura, 1999). In early childhood, key aspects of socialization include types and frequencies of various discipline practices used by caregivers. Thus, our primary aim in the current study was to test whether there were child gender differences in the frequencies of various types of caregiver responses to child misbehavior. We answered this question using a large and very diverse sample of respondents in LMIC. To our knowledge, this is the first study to examine this question with this many representative national samples. By comparison, previous studies have relied on community samples or larger national cohorts from HIC including the United States, Canada, and other non-North American "Western" nations—a major gap in the childrearing and socialization literatures (Henrich, Heine, & Norenzayan, 2010).

There was wide variation in the prevalence of the distinct caregiver responses. From the most to least prevalent (Figure 4), responses included the following: explanation, yelling, spanking with hand, removing privileges, hitting on head, giving something else to do, hitting body, name calling, shaking, hitting with object, and beating with an implement. These 11 indicators were aggregated into four indices based on UN definitions including nonviolence, psychological aggression, physical violence, and severe violence. Analysis of the covariation between child age, gender, maternal education level, and the caregiver response indices (Table 7) showed that child gender and age both had negligible associations with caregiver responses (i.e., coefficients in the ±.02–.05 range), with larger but still modest associations found for maternal education (±.14–.18 range). Although not the focus of the current monograph, it also is worth bearing in mind that we reported considerable between-country variance in the indices in a prior report based on a smaller number of countries in the MICS3 data set (Lansford & Deater-Deckard, 2012).

Child gender accounted for only trivial amounts of variance in caregiver responses, spanning nonviolent to violent behaviors. This was most evident in the data in Tables 8 through 12 in which the ORs representing the gender difference on each response index within each country were presented. Many of the ORs were near 1.0, indicating no difference for girls and boys. Furthermore, in spite of the statistical power afforded by the large samples within each country, only 25 out of 157 estimated ORs were statistically significant. If a more conservative alpha level of $p < .01$ was used to account for inflated type-1 error arising from multiple comparisons, only four of the 157 estimated effects were significant. Thus, although it was clear that boys were more often the recipients of punitive and harsh caregiving behaviors compared to girls, this difference was very small, and the small effect sizes were not consistent across countries or response indices. The overall pattern of harsher treatment of boys compared to girls is consistent with theory and prior research indicating that there may be distinct norms and punishment of behavior deemed inappropriate for females and males (e.g., Lytton, 1990; MacKenzie et al., 2011), but strong evidence for such theories in the current study was thin at best.

The impetus for the current study was based in part on our reading of the seminal meta-analysis by Lytton and Romney (1991) who reported little evidence for child gender differences in caregiving behaviors. One of their exceptions, however, was a small effect of harsher punishment of boys than girls, yet even this effect was not robust across countries. Studies published since this 1991 meta-analysis have shown a similar pattern overall. For example, in the National Survey of Children, parents were asked to report on the frequency of 11 nonviolent and violent verbal and physical caregiver behaviors (Starrels, 1994). There were few significant gender differences, and when present, the effect sizes were small and generally suggestive of slightly higher levels directed at boys than girls. In a large national survey of parents of 0–2 year olds in the United States, there was no statistically significant gender difference, although again the data suggested slightly higher levels of verbal and physical behaviors toward boys than girls (Regalado et al., 2004).

The same pattern has been found in diverse U.S. samples of high-risk families (MacKenzie et al., 2011) and general pediatric practice clients (Barkin et al., 2007). However, some studies of Western samples have shown the gender difference to be significant. A Dutch study found a statistically significant difference showing higher levels of harsh verbal and physical behaviors directed at boys (Jansen et al., 2012). An older study of U.S. families also found a significant difference (Straus & Stewart, 1999). Yet, even in the studies that have reported significant effects, the effect sizes generally have been modest. Thus, the current study's results are very consistent with the empirical literature. Furthermore, they are most consistent with a gender similarities hypothesis (Hyde, 2005), which suggests that variation in socialization experiences and developmental outcomes lies largely within, rather than between, female and male gender groups.

Exploratory analysis of the direction and magnitude of the gender difference effect sizes revealed some evidence of a pattern of a larger gender difference in harsh treatment and severe violence in countries with higher HDIs and more equitable treatment of males and females. As reported in Lansford and Deater-Deckard (2012) and evident in the means shown in Table 8, among the countries with higher HDI (and co-occurring higher levels of gender equality as indicated by the GRS and GII), smaller proportions of both girls and boys were treated harshly compared to countries with lower HDI and less equitable treatment of males and females. Within this context of lower rates of harsh treatment overall in higher HDI countries with more gender equality, boys were more likely to be treated harshly than were girls. We know of no theory or prior empirical research that would predict such an effect. Perhaps, more importantly, the vast majority of the estimated ORs within each country were not significantly different from zero, and the overall gender difference effect size was very modest. Therefore, the results presented in Table 13 should be interpreted with caution and in the broader context of a very small gender difference.

Limitations

This study has limitations that raise additional questions about gender in LMIC. Some general and specific limitations associated with the MICS are addressed in Bornstein, Putnick, Bradley, Deater-Deckard, and Lansford (2016). Thus, there are a number of caveats to consider when interpreting the current study's results. It is important to bear in mind that there are likely to be between- and within-country and culture differences in whether caregivers deem each of the various behavioral responses as appropriate, normative, acceptable, or necessary—variation that can make direct comparisons of countries and cultures more challenging to interpret because respondents' attitudes and beliefs about these behaviors might influence their willingness to report certain practices (i.e., social desirability biases for reporting more severe behaviors). Another limitation of the study was the almost exclusive reliance on female caregivers, typically the biological mothers of the target children in the MICS3 sample. There were very few male caregiver respondents, and as a result we could not examine parent gender differences.

However, it may be the gender composition of the parent–child dyad that matters most (compared to examining child gender on its own, as we have done), when examining gender differences in caregiving behaviors. That is, the largest differences in childrearing practices may be found when comparing fathers of sons to mothers of daughters (Starrels, 1994). Another related matter is that larger gender differences may be evident when one examines within-family differential treatment of sibling girls and boys, which was not an option because we did not have sibling data in the MICS3 data set. More generally, a limitation of prior meta-analyses and reviews (including Lytton & Romney, 1991) and the current work is that the measures are largely devoid of "context"; they capture general aspects of caregiving behaviors that may not capture important context-specific fluctuations or differences in parenting that could be important. If true, one might find larger gender differences in particular contexts—differences that may or may not generalize across broader cultural and national contexts. Finally, an even more fundamental limitation in measurement is that the binary response format of the indicators did not permit more fine-grained analysis of the variation in frequency and timing of the caregiver behavioral responses.

The current study has a number of strengths. Most importantly, we analyzed data on large representative samples of caregivers and young children in many non-Western LMIC, thereby addressing a major gap in the literature identified by many developmental and family science researchers (Henrich et al., 2010; Lytton & Romney, 1991). The MICS3 data set represents a unique resource that could not be built by even a large research team on its own.

Conclusions and Implications

Although our analysis of MICS3 has thoroughly examined mean differences in discipline experiences and exposure to violence, it remains to be seen whether there are meaningful child gender differences in the correlates of these caregiving environment indicators. Future research should more thoroughly examine child gender as a moderator of the links between the wide variation observed in caregiver behaviors and child developmental and health outcomes. In addition, future research also should focus on comparison of temporal trends in the MICS data sets, spanning prior assessments and the current MICS4 assessment that is nearing completion. Testing for potential historical trends in the patterns of child gender differences in caregiving experiences in early childhood would be very illuminating, with respect to hypothesis generation for testing theories about cultural and national influences on child caregiving norms and behaviors. Given the large proportion of both girls and boys who continue to experience psychological aggression and physical violence in their homes, it is clear that the goals of protecting children from all forms of physical or mental violence, injury or abuse outlined in the CRC have not yet been realized fully. The CRC further calls for the establishment of social programs to provide support for children and parents to prevent and intervene in cases of child maltreatment. Our findings suggest that girls and boys are equally in need of such protections and point to particular countries in which efforts are most needed, given high rates of reported psychological aggression and physical violence (as reported in Table 8 and in Lansford & Deater-Deckard, 2012). Furthermore, the current study's findings converge with the extant literature to show that nearly all variation overlaps for girls and boys in every country, regardless of GRS or GII or national HDI. Cultural groups that show large child gender differences in caregiver discipline and punishment of young children are exceptions that prove the rule: on average, young girls and boys are disciplined, punished, and physically abused similarly around the world, and as a result, these caregiving behaviors are not likely to account for group-level gender differences in child attributes and developmental outcomes.

VI. GIRLS' AND BOYS' LABOR AND HOUSEHOLD CHORES IN LOW- AND MIDDLE-INCOME COUNTRIES

Diane L. Putnick and Marc H. Bornstein

> This article is part of the issue "Gender in Low- and Middle-Income Countries," Bornstein, Putnick, Lansford, Deater-Deckard, and Bradley (Issue Authors). For a full listing of articles in this issue, see: http://onlinelibrary.wiley.com/doi/10.1111/mono.v81.1/issuetoc.

States Parties recognize the right of the child to be protected from economic exploitation and from performing any work that is likely to be hazardous or to interfere with the child's education, or to be harmful to the child's health or physical, mental, spiritual, moral or social development.

–Article 32.1, Convention on the Rights of the Child
General Assembly resolution 44/25, 20 November 1989.

Children in impoverished households in low- and middle-income countries (LMIC) often contribute to their family's welfare by managing household responsibilities while parents work outside the home or by engaging in employment themselves. UNICEF (2007a) estimated that one in six children aged 5–14 years was involved in child labor. However, estimates vary widely because of inconsistent definitions of child labor. Some definitions of child labor include only paid work outside the home and others include unpaid work, family work, and excessive household chores as child labor because each type has the same impact on child school attendance, health, and well-being (ILO, 2004,

---

Corresponding author: Diane L. Putnick, Child and Family Research, *Eunice Kennedy Shriver* National Institute of Child Health and Human Development, 6705 Rockledge Drive, Suite 8030, Bethesda, MD 20892. email: putnickd@mail.nih.gov
DOI: 10.1111/mono.12228
© 2015 The Society for Research in Child Development, Inc.

2009). Girls are also more likely to be involved in excessive housework than boys (Huebler, 2008). In this chapter, we use a broad definition of child labor and compare the rates of different types of labor in girls and boys in 38 LMIC.

THREE TYPES OF CHILD LABOR

Child labor is often divided into three major categories: paid or unpaid work outside the home, family work, and housework. Children's work outside the home has received the most empirical attention. Work outside the home is itself divided into three broad sectors of agriculture (69% of economically active children; such as farming, fishing, and forestry), services (22%; such as trade including street selling or begging, domestic, restaurant, and transportation work), and industry (9%; such as manufacturing, mining, construction, and public utility work; Hagemann, Diallo, Etienne, Mehran, 2006). These kinds of work outside the home can be paid or unpaid. Family work consists of any (usually unpaid) work that children do for the family. Often, family work is agricultural (Webbink, Smits, & de Jong, 2010), but it also includes work for any other type of family-owned business. Finally, housework, or household chores, includes childcare, cleaning, cooking, laundry, shopping, fetching water and wood, and home maintenance. Housework is considered to be a hidden form of child labor because it is unpaid and it often goes unreported (Gibbons, Huebler, & Loaiza, 2005; Webbink et al., 2010). UNICEF (2006) considers housework to be child labor if the child engages in 4 or more hours per day (28 hr/week).

CHILD LABOR LEGISLATION

The International Labor Organization (ILO, 2012, p. 1) defines child labor broadly as any "work that deprives children of their childhood, their potential, and their dignity, and that is harmful to physical and mental development." The ILO also established global standards to protect children from child labor. ILO Convention No. 138, ratified by 161 countries, set the minimum age for child labor at 15 (ILO, 1973), and ILO Convention No. 182, ratified by 174 countries, identified the "worst forms" of child labor as slavery, child trafficking, use of children in armed conflict, prostitution, drug trafficking, and any work which is likely to harm the health, safety, or morals of children (ILO, 1999). Because of the wording of ILO Convention No. 182, agricultural work, the most common form of child labor (Hagemann et al., 2006), is often considered to be a "worst form" on account of the risk of injury and exposure to pesticides (Woolf, 2002). Following the introduction of ILO conventions, the number of children engaged in child labor, and especially the number of children working in hazardous conditions, has decreased (Hagemann et al., 2006). However, Dessy and Pallage

(2005) argued that a complete ban on the worst forms of child labor, without programs designed to counter the economic losses of the ban, only punishes families who rely on their child's income to survive.

WHY CHILDREN WORK

Despite hazards associated with child labor, many children still work. For some children, there is little distinction between work and play (Harkness & Super, 1986). Children's play may revolve around the "useful" activities that they see adults do. Consequently, children who watch adults carry wood may also carry smaller bundles of wood as a manner of play that has the benefit of helping the household. Just as children from developed countries pretend to drive the carpool and carry a briefcase around the house, children who live on subsistence farms in LMIC may pull weeds and water plants. Furthermore, children may engage in gendered work behavior because they pattern their play and work habits after the same-sex parent (Bussey & Bandura, 1999; Whiting & Whiting, 1975).

When Nigerian children were asked about the benefits of working, the most common reasons cited were supporting the family and having money to pay for school or to learn a trade (Omokhodion, Omokhodion, & Odusote, 2006). For children in Bangladesh, Guatemala, El Salvador, Ethiopia, Nicaragua, and the Philippines, the two most common benefits of working were earning money and supporting the family (Woodhead, 1999). Parents may employ their children in farm work because they cannot afford to pay outside workers (Dumas, 2007). Working mothers in LMIC may also have limited childcare options, leading them to use their older children to care for younger children (Mehra, Kurz, & Paolisso, 1992). However, the root cause of most child labor is generally accepted to be poverty (Dessy & Pallage, 2005; Jensen & Nielsen, 1997).

CHILD LABOR AND POVERTY

Child labor is more common in LMIC than high-income countries (HIC; Dorman, 2001; Fares & Raju, 2007). The countries included in this study all constitute LMIC (UNICEF, 2006). Although there is considerable variation within individual countries, children and caregivers in LMIC are likely to have a low standard of living (World Bank, 2012) and to command relatively few material resources (Bradley & Putnick, 2012), and they are unlikely to have access to governmentally sponsored social assistance programs (World Bank, 2012). Consequently, children in LMIC may work because their families need them to work to survive. Galli (2001) suggested that child labor contributed somewhere between 10% and 20% of family income, depending on the location. Considering the indirect contributions of unpaid family work (e.g., family farm or business work) and household chores (e.g., childcare), 10%–20% may be a drastic underestimate.

That said, child labor may perpetuate poverty. Children who work or spend many hours taking care of household responsibilities are less likely to attend school (Beegle, Dehejia, & Gatti, 2009; Fares & Raju, 2007; Gibbons, Huebler, & Loaiza, 2005; Guarcello, Lyon, & Rosati, 2008; Huebler, 2008). Furthermore, a study in Ghana suggested that it is not just school enrollment or attendance that are affected by child labor, but also math and reading achievement for those in school. Controlling for a host of family and personal variables, Heady (2003) demonstrated that work outside the home, more so than housework or work at home, had a negative relation with math and reading test performance in 9- to 18-year-olds. Orazem and Gunnarsson (2003) replicated these findings for working children in Latin American countries. Finally, in a retrospective study, Emerson and Souza (2007) explored the impact of age of entry into the labor force on adult men's earnings in Brazil. Controlling for years of education, child labor was associated with lower adult earnings. Therefore, even if the child laborer stayed in school, his adult earnings were diminished compared to a child who delayed entry into the workforce into later adolescence (Emerson & Souza, 2007; see also Knaul, 2001).

BENEFITS AND COSTS OF CHILD LABOR

Under the right circumstances employment can teach children skills, responsibility, and time management that help prepare them for work as adults. Child apprentices may learn critical skills that will allow them to make enough money to support their families or pay for school (Lancy, 2012a). Children who work alongside their same-sex parents may learn important gender roles, rules for appropriate gendered behavior, and solidify their identities as contributing members of their communities (Lancy 2012b). Weisner (1984) suggested that through work, children learn culturally relevant behavior, self-reliance, self-esteem, and compliance. However, children often work out of necessity, and working conditions may not be designed with children's best interests in mind. In addition to the negative economic and educational consequences of child labor already discussed, working children are exposed to a variety of toxins, and such exposure may have serious consequences for growth and health because children are less able to metabolize or eliminate those toxins than adults (Woolf, 2002). In a sample of 83 LMIC, Roggero, Mangiaterra, Bustreo, and Rosati (2007) found that child labor (limited to economically active children, not those working in the household) was associated with mortality and undernourishment, even after controlling for country-level poverty and the adult mortality rate. Farm work in the United States has been recognized as one of the most dangerous occupations for children because of high injury and death rates on the job (American Academy of Pediatrics, 2001). Farm work is also likely to be dangerous in LMIC, but many countries lack the reporting systems necessary to track work-related injury and death (Hurst, 2007). Children working in poor conditions may also suffer from mental health problems, such as depression and anxiety (Fekadu, Hägglöf, & Alem, 2010; Thabet, Matar, Carointero, Bankart, & Vostanis, 2010).

Household chores can serve to teach important skills about how to keep a household functioning. However, like work outside the home, working inside the home presents numerous challenges (ILO, 2004). Many household chores are inappropriate to a child's age or strength, and children may engage in many hours of household chores, leading to fatigue. For example, caring for younger children often requires lifting and carrying them, which can injure even the older child caregiver and put the younger child at risk. Similarly, child caregivers may lack the necessary judgment to adequately protect themselves and their younger siblings from harm. Collecting firewood and water and carrying them long distances can also lead to fatigue and injury in young children. Finally, cooking can lead to burns, cuts, and other injuries in children who do not have the necessary knowledge, strength, and dexterity to safely accomplish such tasks.

GENDER DIFFERENCES IN CHILD LABOR

Overall, boys may engage in more child labor than girls (Fares & Raju, 2007); but the meaning of this difference is challenging to interpret given that girls and boys tend to engage in different kinds of labor. Indeed, one study conducted in Ethiopia showed that 14- and 15-year-old girls and boys spent about the same amount of time per day in family connected labor, but their time was spent in different forms of labor (Pells, 2011). Gender differences in participation rates also vary by country; thus, it can be difficult to infer what participation in various forms of labor may portend for children's overall well-being.

Work Outside the Home

Overall, boys are more likely than girls to work outside the home (Fares & Raju, 2007), and they are more likely to be paid for work (Kolomiyets, 2004), but relative rates depend on the industries and norms in the region under study. Aggregating across multiple countries, girls are more likely to be employed in services (especially domestic work), boys are more likely to be employed in agriculture, and similar percentages of girls and boys are engaged in industry, but gender rates vary considerably by country (Allais, 2009).

Family Work

Based on a sample of 8- to 13-year-old children in 16 LMIC in Africa and Asia, Webbink et al. (2010) concluded that boys spent about 1 hr more per week on family work than girls. Kolomiyets (2004) also noted that a higher proportion of 5- to 14-year-old boys than girls were working for their families in four LMIC. However, family work has not been studied systematically across LMIC.

Housework

Girls are more likely than boys to work inside the home doing household chores, childcare, and elder care (Allais, 2009; Bonke, 2010; Evans, 2010; Webbink et al., 2010), and twice the proportion of girls than boys works more than 28 hr/week doing household chores (Allais, 2009). There is also evidence that the household chores girls and boys do in HIC are gender differentiated (Goodnow, 1988), but there are no available data about the types of household work done in LMIC.

GENDER DIFFERENCES IN CHILD LABOR AS A REFLECTION OF NATIONAL GENDER INEQUALITY

Girls' greater labor rates inside the home and boys' greater labor rates outside the home may reflect macrosystem-level gender inequality. In some LMIC, women's rates of employment and education are quite divergent from men's. Few economic opportunities for adult women may position parents to encourage their girls to take on domestic responsibilities to prepare them for their likely adult responsibilities as homemakers. Similarly, boys may be encouraged to work outside the home to develop skills they could apply to their work as adults. To investigate the link between gendered labor and macrosystem influences, we explored two country-level indicators of gender equality/inequality, controlling for the overall level of human/economic development in the country.

THIS STUDY

Using a sample of 38 LMIC drawn from all regions of the world, we investigate differences between rates of child labor in girls and boys aged

5–14. We include three major types of child labor—work outside the family, work for the family, and household chores—and examine each type separately by gender, to provide a more complete picture of the types of labor engaged in by young girls and boys. Based on sparse previous research, we expected that more boys than girls would engage in child labor overall, in work outside the home, and family work, and that more girls than boys would engage in excessive household chores. Given the paucity of data from many of these countries we could not make specific predictions for every country. Most studies of child labor include only one country or a small selection of countries from a single region. By exploring the rates of child labor across 38 countries, we expand the knowledge base about gender similarities and differences in child labor. Finally, we explore whether differences between labor rates of girls and boys are related to national indicators of gender equality and the overall level of human/economic development in the country.

METHOD

Participants

We evaluate child labor in girls and boys in 233,980 families in 38 countries (Table 14). The randomly selected child from each family averaged 9.27 years of age ($SD = 2.92$, range $= 5$–14), and 49.54% were female. Girls were slightly but not meaningfully older than boys on average, $M = 9.29$, $SD = 2.94$, for girls and $M = 9.25$, $SD = 2.90$, for boys, $t(233{,}735.07) = 3.95$, $p < .001$. Questions were usually answered by the child's biological mother (88.3%). Of the 11.7% that were completed by another mother figure, 98.3% had no biological mother living in the household. Mothers averaged 37.04 years ($SD = 10.23$, range $= 15$–95), and the highest level of education she had completed was none or preschool for 35.6%, primary school/non-standard curriculum/religious school for 29.9%, secondary/vocational/tertiary school for 29.0%, and higher for 5.5%. Mothers of girls were slightly, but not meaningfully, older ($M = 37.14$, $SD = 10.38$) and less educated ($M = 1.04$, $SD = 0.93$) than mothers of boys ($M = 36.93$, $SD = 10.09$, and $M = 1.05$, $SD = 0.93$, respectively), $ts(233{,}089.40$ and $233{,}553.19) = 5.04$ and -4.16, $ps < .001$, respectively.

Procedures

We used the Multiple Indicator Cluster Survey (MICS3), the Gender Relative Status Index (GRS; Beneria & Permanyer, 2010; Permanyer, 2010), the Gender Inequality Index (GII; UNDP, 2011), and the Human

TABLE 14
Sample Descriptive Statistics and Percentages of Children Who Were Engaged in Child Labor by Gender and HDI

Country	n	Child gender Female (%)	Child age M	Child age SD	Mother education[a] M	Mother education[a] SD	Child labor index in the past week Girls (%)	Child labor index in the past week Boys (%)	Child labor index in the past week OR	Child labor index in the past week largest share[b]
High HDI										
Trinidad and Tobago	1,745	51.06	9.69	2.98	1.82	0.78	0.67	1.17	0.57	Fam/work
Montenegro	928	47.20	8.83	2.90	1.90	0.65	7.18	9.13	0.79	Work
Serbia	2,835	48.32	9.00	2.88	1.59	0.82	4.28	4.99	0.84	Work
Belarus	1,943	49.46	9.54	2.95	2.21	0.41	5.53	5.91	0.94	Work
Macedonia	2,712	51.66	8.01	2.95	1.18	0.72	5.78	4.12	1.44*	Work
Albania	2,244	46.43	9.82	2.88	2.46	0.55	8.16	12.15	0.61***	Fam
Kazakhstan	5,935	48.32	10.00	2.89	2.20	0.43	2.34	3.03	0.76	Work/fam
Bosnia and Herzegovina	1,989	50.58	8.89	2.81	1.65	0.62	3.88	5.09	0.74	Fam
Medium HDI										
Thailand	16,263	49.29	9.68	2.81	1.39	0.77	8.41	8.70	0.95	Fam
Ukraine	1,668	48.32	9.58	2.79	2.27	0.67	8.31	11.02	0.74	Fam
Jamaica	1,990	49.05	9.58	2.85	1.99	0.55	4.92	5.15	0.95	Work
Suriname	2,593	50.02	9.25	2.87	1.60	1.18	3.73	4.79	0.76	Work
Georgia	3,753	46.36	9.90	2.95	2.04	0.75	16.80	19.46	0.83*	Work
Syrian Arab Republic	11,486	48.76	9.44	2.98	1.14	0.88	2.13	4.49	0.44***	Fam
Guyana	2,811	49.55	9.39	2.86	1.74	0.99	17.79	18.68	0.97	Fam
Mongolia	3,688	49.30	9.47	3.03	2.18	0.59	15.95	18.29	0.82*	Chores/fam
Vietnam	4,439	47.65	10.07	2.93	1.50	0.76	17.07	16.75	1.02	Fam
Uzbekistan	6,271	48.62	9.77	2.97	2.12	0.32	2.30	3.10	0.73*	Work
Kyrgyzstan	3,025	48.00	9.65	2.89	2.16	0.43	2.34	3.69	0.63*	Chores/fam
Tajikistan	5,016	47.31	9.50	3.00	2.05	0.37	10.03	10.82	0.94	Chores[c]
Laos	4,515	49.57	9.36	2.96	0.79	0.71	11.67	9.53	1.21	Fam
Yemen	2,801	49.30	9.21	2.90	0.35	0.65	23.14	19.56	1.26*	Chores/fam

(*Continued*)

TABLE 14. (Continued)

		Child gender	Child age		Mother education[a]		Child labor index in the past week				
Country	n	Female (%)	M	SD	M	SD	Girls (%)	Boys (%)	OR	largest share[b]
Mauritania	7,415	50.21	8.95	2.93	0.73	0.77	14.23	17.69	0.78***	Fam
Ghana	3,582	49.80	9.31	2.88	0.78	0.96	35.08	35.31	1.01	Fam
Bangladesh	41,168	48.90	9.30	2.83	0.79	0.87	8.33	16.62	0.44***	Chores/fam
Cameroon	5,475	51.56	9.12	2.90	0.94	0.81	32.36	32.53	0.99	Fam
Djibouti	2,790	50.14	9.45	2.95	0.36	0.72	6.35	6.29	1.05	Work
Low HDI										
Nigeria	17,395	50.19	8.87	2.91	0.63	0.88	28.31	29.21	0.96	Fam
Togo	4,545	50.45	9.11	2.88	0.46	0.74	28.96	28.93	1.00	Fam
Gambia	6,025	53.58	9.10	2.94	0.42	0.74	28.64	19.28	1.67***	Fam
Côte d'Ivoire	6,937	49.98	8.96	2.92	0.38	0.66	34.91	36.42	0.93	Fam
Guinea-Bissau	5,220	48.64	9.03	2.88	0.40	0.88	39.07	42.42	0.89*	Fam
Burundi	5,454	51.39	9.32	3.00	0.76	0.55	16.57	17.74	0.90	Chores
Mozambique	9,294	52.00	9.05	2.87	0.76	0.67	21.09	18.85	1.17*	Fam
Central African Republic	6,586	51.15	8.72	2.88	0.63	0.73	48.71	42.75	1.27**	Fam
Sierra Leone	5,603	50.21	8.78	2.91	0.32	0.71	46.30	45.58	1.05	Fam
HDI N/A										
Iraq	11,851	48.82	9.24	3.00	0.98	0.77	7.36	10.04	0.70***	Fam
Somalia	3,990	49.02	8.79	2.87	.41	0.72	56.01	46.12	1.48***	Fam
Total	233,980	49.54	9.27	2.92	1.05	0.96	16.82	18.10	0.88***	Fam

Note. fam, family work; work, work outside the home; chores, household chores.
[a]Mother education is rated as 0 = none or preschool, 1 = primary school, nonstandard curriculum, religious school, 2 = secondary, vocational, tertiary school, and 3 = higher education.
[b]The type of work that accounted for the largest share of child labor. When the largest share differed between girls and boys, we report girls' largest share/boys' largest share.
[c]For boys, there was a tie between chores and work.
*$p \leq .05$.
**$p \leq .01$.
***$p \leq .001$.

Development Index (HDI). Additional information about the MICS3, GRS, GII, and HDI is available in Chapter II (Bornstein et al., 2016).

MICS3 Child Labor Module
The mother of each child between 5 and 14 years indicated whether the child had worked outside the home in the past week (0 = No, 1 = Yes) and whether the child had been paid for this work (0 = No, 1 = Yes). Mothers also estimated the number of hours the child had worked outside the home in the past week. Next, mothers indicated whether the child had engaged in family work (like a family farm or business) or helped with household chores (like shopping, collecting firewood, fetching water, and childcare) in the past week (0 = No, 1 = Yes), and estimated the number of hours the child had engaged in family work and household chores in the past week.

Following UNICEF (2006) we computed a child labor index, combining work outside the home, family work, and excessive housework into a single indicator. Children aged 5–11 were considered to engage in child labor if they had worked for 1 hr or more (for the family or outside the family) and/or had engaged in 28 or more hours of housework. Children aged 12–14 were considered to engage in child labor if they had worked for 14 or more hours (for the family or outside the family) and/or had engaged in 28 or more hours of housework per week. Allowing older children to work up to 2 hr/day without being counted as child labor accounts for the potential benefits associated with small amounts of work in this age group (Larson & Verma, 1999). The age group employed in the current sample and the definitions of child labor employed (i.e., excluding <14 hr of work in preteens, and reasonable hours of household chores for all ages) circumscribed our investigation to child labor that is likely to interfere with healthy child development. Supporting the use of 28 hr as the cut-point for excessive household chores, Allais (2009) and the ILO (2009) both reported that girls who do 28 or more hours of household chores per week are over 20% less likely to be enrolled in school compared to girls who do fewer than 14 hr of chores. The negative impact of 28 hr of household chores on school enrollment for boys was only about half that of girls. In addition to the child labor index, we explored the three components of work (work outside the home, family work, and excessive household chores) separately.

Analytic Plan
First, to determine whether girls and boys engaged in similar types and amounts of labor, we explored the child labor index and three components of work with binary logistic regressions. We modeled main effects and the interaction between child gender and country. Next, the effect sizes for

child gender for each country (i.e., odds ratios) were correlated with the country's HDI and the GRS and GII with and without controlling for the country's HDI.

For the logistic regressions, we used child age and maternal education as covariates. Older children were generally more likely to engage in labor, $rs(233,127–233,573) = -.00$ to $.10$, $ps = ns$ to $.001$. Children from families where the mother had higher education engaged in less labor, $rs(232,776–233,217) = -.06$ to $-.19$, $ps < .001$. There were also large differences in maternal education across countries, $F(37, 233,597) = 3,956.57$, $p < .001$, $\eta^2 = .385$, and controlling for maternal education accounts for across-country differences as well as within-country differences, yielding more precise statistical estimates of gender differences in child labor.

RESULTS

The results supported our hypothesis that more boys than girls engaged in child labor overall as well as labor outside the home and family work, and more girls than boys engaged in excessive household chores. However, the pattern of relations was not consistent across countries, and gender differences were largely unrelated to national indicators of gender equality and sociodemographic development.

Child Labor Index

The gender by country interaction for child labor in the past week was significant, Wald $\chi^2(37) = 809.20$, $p < .001$, as were the main effects of gender, Wald $\chi^2(1) = 118.74$, $p < .001$, OR = .88, and country, Wald $\chi^2(37) = 15,990.58$, $p < .001$. Deconstructing the interaction (Table 14), in 10 countries boys were more likely than girls to have worked in the past week, in 6 countries girls were more likely than boys, and in the remaining 22 countries there was no difference between girls and boys.

The child labor index is an aggregate of work outside the home, family work, and excessive household chores. When we looked at which type of work contributed the most to the child labor index in each country, a distinct pattern emerged (Table 14). In high-HDI countries, the largest share of child labor was either from work outside the home or family work. In medium-HDI countries, there was a mix of work outside the home, family work, and chores (usually only for girls). In low-HDI countries, the largest share of child labor came from family work for girls and boys in every country except Burundi, where chores prevailed for both genders.

In summary, looking across all 38 countries, boys were more likely than girls to have engaged in child labor in the past week (last row of Table 14), but the pattern varied considerably by country. The largest share of child labor, contributed by either work outside the home, family work, or household chores, varied by the economic level of the country. However, in some countries more than one type of child labor was prominent. Next, we explore gender differences in each type of labor.

Work Outside the Home

Work outside the home included any work (paid or unpaid) done for someone outside the household in the past week. The gender by country interaction for work outside the home in the past week was significant, Wald $\chi^2(37) = 259.95$, $p < .001$, as were the main effects of gender, Wald $\chi^2(1) = 92.33$, $p < .001$, $OR = .82$, and country, Wald $\chi^2(37) = 6746.59$, $p < .001$. Deconstructing the interaction (Table 15), controlling for child age, boys were more likely than girls to have engaged in child labor outside the household in the past week in 5 countries, girls were more likely than boys in 1 country (Vietnam), and there was no difference between girls and boys in the remaining 32 countries.

Looking across all countries, boys were more likely than girls to have worked (last row of Table 15), but the pattern varied considerably by country. Some countries had very similar proportions of girls and boys working outside the household (e.g., Yemen and Cameroon), and others had quite different proportions of girls and boys working outside the household (e.g., Syrian Arab Republic and Iraq).

Family Work

Family work included any work done for a member of the household, including family farm or business work, but not household chores. The gender by country interaction for family work in the past week was significant, Wald $\chi^2(37) = 1,095.55$, $p < .001$, as were the main effects of gender, Wald $\chi^2(1) = 326.61$, $p < .001$, $OR = .78$, and country, Wald $\chi^2(37) = 13,563.30$, $p < .001$. Deconstructing the interaction (Table 15), in 13 countries boys were more likely than girls to have done family work in the past week, in 2 countries (Gambia and Central African Republic) girls were more likely than boys, and in the remaining 23 countries there was no difference between girls and boys.

Looking across all countries, boys were more likely than girls to have engaged in child labor for the family farm or business in the past week (last row of Table 15), but the pattern varied considerably by country. Some countries had very similar proportions of girls and boys doing family work (e.g., Montenegro and Guyana), but proportions were quite different in other countries (e.g., Bangladesh and the Gambia).

TABLE 15
PERCENTAGES OF CHILDREN WHO ENGAGED IN WORK OUTSIDE THE HOME, FOR THE FAMILY, OR DOING EXCESSIVE HOUSEHOLD CHORES IN THE PAST WEEK, BY GENDER AND HDI

Country	Work outside the home			Family work			Household chores		
	Girls (%)	Boys (%)	OR	Girls (%)	Boys (%)	OR	Girls (%)	Boys (%)	OR
High HDI									
Trinidad and Tobago	0.11	0.59	0.19	0.45	0.47	0.98	0.11	0.12	0.89
Montenegro	4.17	5.56	0.75	3.94	3.93	1.04	0.23	0.21	1.15
Serbia	3.16	3.91	0.80	0.88	1.58	0.54	0.37	0.07	5.20
Belarus	4.37	4.38	1.01	1.77	2.34	0.75	0.00	0.00	n/a
Macedonia	4.28	3.20	1.36	1.43	1.07	1.39	0.14	0.00	n/a
Albania	2.30	1.91	1.20	6.14	10.48	0.53***	0.29	0.08	2.89
Kazakhstan	1.22	1.24	0.99	0.91	1.60	0.56*	0.66	0.72	0.92
Bosnia and Herzegovina	0.80	1.22	0.64	3.18	4.37	0.71	0.00	0.00	n/a
Medium HDI									
Thailand	2.66	2.40	1.09	5.80	6.32	0.91	0.31	0.36	0.82
Ukraine	3.35	3.48	0.96	5.71	8.70	0.64*	0.37	0.12	3.16
Jamaica	2.77	3.16	0.86	1.23	1.19	1.02	1.23	0.89	1.39
Suriname	1.87	2.68	0.66	1.40	1.86	0.78	0.79	0.32	2.32
Georgia	14.01	15.54	0.88	5.34	6.07	0.87	0.58	0.85	0.69
Syrian Arab Republic	0.43	2.09	0.18***	1.32	2.45	0.53***	0.57	0.34	1.59
Guyana	5.16	6.35	0.82	14.18	14.51	1.00	0.58	0.43	1.68
Mongolia	0.88	1.44	0.59	7.32	9.84	0.71**	9.35	9.14	0.97
Vietnam	1.70	0.99	1.74*	12.72	14.20	0.86	4.02	1.98	2.07***
Uzbekistan	2.13	2.70	0.78	0.66	1.09	0.59	0.00	0.00	n/a
Kyrgyzstan	0.76	1.27	0.59	0.69	1.53	0.45*	0.90	0.95	0.93
Tajikistan	3.92	5.07	0.77	0.97	1.78	0.55*	5.90	5.07	1.23
Laos	1.25	1.67	0.69	8.85	7.55	1.16	2.41	0.92	2.48***

(*Continued*)

GENDER IN LOW- AND MIDDLE-INCOME COUNTRIES

TABLE 15. *(Continued)*

	Work outside the home			Family work			Household chores		
Country	Girls (%)	Boys (%)	OR	Girls (%)	Boys (%)	OR	Girls (%)	Boys (%)	OR
Yemen	2.10	2.11	1.00	10.09	12.31	0.80	13.32	6.32	2.39***
Mauritania	1.27	1.98	0.64*	10.16	13.28	0.75***	3.60	3.22	1.11
Ghana	8.70	7.07	1.27	28.59	30.70	0.92	3.20	1.95	1.70*
Bangladesh	2.05	4.49	0.44***	2.71	11.87	0.20***	3.97	0.87	4.84***
Cameroon	14.13	15.23	0.92	15.85	17.38	0.90	7.99	4.84	1.71***
Djibouti	3.86	4.46	0.90	2.88	2.24	1.33	0.22	0.51	0.39
Low HDI									
Nigeria	10.13	10.62	0.96	20.21	21.20	0.95	2.13	1.93	1.08
Togo	7.85	7.83	1.01	21.10	22.30	0.93	4.14	1.95	2.16***
Gambia	3.87	3.47	1.12	24.46	16.39	1.67***	2.18	1.18	1.67*
Côte d'Ivoire	2.94	3.63	0.80	29.42	33.39	0.83***	6.40	1.91	3.50***
Guinea-Bissau	4.18	4.82	0.89	34.44	39.00	0.84*	4.62	4.00	1.16
Burundi	2.33	1.94	1.18	3.66	5.96	0.61***	12.02	11.11	1.07
Mozambique	1.08	1.64	0.66*	13.62	14.29	0.95	8.76	4.70	2.04***
Central African Republic	15.08	15.01	1.00	34.61	29.78	1.25***	11.08	7.72	1.50***
Sierra Leone	15.81	16.71	0.95	38.61	38.26	1.03	2.01	1.31	1.48
HDI N/A									
Iraq	1.31	3.23	0.40***	4.39	6.58	0.65***	2.44	0.99	2.49***
Somalia	2.62	1.78	1.47	37.63	39.54	0.91	32.63	16.65	2.48***
Total	4.14	4.90	0.82***	10.97	13.04	0.78***	4.01	2.25	1.84***

Note. n/a = statistics not available because of no variance in one or both groups.
*$p \leq .05$.
**$p \leq .01$.
***$p \leq .001$.

117

Household Chores

Household chores were (usually unpaid) work children did for 28 or more hours/week around the household, including childcare, fetching water or wood, cooking, and cleaning. The gender by country interaction for excessive household chores in the past week was significant, Wald $\chi^2(37) = 1,616.61$, $p < .001$, as were the main effects of gender, Wald $\chi^2(1) = 557.23$, $p < .001$, OR = 1.84, and country, Wald $\chi^2(37) = 6,821.30$, $p < .001$. Deconstructing the interaction (Table 15), in 13 countries girls were more likely than boys to have done excessive household chores in the past week, and in the remaining 21 countries for which tests could be computed there was no difference between girls and boys. For four countries (Belarus, Macedonia, Bosnia and Herzegovina, and Uzbekistan), no boys and/or no girls engaged in 28 or more hours of household chores, and statistics could not be computed.

Looking across all countries, girls were more likely than boys to have done excessive household chores in the past week (last row of Table 15). In no country were boys significantly more likely than girls to do excessive household chores, but girls' and boys' engagement was similar in some countries (e.g., Trinidad and Tobago and Burundi).

Relations Between Gender Effect Sizes and National Indices

To assess whether differences between participation in child labor of girls and boys reflected national gender disparities and sociodemographic development, we computed correlations of the effect sizes for child gender for each country with national level GRS, GII, and HDI scores (Table 16). Larger effect sizes indicate that girls are more likely than boys to engage in the activity, and smaller effect sizes indicate that boys are more likely than girls to engage in the activity. Child labor was unrelated to national indicators of gender equality. In countries with lower sociodemographic development, girls were more likely than boys to engage in child labor overall and to engage in excessive household chores

TABLE 16

CORRELATIONS OF CHILD GENDER EFFECT SIZES WITH COUNTRY-LEVEL GENDER AND SOCIO-DEMOGRAPHIC DEVELOPMENT

Labor in the past week	GRS	GII	HDI
Child labor	−.21/.07	.27/.13	−.39*
Work outside the home	.17/.32	−.17/−.43*	−.11
Family work	−.26/−.13	.16/−.07	−.26
Household chores	−.19/−.22	.32/.49*	−.03

Note. GRS, Gender Relative Status Index; GII, Gender Inequality Index; HDI, Human Development Index. Correlations after the slash control for the 2009 Human Development Index.
*$p \leq .05$.

in the past week. However, the countries with lower gender equality also tended to have lower overall sociodemographic development. To remove the variance in the gender indices associated with overall economic level of the country, we controlled the correlations with the GRS and GII for the HDI, and two relations became significant. Controlling for the HDI, in countries with better national gender equality (as measured by the GII only), girls were more likely than boys to work outside the home in the past week, and boys' engagement in excessive household chores approached that of girls.

DISCUSSION

The incidence of child labor varied greatly across countries. In some countries, fewer than 1% of children engage in child labor, but in other countries, as many as half of 5- to 14-year-old children engage in child labor. Overall, these findings for LMIC support the existing western HIC literature on gender differences in child labor. Considering all types of child labor at once (as measured by the child labor index), a slightly higher percentage of boys worked than girls across all 38 LMIC, but there were significant gender differences in fewer than half of the countries, and in some countries girls worked more than boys. Overall, more boys in this study worked outside the home and did family work, and more girls worked inside the home. However, these patterns were not universal across all countries either. In some countries, more girls worked outside the home and did family work than boys. The pattern of relations for excessive household chores was somewhat more consistent. There were gender differences in one-third of the countries, with a higher percentage of girls doing excessive chores than boys, and in no country did significantly more boys than girls do excessive chores.

Gender Differentiated Work

The global pattern of gender relations suggests that parents allow their children to work in ways that reflect macrosystem influences (e.g., current and future gender-differentiated roles in society). In many LMIC, girls will become mothers and housekeepers, and boys will work outside the home. Hence, their patterns of child labor may reflect the general patterns of adult time use. However, the gender difference effect sizes were generally small, and we did not find consistent, strong relations between gender differences in child labor and gender inequality indices at the national level. When controlling for the overall economic level of the country, the only significant findings were that girls were more likely than boys to work outside the home and girls' and boys' engagement in excessive household chores was more similar in countries with better national gender equality.

The findings of this study support the importance of considering excessive household chores (≥ 28 hr/week) as child labor. Girls were sometimes more likely to engage in household chores than boys. In all countries, the average number of hours spent doing household chores was below the threshold of 28 hr (e.g., 4 hr/day), but sometimes a large percentage of children in a country met the threshold. For example, in Somalia, 33% of girls and 17% of boys spent 28 hr/week or more on household chores (even higher percentages did family work), but fewer than 3% of girls and boys worked outside the home in Somalia (Table 15). Any intervention designed to reduce or eliminate child labor should be informed by the types of child labor in which children are employed as well as the reasons for their employment.

One striking example of a country that did not follow the overall pattern of gender relations across LMIC was the Gambia. More girls than boys in the Gambia were engaged in child labor overall as well as every individual type of labor (work outside the home, family work, and household chores; although the difference was not significant for work outside the home). Kea (2007) explored girls' work in Brikama, the Gambia, explaining that there is a strong cultural expectation for girls to work both in the household and on the farm. Girls' higher rates of child labor in the Gambia can be explained by a host of macrosystem factors, including the reliance of local economies on crop farming, cultural norms of gendered behavior (e.g., women do farm work and men do more skilled jobs), the introduction of double-shift schooling that allows children to attend school for part of the day and then work for the rest of the day, and the cultural practice of "loaning" girls to relatives or patrons to live and work in other households (Kea, 2007).

Variability Across Countries

The variability in girls' and boys' labor across countries was striking. A relatively small percentage (<12%) of children in high-HDI countries was engaged in child labor. In low-HDI countries, children were more likely to engage in labor (most >20%; Table 15). Each HDI group contained countries where more girls than boys engaged in labor and more boys than girls engaged in labor. Smaller percentages of children in high-HDI than low-HDI countries also engaged in family work and excessive household chores, but work outside the home seemed to be less tied to HDI. Looking across types of labor, countries varied in whether work outside the home, family work, or excessive household chores accounted for the largest percentage of work. For example, Georgia, Vietnam, and Burundi all had child labor rates in the 15–20% range, but the relative contributions of different types of work diverged. In Georgia, the largest share of child labor came from work outside the home; in Vietnam, the largest share of child labor came from family work; and in Burundi, the largest share of child labor came from excessive household chores. This inherent variability highlights the need to assess the prevalence of specific types of child labor, working conditions, and motivations associated with child labor in each country.

Limitations

This study has limitations that raise additional questions about gender in LMIC. Some general and specific limitations associated with the MICS3 are addressed in Bornstein, Putnick, Deater-Deckard, Lansford and Bradley, Chapter VII (2016). Information that was gathered on child labor in the MICS3 is somewhat incomplete. We do not know the sector of work a child is doing (e.g., agricultural, trade, manufacturing), their working conditions, the types of tasks in which they engage on the job (e.g., operating machinery, childcare, cleaning), the psychosocial impact on the child (e.g., stressful and depressing vs. motivating and self-esteem building), and what factors drove the child to work. We might have found more gender differentiated work within the broad categories of work outside the home, family work, and household chores if the MICS collected more detailed data about the work (e.g., girls do more commercial sewing, weeding, and childcare, and boys do more mining, planting, and firewood collection). Another limitation is the seasonality of data collection. Data for some children may have been collected during school breaks or critical harvesting times, which could lead to overestimates of some kinds of work in some areas. Potential overestimates may also be offset by the parent-report nature of the MICS3. Child labor is a sensitive subject (especially in the context of laws governing child labor, which some countries have in place), so reporter bias and underreporting may be an issue.

Conclusions and Implications

More in-depth research is needed to document the impact of varying amounts and types of child labor on child development. In some countries, child labor could have a positive impact on children's psychosocial well-being as well as their future earnings and job prospects because they have few alternatives available for education or high-level employment. The link between education and child labor also needs to be explored across countries (Putnick & Bornstein, 2015). For example, although child labor may decrease school attendance and performance (Beegle et al., 2009; Fares & Raju, 2007; Gibbons et al., 2005; Guarcello et al., 2008; Heady, 2003; Huebler, 2008; Orazem & Gunnarsson, 2003), child labor may not have detrimental effects on the child if the labor is paired with continued education, or if it is directly relevant to a future career. These effects are most likely moderated by the country of residence and/or the family's socioeconomic status.

Much more research is also needed to understand factors that encourage and discourage child labor. There may be common factors, such as poverty, but there are certainly also country-, community-, and family-specific factors that influence the decision to put a child to work. A thorough investigation of these factors, such as that done by Kea (2007) for one community in the Gambia (see also Admassie, 2003, for Ethiopia), is needed for each country/community to inform effective interventions. To date, some governmental and nongovernmental organizations (NGOs) have focused on global strategies to reduce child labor. One global strategy has been to set a minimum age for labor, another to ban child labor altogether (ILO, 1973, 1999). These strategies will likely fail to eradicate child labor and improve living conditions for children (Budhwani, Wee, & McLean, 2004; Levine, 2011; Morrow, 2010) because a host of factors promotes or maintains child labor, including (but not limited to) the unavailability or prohibitive costs of quality schooling, gender-based cultural norms, the unavailability of alternative labor sources, and individual family needs. Another more promising global strategy for reducing child labor is to improve access to schooling. Dessy (2000) argued that free and compulsory education could improve later job prospects and encourage families to choose school over work, but some incentives may be needed to offset immediate family losses associated with removing children from the workforce. Free education may also discourage child labor because many children work to pay for school (Omokhodion et al., 2006). Educating girls, in particular, may be the best long-term strategy for reducing child labor. Leinberger-Jabari, Parker, and Oberg (2005) and the ILO (2009) suggested that educating girls would have a positive cascading effect on the economy and human development (at least in the long-term) because more educated girls delay marriage and childbearing, are less likely to be poor, have children with fewer health and growth problems, and ensure that their offspring become educated as well.

The MICS3 yields comparable estimates of the percentages of girls and boys working outside the home, doing family work, and doing excessive household chores. For several countries, this study provides the first globally comparable estimates of the burden of child labor in girls and boys. However, this study is just a first step to describing and comparing child labor in girls and boys in LMIC. Only with a full understanding of the scope of child labor across types, countries, and genders can local governments and NGOs specifically target the types of child labor that affect girls and boys, work to protect children from ill effects, and promote positive effects of employment in children at a young age.

VII. GENDER IN LOW- AND MIDDLE-INCOME COUNTRIES: REFLECTIONS, LIMITATIONS, DIRECTIONS, AND IMPLICATIONS

Marc H. Bornstein, Diane L. Putnick, Kirby Deater-Deckard, Jennifer E. Lansford, and Robert H. Bradley

> This article is part of the issue "Gender in Low- and Middle-Income Countries," Bornstein, Putnick, Lansford, Deater-Deckard, and Bradley (Issue Authors). For a full listing of articles in this issue, see: http://onlinelibrary.wiley.com/doi/10.1111/mono.v81.1/issuetoc.

States Parties agree that the education of the child shall be directed to:

The preparation of the child for responsible life in a free society, in the spirit of understanding, peace, tolerance, equality of sexes, and friendship among all peoples, ethnic, national and religious groups and persons of indigenous origin....

–Article 29.1d, Convention on the Rights of the Child
General Assembly resolution 44/25, 20 November 1989.

GENDER THEORY

Social science theories have long been concerned with questions of whether girls and boys, females and males, are qualitatively and quantitatively similar or different in their psychological characteristics and how similarities as well as differences arise. Historically, most investigators have emphasized gender differences. From the moment of gender assignment at birth, the

---

Corresponding author: Dr. Marc H. Bornstein, Child and Family Research, *Eunice Kennedy Shriver* National Institute of Child Health and Human Development, Suite 8030 6705 Rockledge Drive, Bethesda, MD 20892-7971. email: Marc_H_Bornstein@nih.gov
DOI: 10.1111/mono.12229
© 2015 The Society for Research in Child Development, Inc.

social world often interacts differently with the developing individual, depending on her or his gender. That is, children's personality, interests, skills, and perceptions relative to gender are promoted from the culture and through the parents. Parents often describe their newborn infants' attributes and characteristics in gender-stereotyped ways within hours of the child's birth (Rubin, Provenzano, & Luria, 1974), and as early as kindergarten children demonstrate knowledge of gender-role stereotypes (Williams & Best, 1982/1990). Many family studies indicate that parents treat girls and boys differently, encouraging girls and boys to accept distinctive and often "traditional" gender roles. Lytton and Romney's (1991) meta-analysis of 172 studies in diverse domains revealed that the only significant effect of socialization was for parental encouragement of gender-typed behaviors in children. Caregiver motivations in regard to gender appear to be rooted in concerns for the upbringing of children in ways that render them expected, typical, and mentally healthy and adjusted members of their broader society, and so phenotypic gender-associated characteristics in beliefs and behaviors have been attributed to socialization. A common interpretation of gender differences is that they reflect differential societal expectations as to what constitutes culture-specific appropriate feminine and masculine beliefs and behaviors. Gender expectations appear to be deeply ingrained; but historical shifts in political and economic—even climatic—conditions are forcing adjustments in what is expected and how expectations are insinuated in the everyday lives of children. Together, these streams may converge to highlight gender singularities in psychological functioning.

That said, except for XX versus XY chromosomes, hormones, and differential reproductive functions, persons of the two genders are essentially similar, the broad distributions of human characteristics overlap, and in many ways in their caregiving parents are indifferent to child gender, putting the child first. Variations in child behavior may be less important than adult expectations, at least early in development. In consequence, investigators today have begun to focus on similarities in the genders on the twin observations that variation within each gender is wide and often trumps between-gender variation and so often fails to support different developmental and psychological processes for many characteristics between females and males (Hyde, 2005, 2014).

WHAT MICS3 DATA REVEAL ABOUT CHILD GENDER IN LMIC

The first substantive chapter in this monograph of the SRCD focused on child growth. Child morbidity and mortality are perennial caregiving concerns, so much so that they are explicitly addressed in the UN Millennium Goals. In every society caregivers are vested with the responsibility for promoting children's wellness and preventing their illness. Bradley and Putnick in Chapter III (2016) compared growth (height-for-age and stunting, weight-for-age and underweight, and weight-for-height and wasting) as well as mortality in girls and boys and assessed associations between these indices and housing quality and household material resources for girls and boys in under-researched LMIC. Their analyses shed light on how varying conditions in LMIC relate to putative gender disparities in survival and growth. Having more material resources in the household was associated with less mortality and better growth, but the strength of these effects varied by country. What the findings from this study showed, however, was that household quality and material resources accessible at home were differentially associated with indicators of growth in girls and boys, granting those relations were small and varied by country. With respect to child gender, these authors found evidence that boys may be at greater risk of mortality and growth problems than girls, especially in the poorest countries where the biological advantages enjoyed by girls may help them survive and grow in conditions of severe want (see also Svedberg, 1990). Furthermore, poorer home environment conditions and material resources across all countries had small but stronger relations with boys' than girls' weight-for-height and wasting status (indicators of acute, but generally short term, undernourishment). Although fairly consistent, all the gender differences unearthed were small, and evidence emerged that the degree to which conditions favored girls depended on the average level of wealth in a country.

The second substantive chapter focused on mothers' and fathers' caregiving of girls and boys (Bornstein & Putnick, 2016). Caregiving responsibilities toward young children include engaging girls and boys in affective interpersonal exchanges and stimulating them to understand their wider natural and designed environments. Overall, Bornstein and Putnick in Chapter IV (2016) found that more mothers than fathers engage in caregiving activities with their young children in almost every country studied. Child gender differences, however, were small and inconsistent across countries. When there were gender differences, they tended to favor boys. For example, more boys than girls were taken outside the home in 15 countries, played with in 7 countries, and named, counted, and drawn with in 5 countries. Furthermore, some evidence of differential treatment of girls and boys by mothers and fathers emerged, but those effects tended to be small and inconsistent across countries as well.

Properly socializing young children also entails managing and setting limits on children's behavior. Deater-Deckard and Lansford in Chapter V (2016) examined gender similarities and differences in the prevalence of 11 parental responses to children, including nonviolent discipline (reasoning, distraction), psychological aggression (yelling, name calling), and various forms of physical punishment and violence (spanking, hitting, beating with implement) as well as caregivers' endorsement of the need to physically punish young girls and boys. In the whole sample, fewer than one in five caregivers in LMIC reported using only nonviolent responses, whereas two-thirds reported using psychological aggression, and nearly two-thirds reported resorting to physical violence, but fewer than one in five severe violence. Reported use of disciplinary behaviors varied widely by country. Nearly one-third of mothers endorsed the need for physical punishment, however. Consistent with the literature on families in HIC (McKee et al., 2007; Pinderhughes, Dodge, Bates, Pettit, & Zelli, 2000), boys in LMIC tended to receive harsher treatment than girls, but again the size of this effect was modest.

Many parents in LMIC allow their children to work as a means of supporting the family. UNICEF (2007a) estimated that one in six children aged 5–14 is involved in child labor. The percentages of girls and boys who participate in different types of child labor have been incompletely documented in LMIC. Putnick and Bornstein in Chapter VI (2016) found that the incidence of child labor varied greatly across LMIC: In some LMIC fewer than 1% of children engaged in child labor, but in other LMIC as many as half of 5- to 14-year-olds engaged in child labor. Across LMIC, a slightly greater percentage of boys than girls was involved in child labor as measured by an index that combined work outside the home, family work, and excessive household chores. However, gender differences were noted in fewer than one-half of the countries, and girls worked more than boys in several countries. In general, girls were slightly more likely to do housework or childcare than boys. By contrast, boys were slightly more likely to work outside the home or do family work than girls. That said, none of these patterns was observed in all LMIC.

Child Gender: Good News

Overall, we found that most gender effects (when there were any) were small. Moreover, there were not consistent gender differences across countries in growth and mortality, experiences being parented and disciplined, and having to engage in child labor. Most gender-related patterns varied considerably by country. The "good news" in these findings is, then, that young girls and boys are normally treated mostly equally in contemporary 21st-century LMIC. This finding is somewhat surprising from a gender difference framework, but accords well with a gender similarities perspective.

What accounts for the pervasive gender similarities observed in these LMIC MICS data? It is possible that gender biases are specific or more pronounced in Western, educated, industrialized, rich, and democratic societies that have heretofore provided the large data base in psychological and developmental science (Henrich et al., 2010). Alternatively, the absence of large or even moderate gender differences might indicate that caregivers in these LMIC possess ethnotheories that prompt similar treatment of young girls and boys. Children's basic needs pertaining to survival, early competence development, and adaptive functioning may be so pervasive that LMIC parents may typically share a strong belief that girls and boys alike are children who should be treated the same. The lack of differences may be due to less gender differentiation in home life among LMIC (than is sometimes recognized in HIC: Costa, Terracciano, & McCrae, 2001) as a consequence of very limited household and community resources to address more than the most basic human needs (Pells, 2010). In effect, in well-resourced societies, where child survival is not a typical worry, parents in some sense enjoy the luxury to more fully enact values connected to gender differentiation although their children are young. By contrast, in poorly resourced societies, where child survival is an issue, gender differentiation per se may be less significant. So much is fragile in the first years of life for children in LMIC that cultural proclivities *re* gender may not manifest themselves so strongly early on (Lancy, 2014). Another possibility is that gender differentiated treatment occurs in more subtle ways in LMIC than is captured by the MICS. For example, caregivers may be equally likely to take a boy and a girl outside, but they may be more likely to take a boy to a place where he may benefit more.

We studied children mostly in the 0- to 5-year age range. Here, we found a greater preponderance of gender similarities. It is possible that more systematic gender differences in children's experiences and treatment begin later in development, as children gradually assume adolescent and adult roles (Cappa, Wardlaw, & Morgan, 2011; UNICEF, 2011). Some cultures might not differentiate the genders until the advent of puberty and rites of passage and initiation into the adult world. For example, with respect to child labor, where the children were older (child labor included 5- to 14-year-olds), more and larger gender differences emerged. However, the research available suggests that gender differences entail more the nature of the labor than the amount of time spent engaged in labor per se (Pells, 2011). The societal tendency to assort by gender is complex. Later in development, gender segregation is pervasive, and gender proclivities, expectations, and interactions (as in interests and occupations) become distinguished so much that older girls and boys have been described as "growing up in separate cultures" (Maccoby & Jacklin, 1987). Also, we tend to assume that parents and other adults are responsible for gender differentiation in children, but girls and boys elicit socialization, and girls and boys, particularly when older, may evoke different forms of socialization.

Comparative studies in child experience and parenting have long been a focus of scholarly inquiry, as here, but research has only recently begun to attend to how historical social change affects patterns of child socialization.

There are numerous macro-level currents throughout the modern world (e.g., increased education, exposure to mass media, improvements in community infrastructure, internal and external migration, democratization) that are moving societies toward more egalitarian social and economic relations between the genders. Around the globe, families are today shaped by homogenizing economic and social forces (from urbanization to individualism to egalitarianism) such that some traditional distinctions (perhaps those surrounding gender) may be waning (Greenfield, 2009; Inglehart, 1997; Rendall, 2013). Female education and maternal employment outside the home, which are on the rise worldwide, are also associated with reductions in gender stereotyped beliefs and behaviors (Ruble, Martin, & Berenbaum, 2006). For example, urban, educated Indian and Chinese mothers profess autonomy goals for their children that emulate those of mothers from traditionally independent-minded nations of Germany and the United States (Keller et al., 2006). Thus, economic and ecological shifts relative to historical time may be reshaping parents' socialization goals vis-à-vis child gender, in the present case de-emphasizing traditional gender mores and hierarchy to redirect caregiving toward more gender egalitarian child-centered parenting.

Child Gender: Bad News

At the same time, we found some evidence that boys were at slight disadvantages relative to girls in growth and mortality, harsh discipline, and child labor for the family and outside the family, and girls were at slight disadvantages relative to boys in some forms of caregiving and assignment of excessive household chores. If gender inequality is taken as bad news, any small, but consistent, girl–boy differences distributed over an estimated 650,000,000 young LMIC children could add up to meaningful gender divergences. Considering the prevailing view that girls are at greater disadvantages than boys (UNICEF, 2007b), our mixed findings are noteworthy and raise the question of why girls and boys may be at slight (if consistent) disadvantages in some domains. Each domain we investigated might carry a different likely explanation.

In terms of mortality and growth, some authorities point to genetic disadvantages for boys (Klein, 2007; United Nations, Department of Economic and Social Affairs, Population Division, 2011). However, genetics explains only so much. Parents typically hold different cognitions about healthy development in their girls and boys, even when infants do not differ in other physical characteristics, such as weight, length, or Apgar score (Rubin, Provenzano, & Luria, 1974). For example, in the West mothers underestimate motor skills of infant girls and overestimate those of infant boys, even when objective tests show no gender differences in children's motor performance (Mondschein, Adolph, & Tamis-LeMonda, 2000).

Engaging in caregiving activities, such as playing out of doors, more with boys than girls may reflect cultural beliefs about appropriately gendered behavior and social learning. For example, more boys may go outside than girls because men spend more time outdoors and women spend more time indoors. Also, parental cognitions may play a role. Parents in some countries may perceive their boys as benefitting more from parent–child play than their girls or simply think that boys are more "active" and, thus, could use some relief by being allowed outside for more vigorous activity. It is important to bear in mind in this connection that siblings often play instrumental roles in socializing each other and there are societal differences in how much older siblings are involved in the care of younger siblings (Whiteman, Becerra, & Killoren, 2009).

Harsher disciplining practices for boys than girls may emanate from boys' greater levels of (even mild) externalizing behavior than girls (Seedat et al., 2009) or, perhaps, from the belief that boys require more control (physical punishment) than do girls to elicit appropriate behavior, which Deater-Deckard and Lansford in Chapter V (2016) found to be endorsed slightly more by parents of boys than girls.

Child labor differences may reflect societal expectations of future adult roles and responsibilities or beliefs about what girls and boys can accomplish. For example, boys may be more likely to work in manual labor positions for the family or outside the home because parents believe that boys are stronger than girls and can handle the work better. More girls than boys may engage in excessive household chores because chores are common activities and situations around the world that reinforce existing gender differences in adult roles. For example, Bornstein and Putnick in Chapter IV (2016) reported a consistent gender difference in parental caregiving of young children, and mothers still do the bulk of the housework, even in HIC (Bianchi, Milkie, Sayer, & Robinson, 2000). Because of these general predilections, caregivers may just feel that it is proper to engage girls in such activities.

Socialization messages are often delivered consistently in different social contexts via different social channels. Through themacity, diverse processes of socialization work in concert with one another (Quinn & Holland, 1987). Studies of children's household work indicate patterns that are pertinent to a thematic consideration of gender socialization. Psychodynamic mechanisms like introjection and internalization have been posited to account for developmental phenomena, such as gender socialization. So children seeing mothers and fathers at work may internalize their roles. Mothers and fathers typically model a traditional gender-stereotyped division of labor in their own household work for imitation (Coltrane, 2000). Tradition has dictated that mothers are more responsible for their children's day-to-day well-being, and fathers are more often out-of-home breadwinners and role models (Bird, 1997; Pleck, 2010). To the extent that mothers, fathers, or other caregivers are important and influential figures in children's lives, often to be emulated or feared, they shape children's impressions of what it means to be a woman or a man, for example, simply by acting like a woman or a man (Bussey & Bandura, 1999). In this view, children may acquire new behaviors without ever performing them overtly and without ever being rewarded, but merely by observing behaviors being performed by parents (Bandura, 1989). Girls usually identify with mothers and adopt female behaviors, boys with fathers and male behaviors. In a related way, attachment research assumes that, on the basis of repeated patterns of interaction, children develop enduring representations of their socioemotional relationships (Fraley & Shaver, 2000; Mikulincer, Shaver, & Pereg, 2003). Children who work alongside their same-gender parents internalize roles and rules for appropriate gendered behaviors and identities as members of their communities (Lancy & Grove, 2010).

An instruction and scaffolding view of socialization reflects more of an interactive, bidirectional process. Vygotsky (2005) emphasized the crucial importance of social interaction in socialization, contending that the more advanced partner (the socializer) influences the less advanced partner (the socializee) through their social–cognitive interactions. Wood, Bruner, and Ross (1976) identified the teaching roles adults adopt in interactions with children under the rubric of "scaffolds." Mothers and fathers tend to scaffold children's learning differently, and they encourage girls' and boys' participation in different learning activities and chores in anticipation of their expected later gender roles in adulthood (Coltrane, 2000; Leaper, 2002; Raley & Bianchi, 2006). Hence, girls work more inside the home and boys work more outside the home. That said, as family size has decreased and women's participation in the paid labor force has increased, parent–child relationships have evolved, such that fathers often provide more direction for daughters than was previously the case (Crespi, 2003).

A related direct avenue of socialization is posited to flow through parents' differential treatment, which may assume various forms (Chodorow, 1978). One type operates through parenting cognitions; for example, parents may possess different beliefs or expectations about girls and boys across a wide array of domains. Parents tend to expect boys to do better than girls in science and math (Eccles, Freedman-Doan, Frome, Jacobs, & Yoon, 2000; Tenenbaum & Leaper, 2003), again despite a lack of actual gender differences in performance (Hyde, Lindberg, Linn, Ellis, & Williams, 2008; Tenenbaum & Leaper, 2003). On outings to museums, parents focus on explanations of scientific content with their boys more than with their girls and so may foster boys' greater interest in and knowledge about science (Crowley, Callanan, Tenenbaum, & Allen, 2001). These messages are hypothesized to influence children's self-concepts, motivation, and choices. The resort to harshly discipline more boys than girls and play with more boys than girls may reflect parents' cognitions about differential needs and capabilities of their boys and girls.

Another type of differential treatment occurs through parenting practices, parents' direct active or passive interactions with children. Mischel's (1970) social learning perspective called attention to parents' (and others') direct reinforcement of children's conformity to expected or desired norms, as with respect to gender when adults compliment a girl when she nurtures a toy doll and a boy when he builds a model airplane. Children's execution of different behaviors often depends on rewards or injunctions associated with their outcomes. For example, girls and boys may be differentially complimented for engaging in age-appropriate chores and jobs for the family.

Finally, an understudied route by which gender socialization proceeds is through the types of opportunities parents provide or promote. Access to certain settings affords children chances to develop specific conceptions of themselves and to engage in particular activities. It also affords them opportunities to receive encouragement for repeating those activities. Parents, therefore, instill gender orientations in their children by placing girls and boys in gender-distinctive roles and contexts (e.g., rooms with certain furnishings; Pomerleau, Bolduc, Malcuit, & Cossette, 1990). For example, parents tend to allocate gender-typed chores to children, typically assigning childcare and cleaning to daughters and allotting maintenance work to sons (Huebler, 2008; Pinzas, 2008; Raley & Bianchi, 2006). The availability of feminine-stereotyped toys to girls prompts caregiving behaviors (e.g., feeding a doll), whereas the availability of masculine-stereotyped toys to boys prompts instrumental behaviors (e.g., constructing a model). Stereotyped girls' toys (dolls) provide girls with practice in learning rules, imitating behaviors, and using adults as sources of help for certain outcomes, whereas stereotyped boys' toys (models) refine visual/spatial skills, problem solving, independent learning, self-confidence, and creativity (Martin & Dinella, 2002). At a more basic level, parents may differentially allocate household resources, such as like food and equipment, based on child gender, which may have consequences for child mortality and growth.

Traditionally, the socialization processes asserted to convey intergenerational transmission of beliefs and behaviors include identification, conditioning, reinforcement, modeling, teaching and scaffolding, and the provision of opportunity. On these accounts, it has been easy to assume that parents and other adult socializers are responsible for gender-differentiated conduct in children. However, it is also the case that children actively participate in gender-organized activities, and daughters elicit more feminine stereotypes (affection) and sons more masculine ones (building). Gender is one of the first social categories that children learn. By 4 months of age infants can distinguish female from males faces (Quinn, Yahr, Kuhn, Slater, & Pascalis, 2002), and by 8 months of age infants already exhibit preferences for gender-typed toys (Alexander, Wilcox, & Woods, 2009). Children generally prefer gender-stereotyped clothes and being delegated with gender-stereotyped chores (Schuette & Killen, 2009). Child characteristics and parent influences interact to consolidate gender variation in children. Child effects on parents are in play and coexist with parent effects on children (Lerner et al., 2015), and these mutual influences interact to consolidate socialization in children (Bornstein, 2013). The principle of transaction in child development acknowledges that characteristics of an individual shape his or her experiences, while, reciprocally, experiences shape the characteristics of the individual through time (Bornstein, 2009). In the end, forces pertaining to the expression and treatment of child gender run in both directions—parent-to-child and child-to-parent. This consistency is presumably mutually reinforcing to child gender identification and development.

Child Gender: Worse News

In this monograph of the SRCD, we focused on between-gender similarities and differences rather than country-level effects in our variables of interest. However, the data showed considerable between- and within-country variation as well as overall low levels of some child experiences. On the first, for example, Putnick and Bornstein in Chapter VI (2016) found in some countries that very few children worked, whereas in other countries nearly half of children worked. When considering types of labor, countries also varied in whether work outside the home, family work, or excessive household chores accounted for the largest percentage of child labor. Similarly, discipline practices and violence toward children varied greatly across countries. Humans are not monolithic entities. Within a given context, social-structural variations in gender relations likely depend on people's education, social class, ethnicity, and religion, or other specific characteristics. In the United States, for example, gender emphases appear to vary depending on sociodemographic factors, such as income, education, ethnicity, and family configuration (Chow, Wilkinson, & Baca Zinn, 1996; Hilton & Haldeman, 1991; Leaper & Valin, 1996; Reid & Comas-Diaz, 1990), as well as structural factors, such as marital status or maternal employment (Etaugh, 1993; Leaper, Leve, Strasser, & Schwartz, 1995; Risman, 2001; Stevenson & Black, 1988). Within-family variations, such as number of siblings, birth order, and gender of siblings, matter as regards the roles that children are assigned and the opportunities they may have (Dammert, 2010). Each of these factors influences the relative amounts of power, status, and resources that women and men may enjoy in a society (Kimmel, 2000). What remains unclear is how these factors will coalesce as various macro-level factors shift in the future in LMIC. In some societies, countervailing forces appear to be at play (e.g., economic downturns here, political or religious upheavals there). Thus, among the caveats to consider when interpreting our results, it is important to bear in mind that within- as well as between-country differences are likely in whether caregivers deem gendered activities as appropriate, normative, acceptable, or necessary.

The most concerning news by far in our data arrives in considering the general levels of certain experiences of children in LMIC. For example, Bornstein and Putnick in Chapter IV (2016) found that more primary caregivers played, sang songs, and took their young children outside than read, told stories, and named, counted, and drew with them. However, the base rates of all these kinds of caregiving were low across LMIC. If the reported levels of caregiving by mothers and fathers are proportionally reflective of the totality of growth-promoting caregiving available from all "significant other" caregivers in the household, then the base rates of all these behaviors are low in comparison with findings in HIC contexts. For example, in the United States 70% of 4- to 9-month-old infants are read to at least three times/week and only 9% are never read to (Kuo, Franke, Regaldo, & Halfon, 2004). Similarly, 65% of 0- to 2-year-olds in the United States are sung to or told stories every day in a given week (Murphey, Cooper, & Forry, 2013).

Rates for certain forms of caregiving in LMIC may well be low because of limited resources, caregiver stress, or the presence of siblings. Challenging in optimal circumstances, caregiving (beyond actions connected to immediate needs) is rendered even more difficult when family, community, and national resources are severely restricted (Edin & Lein, 1997; Magnuson & Duncan, 2002). Moreover, in LMIC more young children are likely to be sick and malnourished, which diminishes the likelihood they will receive some kinds of caregiving. The stresses on caregivers in LMIC stemming from day-to-day struggles to secure resources, and the stresses of trying to cope with living in deteriorated dangerous circumstances, tend to undermine effective caregiving (McLoyd et al., 2006). Compared to middle-SES parents, low-SES parents even in HIC are less likely to read to young children or provide appropriate play materials in the home (Bradley, Corwyn, McAdoo, & Garcia Coll, 2001). Compared to middle-SES mothers, low-SES mothers even in HIC converse less with their children and do so in less sophisticated ways (Hart & Risley, 1995; Hoff, Laursen, & Tardif, 2002). In situations where survival or basic health is deemed critical, it may be the case that some parents delay focusing on building psychosocial competencies pending their ensuring the continued existence and health of the child. The interplay of all these reasons is likely strong in LMIC where children and adults are most at risk. Many LMIC suffer dearths of social, economic, and psychological capital. Literatures from around the world have pointed to numerous noxious links between economic privations and diminished levels of child well-being. Young Lives, a study of four LMIC, revealed that children living in low-resource contexts tend to exhibit impaired socioemotional and cognitive outcomes as evidenced, for example, in low self-esteem and reduced educational aspirations (Dercon & Krishnan, 2009).

Across countries, children experienced harsh treatment by their caregivers. Only 17% of caregivers in the entire sample reported that their child had experienced only nonviolent discipline in the past month. In contrast, 67% reported that their child had experienced psychological aggression, 63% reported physical violence, and 17% reported severe violence. These behaviors varied widely across countries, but within each country they varied little by gender. The findings suggest that many countries still have much progress to make to promote children's right to protection from abuse as envisioned by the CRC.

CHILD GENDER AND INDEXES OF NATIONAL GENDER EQUALITY AND SOCIOECONOMIC DEVELOPMENT

Countries across the globe qua macrosystems vary greatly in whether and how well they promote gender equality, and the "culture" of gender equality in a nation may have repercussions for gender similarities and differences at national and family levels. Gender inequality reportedly erodes national achievement (Gaye, Klugman, Kovacevic, Twigg, & Zambrano, 2010). Here, we found that two (albeit related) measures of national gender equality in LMIC did not systematically relate to measures of child growth and mortality or to reports of parenting practices and discipline. This was true even though there was adequate variation in these indices across countries (see Chapter II), and so restricted range is not a limiting issue. However, it is well to remember that our unit of analysis in these correlations was country, so that correlations with the GRS, GII, and HDI were perforce underpowered. In LMIC with worse national gender equality, girls were less likely to work outside the home than boys, more likely to engage in excessive household chores than boys, and the gap in rates of physical violence between girls and boys narrowed. Conversely, boys were more disadvantaged relative to girls in weight-for-age and wasting.

Several national measures of gender equality or inequality are available. We chose the GII and GRS because they include macrosystem indicators of interest (e.g., equality in empowerment, income, education, health), distinguish between female and male advantages, and are available for a large number of the countries in this MICS3 sample. Other indices we considered but excluded were the Gender-Related Development Index (GDI; UNICEF, 2009), Gender Equality Index (GEI; White, 1997), Gender Inequality Index (GI; Forsythe et al., 1998), Relative Status of Women (RSW; Dijkstra & Hanmer, 2000), Standardised Index of Gender Equality (SIGE; Dijkstra, 2002), Gender Equity Index (GEI; Social Watch, 2009), Global Gender Gap Index (GGI; Hausmann, Tyson, & Zahidi, 2010), and Multidimensional Gender Equality Index (MGEI; Permanyer, 2008). We excluded these indices because of computational problems (e.g., not distinguishing between advantages for females or males, out of range values), complicated interpretation (e.g., ranked or comparative indices with floating means), and missing data (e.g., values were only available in a small number of our LMIC). Of course, still other national measures of gender equality could relate to ours or to other domains of psychological functioning or development. Using the Gender-Related Development Index, a United Nations database that indexes gender inequality for participating nations, Eagly and Wood (1999) found correlations between gender inequality and the magnitude of gender differences in mate preferences. Nations with larger gender gaps in power had larger gender gaps in mate preferences (see also Zentner & Mitura, 2012).

As might be expected, we found that the two national measures of gender equality were related to the one national measure of socioeconomic development. That measure, the Human Development Index, proved somewhat more informative. In terms of mortality and growth, gender disparities (favoring girls) were most prevalent in low-HDI countries where socioeconomic resources tend to be scarce. Associations between effect sizes for gender differences in growth and mortality and the HDI revealed that in low-HDI countries boys tend to be disadvantaged compared to girls; but in higher-HDI countries, the gap between girls and boys diminishes, or even reverses. Gender differences in parenting were also related to national HDI such that in lower-HDI countries parents were more likely to take boys than girls outside, name, count, and draw with boys than with girls, and read more to boys than to girls. Although the magnitude of gender differences in discipline varied by country, larger gender differences tended to emerge for more severe forms of physical punishment in countries with higher HDI levels. Finally, in countries with lower HDI, girls were more likely than boys to engage in child labor overall.

STRENGTHS AND LIMITATIONS OF THE MICS AND COUNTRY-LEVEL MEASURES OF GENDER EQUITY AND NATIONAL DEVELOPMENT

The MICS provides a unique data set about child gender as well as children generally and their lives in the developing world of LMIC. Even so, the data have limitations that need to be acknowledged. Thus, there are a number of caveats to consider when interpreting our results. Here, we briefly discuss several salient limitations and strengths of the MICS per se and their implications for understanding gender similarities and differences among children in LMIC.

Caregiver Report

The MICS relies on reports of specific caregivers. That is, items in the MICS are reports of mothers (or occasionally children's other principal female caregiver) about target children, and so are not observations of behaviors, and the MICS contains no controls on such reports (as for social desirability bias, for example; Bornstein et al., 2015). For certain purposes, observations of actual practices might constitute a stronger data base. However, observation can also change behavior (as people display reactance and may do so differently in different social groups), and so, just as reporters may misrepresent the treatment of girls and boys, it is sometimes difficult to observe whether girls and boys are actually treated similarly or differently. For other purposes, such as here, it is well to remember that caregiver reports constitute the social milieu of child rearing (Bornstein, 2014b). Self-reports presumably reflect knowledge about what one has actually done; by contrast, reports about others reflect less detailed knowledge. Mothers are especially involved with daughters (Starrels, 1994), which may serve as a source of bias. Reporters sometimes also misestimate other people's behaviors, and the field of father research, for example, has suffered from misuse and misinterpretation of maternal reports of fathers' behaviors. MICS reports on fathers (or other caregivers) must be understood in this light. Furthermore, MICS data might underestimate children's experiences in the sense that actual numbers are probably greater because more individuals contribute to a child's life than just the mother (or another principal female caregiver). In the "distributed model" of socialization, which may be more normative in LMIC, siblings and extended family as well as others contribute to child caregiving (Bornstein, 2015; Clarke-Stewart & Allthusen, 2002; Leinaweaver, 2014; Marfo, 2011; Smith & Drew, 2002; Zukow-Goldring, 2002). By limiting reports to those provided by a principal caregiver, the MICS may underestimate the amount and depth of experiences of children. Additional research with all child caregivers is needed to determine the full scope of young girls' and boys' lives. Finally, some topics, such as child labor and discipline, are personal or sensitive (especially in the context of restrictive laws), so that reporter bias and underreporting may be an issue for these topics. That said, the MICS uses a limited number of specific but presumably universal (etic) items that reference specific domains associated with specific individuals within specific time periods. Therefore, MICS items probably constitute reasonably accurate report records. It can be useful to tally children's experiences, and MICS items are informative and helpful indicators in this regard.

Questionnaire Data

Because of the global nature and the massive scale of the MICS survey, the information gathered is perforce somewhat incomplete. Questions in the MICS are all close-ended and specific, and its predominant binary response format does not permit more fine-grained analyses (e.g., of frequency or duration; see, e.g., Robinson, Little, & Biringen, 1993). For example, the MICS did not ask why or where children were taken out or about the sector of child labor (e.g., agricultural, trade, manufacturing) or children's working conditions or the reasons children were disciplined. One caregiving item included "name, count, draw"; it could be that caregivers emphasize "name" with girls and "count" with boys. In addition, next to quantitative aspects of caregiving, qualitative aspects matter a great deal. Thus, caregivers of girls and boys could equate in their frequencies of play, yet caregivers of boys might solicit sequences of high-level play that challenge and advance a boy's skills, whereas caregivers of girls demonstrate low-level play that does not advance a girl's skills. It is important also to take the context of parenting into consideration. For example, parents may encourage achievement similarly in girls and boys; however, if the subject matter of achievement (sports versus mathematics versus sewing) is taken into account perhaps different patterns would emerge. In short, some MICS items may not capture more subtle ways that gender is socialized. An extensive but "common-denominator" questionnaire such as MICS is clearly challenging to administer, especially in LMIC. However, the MICS benefits from comparable methods executed under rigid quality control, and well-trained national civil workers, demographers, and others from 41 widely varying participating LMIC worked diligently toward valid MICS development and administration to nationally representative large samples.

Time

The MICS surveyed families at only one point in time; thus, MICS indicators are cross-sectional, precluding longitudinal analyses as well as causal interpretations. Context is dynamic and changes across time, so MICS items are subject to seasonality as well as historical time effects (as on the prevalence of certain diseases and infections). Whether and how often children are taken outside may vary depending on the geographical location of the country (in warmer climate LMIC, more of life may take place out of doors), and data for some children may have been collected during school breaks or critical harvest times (which could lead to overestimates of some kinds of work in some areas). The MICS provides only a snapshot of how gender is implicated in parenting practices and health outcomes, but gender too develops dynamically. Under the assumption that social definitions of gender evolve over time, changes in average levels of certain individual variables likely change over time as well, so that gender-related issues become more salient with age (Lanvers, 2004).

Sampling

At the same time that an impressive number of participants (~2,000,000) in a substantial number (41) of underresearched LMIC are represented in our MICS data, sample sizes vary across countries, not all countries provided all data, not all regions of the majority world of LMIC are represented, and comparable data from minority HIC around the world are lacking (although some chapters in this monograph of the SRCD include, as available, reports of comparable data from HIC). It is important to acknowledge as well that reports in this monograph focus on children in a narrow age range (e.g., usually under 5 years), and so other patterns of findings might apply with children of different ages. Here, we studied one child per family, but families differ in their numbers of children and so in turn the distribution of caregiving activities and so forth. Nonetheless, the MICS includes a proper sampling of large nationally representative data. Another related matter is that larger gender differences may be evident in within-family differential treatment of sibling girls and boys.

Directions of Effects

Thinking about child gender from a MICS point of view highlights parents and societies as possible agents of influence over child gender. Parents and other socializers promote gender-appropriate beliefs and behaviors that come to define "girlhood" and "boyhood." Parents and others provide children with many types of socialization experiences vis-à-vis gender, modeling gender roles, differentially treating daughters and sons, and so forth. It is easy to assume that these socializers are responsible for gender in children, but it is also the case (as mentioned earlier) that daughters and sons elicit socializer behavior. That is, child effects constitute important determinants. Besides evocative effects, the two genders might also be similar or different in their susceptibility to forces of socialization.

The Whole Child

Substantive chapters in this monograph of the SRCD serially examined gender similarities and differences in child mortality and growth, caregiving, discipline and violence, and labor, but we acknowledge that girls and boys function and develop as integrated organisms and in a holistic fashion. The multiple domains of development that intersect child gender are themselves intertwined (Lerner et al., 2015). The MICS does not contain information on all aspects of child gender or development. In general, girls are monitored more than boys, for example (McHale, Updergraff, Jackson-Newsom, Tucker, & Crouter, 2000; Pettit, Laird, Dodge, Bates, & Criss, 2001). Accordingly, future waves of the MICS might profitably collect data on more aspects of child psychology and child development (as in the MICS4 and 5) and focus on cross-domain analyses.

Culture

The MICS recruited and obtained data from nationally representative samples. However, "culture" is conspicuous by its absence. Every culture is characterized (and distinguished from others) by thoroughgoing, deep-seated, and consistent themes that inculcate what one needs to know, to think, and to behave as an appropriately functioning member of the culture. One major domain of this thematicity is certainly gender. Thus, parents' and other caregivers' cognitions and practices likely communicate about gender in many convergent ways, from modeling gender roles to treatment of girls and boys. Cultural norms and values likely undergird social processes related to gender (Chen & French, 2008; French, Lee, & Pidada, 2006). The number of countries studied here precluded reference to individual cultural or national literatures. However, MICS users' ability to interpret and contextualize findings might be enhanced by a richer ethnographic understanding of the beliefs, customs, policies, and laws about gender in each location. The samples here do not represent culturally similar groups and also are diverse within their national populations. The fact that our results are so consistent, even in the face of the great variance of the large number of sampled LMIC, testifies to their robustness and universality.

An important consequence of sacrificing cultural depth for comparative breadth here is that the measures do not allow the investigator to delve into the cultural or developmental mechanisms that create differential contexts or influence children's gender. MICS items could have different meanings in different cultures. Fully understanding children's experiences and their meaning often requires situating them in context (Bornstein, 1995). The same experience can have the same or different meanings in different contexts, just as different experiences can have the same or different meanings in different contexts. In one context caregivers could display socioemotional involvement in girls predominately through singing, whereas in another context caregivers could demonstrate similar affection by playing with boys. These different displays may serve the same socioemotional functions to children of the two genders.

Country-Level Measures

No one measure of national gender equality is satisfactory. Each measure depends on the available data and draws from a theoretical framework of what may be considered important indicators of gender equality. The GRS was developed because previously available indicators of global gender equality either did not distinguish between advantages for women and advantages for men or used mathematical formulations that led to biased results (Beneria & Permanyer, 2010). The GRS addressed both of these problems, but is still limited by the types and availability of its components—female and male life expectancy, adult literacy rate, gross enrollment in school, and estimated earned income. The GII was released for the first time in 2010 and has generated too little literature to fully evaluate its validity. However, Else-Quest and Grabe (2012) criticized the GII on the grounds that a multidimensional indicator may dilute effects when it would be preferable to choose a single, theoretically justified indicator of gender equity. Additionally, Permanyer (2013) noted that the computation of the GII is overly complicated and that LMIC are penalized for a high maternal mortality ratio and adolescent fertility rate, which may have more to do with the overall economic level of the country than gender discrimination. Furthermore, while women's health is included in the indicator, men's health is not. As for its virtues, the GII is the only measure of gender equality that includes indicators of female reproductive health, which has the most influential effect on country rankings (Gaye et al., 2010). Female reproductive health may be a particularly relevant indicator for this investigation because maternal mortality puts children at risk, as does having a teenage mother. Like the GRS, the availability and quality of data used to compute the GII is an issue. Unfortunately, the GRS and GII were missing data for a proportion of the LMIC used in this monograph. It is also possible that the measures of national gender equality used here are too blunt, inappropriate, or disparate to tap culturally specific expectations associated with gender roles (Else-Quest & Grabe, 2012). For example, it may be that differences in adult female and male literacy rates or relative representation in parliament (macrosystem indices) are too far removed from microsystem issues associated with child mortality, growth, caregiving, discipline, or labor to be direct or predictive. Moreover, LMIC vary in their homogeneity. Thus, country-level indicators of gender inequality may reflect the overall climate in which a child develops, but still not capture the complex reasons why parents choose different forms of, say, child labor for their girls and boys.

For its part, the HDI has been criticized on technical grounds that it is unlikely that equally weighting its constituent indices adequately conveys what countries afford their citizens for countries where there is considerable wealth. Neither does the HDI consider the extent to which countries have policies that lead to a sustainable future (Sagar & Najam, 1998). However, the HDI has a record of relations with a number of important indicators of health and well-being (Bray, Jemal, Grey, Ferlay, & Forman, 2012; Britto & Ulkuer, 2012).

Offsetting many of these limitations are the facts that MICS data were collected in large numbers of underserved, underresearched LMIC using a standard protocol that allowed us to make unique gender comparisons, information that is almost completely lacking in the contemporary developmental science literature.

POLICY IMPLICATIONS OF THE MICS

Generally speaking, gender stereotypes are thought to shape adults' perceptions of children, and child gender thought to encourage different parental cognitions and practices (Bornstein, 2015). Adults' gender conceptions and labeling of children help to determine how the social worlds and developmental trajectories of girls and boys are uniquely organized. The prevailing view is that girls (in LMIC and elsewhere) are at a disadvantage compared to boys (UNICEF, 2007b). Across all domains studied here, we found that girls and boys were mostly equal. Boys have more growth problems, are disciplined more harshly, work more for the family and outside the home, and die in greater numbers. Girls are less likely than boys to receive some forms of enriching caregiving and work more inside the home. At least in the earliest years and in the developmental domains reported here, the widespread belief that girls are consistently poorly treated relative to boys appears to be misplaced. In effect, even in societies (and families) where there may be favoritism for male offspring, the supposed gender advantage does not directly translate to better experiences for young boys versus girls in all areas of life. Social policy should attend to the small, but perhaps consistent and so possibly meaningful, disadvantage for boys in some domains of development.

Gender roles unfold within the context of societal stereotypes about females and males. Gender stereotypes also often become rationalizations that further justify differential gender role distributions (Hoffman & Hurst, 1990; Williams & Best, 1982), and contextual information about being female or male can lead to the creation of gender schemas that facilitate gender-related views of life (Martin, 2000) and eventuate in differential treatment of girls and boys. Parents in different cultures are believed to engage in child socialization practices intended to cultivate values and behaviors that promote adaptation to the social, economic, and ecological conditions of their society (Super & Harkness, 1986; Quinn, 2005). However, there are cultural differences in which values are prioritized to define optimal endpoints of child development (Greenfield, Keller, Fuligni, & Maynard, 2003; Harkness & Super, 1996; LeVine, 2003).

Although the two genders of young children were not treated consistently differently across LMIC, overall levels of certain variables for both girls and boys in LMIC warrant discussion in terms of policy. For example, book reading, a developmentally important experience, was a caregiving practice that seems relatively neglected. Notably, prevalence of kinds of caregiving that did not require caregiver literacy or the availability of costly materials was greater. Thus, caregivers should be alerted to the fact that young children benefit from naming or storytelling and "behavioral investment" in these kinds of caregiving early in life likely promote the development of important child capabilities and longer term educational achievement (Gottfried,

Schlackman, Gottfried, & Boutin-Martinez, 2015). Ideally, all caregivers would engage in all kinds of positive caregiving because each caregiving practice provides the child with important life experiences that stimulate his or her developing brain and foster cognitive and socioemotional skills.

Other specific issues we studied prompt additional specific policy implications. For example, child labor is prominent in LMIC, but the short-term advantage it affords families may perpetuate poverty. Children who work or spend many hours attending to household responsibilities are less likely to attend school. Controlling for years of education, child labor is associated with diminished adult earnings (Emerson & Souza, 2007; Knaul, 2001). Our findings also support the importance of considering excessive household chores (>28 hr/week) as child labor. Girls were more likely to engage in excessive household chores than boys. However, the variability in our data highlights the need to assess the prevalence of specific types of child labor, working conditions, and motivations associated with child labor.

Across all domains of study, a strategy that shows the most promise for improving children's outcomes is increasing access to education. Having parents (especially mothers) who are better educated appears to improve the likelihood that children will be better nourished, gain greater access to needed health care, and be offered better educational opportunities (Ahmed, Creanga, Gillespie, & Tsui, 2003; Abuya, Ciera, & Kimani-Murage, 2012; Burchi, 2012; Currie & Moretti, 2003; Wachs, 2008). Maternal education is regularly associated with important caregiving beliefs and behaviors; for example, more-educated parents spend more time with their children (Guryan, Hurst, & Kearney, 2008) and possess more knowledge about child rearing and child development (Bornstein & Hahn, 2014). Better educated mothers have more knowledge about factors that reduce the risks of illness, and they implement practices at home to improve health. Educated parents provide their children with better social environments (Zadeh, Farnia, & Ungerleider, 2010), they utilize household resources in ways that foster child growth and well-being (Bornstein et al., 2015), they are less likely to resort to harsh discipline (Straus & Stewart, 1999), and they are less likely to place their children into the labor force early (Leinberger-Jabari, Parker, & Oberg, 2005). Educating girls would, therefore, have positive cascading effects on human development and national economies (at least in the long term) because more educated girls delay marriage and childbearing, are less likely to be poor, have children with fewer health and growth problems, and ensure that their offspring become educated as well (ILO, 2009; Leinberger-Jabari et al., 2005). Economic development and schooling are especially influential in positive cultural change (Kashima et al., 2009; Inglehart & Baker, 2000). In short, the affirmative characteristics of caregiver (especially maternal) education vis-à-vis child development are profound and pervasive.

Engendering Development (World Bank, 2001) called for policies to address gender imbalances in "rights, resources, and voice," recommending that institutional structures be redesigned to promote gender equality. Gender equity is a humanitarian goal in its own right, as inequity anywhere reflects social failure. For example, gender inequality in education and access to resources may prevent reductions of child mortality and expansion of education of the next generation. Furthermore, gender inequality instrumentally penalizes development goals, undermines economic growth, and obstructs progress in the whole society (Osmani & Sen, 2003).

CONCLUSIONS

Psychological and developmental science have long been fascinated with the idea of gender differences, believing that gender differences are large and immutable. The "gender similarities hypothesis" (Hyde, 2005, 2014) raises the possibility of theorizing gender similarities. Our data largely (although not entirely) support similarities between the genders in LMIC. Variation in socialization experiences in young children and their developmental outcomes lies within, rather than between, female and male gender groups, likely reflecting other values and beliefs parents have and the broader set of affordances of family life. The gender difference effects we observed in LMIC were consistently small, even if some (disfavoring boys) were fairly consistent. Most studies in developmental science include only one region, one country, or a small selection of countries. In this monograph of the SRCD, we analyzed data on large nationally representative samples of young children and caregivers in many LMIC, thereby addressing major gaps in the developmental literature having to do with child gender, development domains, and underresearched populations. By exploring child gender across developmental domains in LMIC, we expand the knowledge base about gender similarities and differences in early childhood. In this regard alone, the MICS data set represents a unique resource. Multinational inquiry provides a strong medium to explore and distinguish uniformity and diversity in child gender.

Whether women and men are fundamentally similar or different has been long debated, and an Andes of research has been conducted on gender. If the primary concern of developmental science is to identify factors connected to child well-being, our data suggest that emphases on early child gender differences may be greater than is useful for guiding practice or policy. That does not mean that some gender-related differences do not have significant consequences and, thus, are important to carefully delineate. It is telling and paradoxical that, in spite of the fact that young girls and boys are biologically and psychologically more similar than different, children growing up in traditional or modern societies alike can expect to live qualitatively different lives based on their gender. This developmental paradox should stimulate future theory and research. Cultural forces might influence how people think about themselves in terms of gender, their perceptions of femininity and masculinity generally, children's gender-related socialization, and pressures to conform ultimately to distinctive gender roles. The cultural forces that bring about gender contrasts in a society manifest in many guises and include the statuses of women and men, the social division of labor, relative involvement of caregiving, economic opportunities, and religious values.

The Convention on the Rights of the Child (CRC; Limber & Flekkoy, 1995) supposes an ecological perspective in stipulating rights, with prominent place given to contexts of development. Furthermore, Implementing Child Rights in Early Childhood (General Comment No. 7) underscores "Ensuring (child) survival and physical health are priorities" (United Nations, 2006, p. 4), and the post-2015 Sustainable Development Goals (SDGs; United Nations General Assembly, 2015) renewed a global commitment to gender equality for children. All children have rights to high-standard nutrition and health care, to an environment that supports their thriving, to nurturing and stimulating caregiving, to freedom from neglect and abuse, and to equivalent treatment vis-à-vis work regardless of their gender.

REFERENCES

> This article is part of the issue "Gender in Low- and Middle-Income Countries," Bornstein, Putnick, Lansford, Deater-Deckard, and Bradley (Issue Authors). For a full listing of articles in this issue, see: http://onlinelibrary.wiley.com/doi/10.1111/mono.v81.1/issuetoc.

Abou-Ali, H. (2003). *The effect of water and sanitation on child mortality in Egypt.* Sweden: Göteburg University.

Abrams, D., Sparkes, K., & Hogg, M. A. (1985). Gender salience and social identity: The impact of sex of siblings on educational and occupational aspirations. *British Journal of Educational Psychology,* **55**, 224–232.

Abrams, D., Wetherell, M., Cochrane, S., Hogg, M. A., & Turner J. C. (1990). Knowing what to think by knowing who you are: Self-categorization and the nature of norm formation, conformity and group polarization. *British Journal of Social Psychology,* **29**, 97–119.

Abu-Ghaida, D., & Klasen, S. (2004). *The economic and human development costs of missing the Millennium Development Goal on gender equity.* Washington, DC: World Bank.

Abuya, B. A., Ciera, J., & Kimani-Murage, E. (2012). Effects of mother's education on child's nutritional status in the slums of Nairobi. *BMC Pediatrics,* **12**, 80.

Adair, L. S. (1999). Filipino children exhibit catch-up growth from age 2 to 12 years. *Journal of Nutrition,* **129**, 1140–1148.

Adams, S., Kuebli, J., Boyle, P. A., & Fivush, R. (1995). Gender differences in parent-child conversations about past emotions: A longitudinal investigation. *Sex Roles,* **33**(5–6), 309–323.

Admassie, A. (2003). Child labour and schooling in the context of a subsistence rural economy: Can they be compatible? *International Journal of Educational Development,* **23**, 167–185.

Aerts, D., Drachler, M., & Giugliani, E. R. (2004). Determinants of growth retardation in southern Brazil. *Cadernos Saude Publica,* **20**, 1182–1190.

Corresponding author: Marc H. Bornstein, Child and Family Research, *Eunice Kennedy Shriver,* National Institute of Child Health and Human Development, National Institutes of Health, Suite 8030, 6705 Rockledge Drive, Bethesda MD 20892-7971; email: Marc_H_Bornstein@nih.gov.
DOI: 10.1111/mono.12230
© 2015 The Society for Research in Child Development, Inc.

Agha, S. 2000. The determinants of infant mortality in Pakistan. *Social Science, Medicine*, **51**, 199–208.

Ahmed, S., Creanga, A. A., Gillespie, D. G., & Tsui, A. O. (2013). Economic status, education and empowerment: Implications for maternal health service utilization in developing countries. *PLoS ONE*, **5**, e11190.

Alexander, G. M., & Wilcox, T. (2012). Sex differences in early infancy. *Child Development Perspectives*, **6**, 400–406.

Allais, F. B. (2009). *Assessing the gender gap: Evidence from SIMPOC surveys*. Geneva: International Labour Organization. Retrieved from http://www.ilo.org/ipecinfo/product/viewProduct.do?productId=10952

Allison, P. D. (2008). *Convergence failures in logistic regression* (Paper 360-2008). Retrieved from http://www2.sas.com/proceedings/forum2008/ 360-2008. pdf

American Academy of Pediatrics. (2001). Prevention of agricultural injuries among children and adolescents. *Pediatrics*, **108**, 1016–1019.

Anker R. (1997). Theories of occupational segregation by sex: An overview. *International Labour Review*, **136**, 315–40.

Annerbäck, E.-M., Svedin, C.-G., & Gustafsson, P. A. (2010). Characteristic features of severe child physical abuse—A multi-informant approach. *Journal of Family Violence*, **25**, 165–172.

Antill, J. K., Goodnow, J. J., Russell, G., & Cotton, S. (1996). The influence of parents and family context on children's involvement in household tasks. *Sex Roles*, **34**, 215–236. doi: 10.1007/BF01544297

Archer, J. (2004). Sex differences in aggression in real-world settings: A meta-analytic review. *Review of General Psychology*, **8**, 291–322.

Aribibhola, A. (2008). Housing policy formulation in developing countries: Evidence from programme implementation from Akure, Ondo State, Nigeria. *Journal of Human Ecology*, **23**, 125–134.

Arnett, J. J. (2008). The neglected 95%: Why American psychology needs to become less American. *American Psychologist*, **63**, 602–614.

Awasthi, S., Glick, H. A., & Fletcher, R. J. H. (1996). Effects of cooking fuels on respiratory diseases in preschool children in Lucknow India. *American Journal of Tropical Medicine & Hygiene*, **55**, 48–51.

Azariadis, C., & Drazen, D. (1990). Threshold externalities in economic development. *Quarterly Journal of Economics*, **105**, 501–526.

Bakeera, S. K., Wamala, S. P., Galea, S., State, A., Peterson, S., & Pariyo, G. W. (2009). Community perceptions and factors influencing utilization of health services in Uganda. *International Journal for Equity in Health*, **8**(25). doi: 10.1186/1475-9276-8-25

Bandura, A. (1989). Regulation of cognitive processes through perceived self-efficacy. *Developmental Psychology*, **25**, 729–735.

Barkin, S., Scheindlin, B., Ip, E., Richardson, I., & Finch, S. (2007). Determinants of parental discipline practices: A national sample from primary care practices. *Clinical Pediatrics*, **46**, 64–66.

Barnard, K. E., & Solchany, J. E. (2002). Mothering. In M. H. Bornstein (Ed.), *Handbook of parenting: Vol. 3. Being and becoming a parent* (2nd ed., pp. 3–26). Mahwah, NJ: Erlbaum.

Barry, H. III, Bacon, M. K., & Child, I. L. (1957). A cross-cultural survey of some sex differences in socialization. *Journal of Abnormal and Social Psychology*, **55**, 327–332.

REFERENCES

Bartlett, S. (2005). Water, sanitation and urban children: The need to go beyond "improved" provision. *Children, Youth & Environments*, **15**, 115–137.

Beegle, K., Dehejia, R., & Gatti, R. (2009). Why should we care about child labor? The education, labor market, and health consequences of child labor. *The Journal of Human Resources*, **44**, 871–889.

Belsky, J., Gilstrap, B., & Rovine, M. (1984). The Pennsylvania Infant and Family Development Project: I. Stability and change in mother-infant and father-infant interaction in a family setting at one, three, and nine months. *Child Development*, **55**, 692–705.

Benenson, J. F. (1996). Gender differences in the development of relationships. In G. G. Noam & K. W. Fischer (Eds.), *Development and vulnerability in close relationships* (pp. 263–286). Mahwah, NJ: Erlbaum.

Beneria, L., & Permanyer, I. (2010). The measurement of socio-economic gender inequality revisited. *Development and Change*, **41**, 375–399.

Berkman, D. S., Lescano, A. G., Gilman, R. H., Lopez, S. L., & Black, M. M. (2002). Effects of stunting, diarrhoeal disease, and parasitic infection during infancy on cognition in late childhood: A follow-up study. *Lancet*, **359**, 564–571.

Best, D. L. (2010). Gender. In M. H. Bornstein (Ed.), *Handbook of cultural developmental science* (pp. 209–222). New York, NY: Psychology Press.

Best, D. L., & Williams, J. E. (1997). Sex, gender, and culture. In J. W. Berry, M. H. Segall, & C. Kagitcibasi (Eds.), *Handbook of cross-cultural psychology: Vol. 3 Social behavior and applications* (pp. 163–212). Boston, MA: Allyn & Bacon.

Bianchi, S. M., Milkie, M. A., Sayer, L. C., & Robinson, J. P. (2000). Is anyone doing the housework? Trends in the gender division of household labor. *Social Forces*, **79**, 191–228.

Bird, C. (1997). Gender differences in the social and economic burdens of parenting and psychological distress. *Journal of Marriage and the Family*, **59**, 809–823.

Bisai, S., & Mallick, C. (2009). Growth pattern and prevalence of underweight, stunting and wasting among infants of Kolkata, West Bengal, India. *The Internet Journal of Biological Anthropology*, **3**, 2.

Bloch, M. N., & Adler, S. M. (1994). African children's play and the emergence of the sexual division of labor. In J. L. Roopnarine, J. E. Johnson, & F. H. Hooper (Eds.), *Children's play in diverse cultures* (pp. 148–178). Albany: State University of New York Press.

Bonke, J. (2010). Children's housework—Are girls more active than boys? *International Journal of Time Use Research*, **7**, 1–16.

Bornstein, M. H. (1980). Cross-cultural developmental psychology. In M. H. Bornstein (Ed.), *Comparative methods in psychology* (pp. 231–281). Hillsdale, NJ: Erlbaum.

Bornstein, M. H. (1991). Approaches to parenting in culture. In M. H. Bornstein (Ed.), *Cultural approaches to parenting* (pp. 3–19). Hillsdale, NJ: Erlbaum.

Bornstein, M. H. (1995). Form and function: Implications for studies of culture and human development. *Culture & Psychology*, **1**, 123–137.

Bornstein, M. H. (Ed.). (2002). *Handbook of parenting* (2nd ed., Vols. 1–5). Mahwah, NJ: Erlbaum.

Bornstein, M. H. (2006). Parenting science and practice. In W. Damon (Series Ed.) & K. A. Renninger & I. E. Sigel (Vol. Eds.), *Handbook of child psychology: Vol. 4. Child psychology in practice* (6th ed., pp. 893–949). New York, NY: Wiley.

Bornstein, M. H. (2007). On the significance of social relationships in the development of children's earliest symbolic play: An ecological perspective. In A. Göncü & S. Gaskins (Eds.), *Play and development* (pp. 101–129). Mahwah, NJ: Erlbaum.

Bornstein, M. H. (Ed.). (2010). *The handbook of cultural developmental science. Part 1. Domains of development across cultures. Part 2. Development in different places on earth.* New York, NY: Psychology Press.

Bornstein, M. H. (2013). Parenting × gender × culture × time. In W. B. Wilcox & K. K. Kline (Eds.), *Gender and parenthood: Biological and social scientific perspective* (pp. 91–119). New York, NY: Columbia University Press.

Bornstein, M. H. (2014). Parents' reports about their children's lives. In G. B. Melton, A. Ben-Arieh, J. Cashmore, G. S. Goodman, & N. K. Worley (Eds.), *The SAGE handbook of child research* (pp. 486–533). Los Angeles, CA: SAGE.

Bornstein, M. H. (2015). Children's parents. In M. H. Bornstein & T. Leventhal (Eds.), *Ecological settings and processes in developmental systems.* Volume 4 of the *Handbook of child psychology and developmental science* (7th ed., pp. 55–132). Hoboken, NJ: Wiley.

Bornstein, M. H., & Hahn, C.-S. (2014). Mothers' knowledge about child development and childrearing: National and cross-national studies. Unpublished manuscript, National Institute of Child Health and Human Development.

Bornstein, M. H., & Lansford, J. E. (2010). Parenting. In M. H. Bornstein (Ed.), *Handbook of cultural developmental science* (pp. 259–278). New York, NY: Psychology Press.

Bornstein, M. H., & Putnick, D. L. (2012). Cognitive and socioemotional caregiving in developing countries. *Child Development*, **83**, 46–61.

Bornstein, M. H., & Putnick, D. L. (2016). Mothers' and fathers' parenting practices with their daughters and sons in low- and middle-income countries. *Monographs of the SRCD*, **81**(1), 61–78.

Bornstein, M. H., Putnick, D. L., Bradley, R. H., Deater-Deckard, K., & Lansford, J. E. (2016). Gender in low- and middle-income countries: Reflections, limitations, directions, and implications. *Monographs of the SRCD*, **81**(1), 124–145.

Bornstein, M. H., Putnick, D. L. Bradley, R. H., Deater-Deckard, K., Lansford, J. E., & Ota, Y. (2016). Gender in low- and middle-income countries: General methods. *Monographs of the SRCD*, **81**(1), 26–34.

Bornstein, M. H., Putnick, D. L., Bradley, R. H., Lansford, J. E., & Deater-Deckard, K. (2015). Pathways among caregiver education, household resources, and infant growth in 39 low- and middle-income countries. *Infancy*, **20**(4), 353–376.

Bornstein, M. H., Putnick, D. L., Lansford, J. E., Pastorelli, C., Skinner, A. T., Sorbring, E., et al. (2015). Mother and father socially desirable responding in nine countries: Two kinds of agreement and relations to parenting self-reports. *International Journal of Psychology*, **50**, 174–185.

Bornstein, M. H., Rebello Britto, P., Nonoyama-Tarumi, Y., Ota, Y., Petrovic, O., & Putnick, D. L. (2012). Child development in developing countries: Introduction and methods. *Child Development*, **83**, 16–31.

Boyle, M. H., Racine, Y., Georgiades, K., Snelling, D., Hong, S., Omariba, W., et al. (2006). The influence of economic development level, household wealth and maternal education on child health in a developing world. *Social Science & Medicine*, **63**, 2242–2254.

Bradley, R. H. (2004). Chaos, culture, and covariance structures: A dynamic systems view of children's experiences at home. *Parenting: Science and Practice*, **4**, 243–257.

REFERENCES

Bradley, R. H. (2015). Children's housing and physical environments. In M. H. Bornstein & T. Leventhal (Eds.), *Ecological settings and processes in developmental systems*. Volume 4 of the *Handbook of child psychology and developmental science* (7th ed., pp. 455–492). Hoboken, NJ: Wiley.

Bradley, R. H., Corwyn, R. F., McAdoo, H. P., & Garća Coll, C. (2001). The home environments of children in the United States part I: Variations by age, ethnicity, and poverty status. *Child development*, **72**, 1844–1867.

Bradley, R. H., & Putnick, D. L. (2012). Housing quality and access to material and learning resources within the home environment in developing countries. *Child Development*, **83**, 76–91.

Bradley, R. H., & Putnick, D. L. (2016). The role of physical capital assets in young girls' and boys' mortality and growth in low- and middle-income countries. *Monographs of the SRCD*, **81**(1), 35–60.

Bray, F., Jemal, A., Grey, N., Ferlay, J., & Forman, D. (2012). Global cancer transitions according to the Human Development Index (2008–2030): A population-based study. *The Lancet Oncology*, **13**(8), 790–801.

Britto, P. R., & Ulkuer, N. (2012). Child development in developing countries: Child rights and policy implications. *Child Development*, **83**, 92–103.

Brody L. (1999). *Gender, emotion and the family*. Cambridge, MA: Harvard University Press.

Brody, L. R. (2000). The socialization of gender differences in emotional expression: Display rules, infant temperament, and differentiation. In A. H. Fischer (Ed.), *Gender and emotion: Social psychological perspectives*. New York, NY: Cambridge University Press.

Bronfenbrenner, U., & Morris, P. A. (2006). The bioecological model of human development. In R. M. Lerner & W. Damon (Eds.), *Handbook of child psychology: Vol. 1. Theoretical models of human development* (6th ed., pp. 793–828). Hoboken, NJ: Wiley.

Budhwani, N. N., Wee, B., & McLean, G. N. (2004). Should child labor be eliminated? An HRD perspective. *Human Resource Development Quarterly*, **15**, 107–116.

Bugental, D. B., & Grusec, J. E. (2006). Socialization processes. In W. Damon (Series Ed.) & N. Eisenberg (Vol. Ed.), *Handbook of child psychology: Vol. 3. Social, emotional, and personality development* (6th ed., pp. 366–428). New York, NY: Wiley.

Burchi, F. (2012). Whose education affects a child's nutritional status? From parents' to household's education. *Demographic Research*, **27**, 681–704.

Burgner, D., Jamieson, S. E., & Blackwell, J. M. (2006). Genetic susceptibility to infectious diseases: Big is beautiful, but will bigger be even better? *Lancet Infectious Diseases*, **6**, 653–663.

Buss, D. M., & Schmitt, D. P. (1993). Sexual strategies theory: An evolutionary perspective on human mating. *Psychological Bulletin*, **100**, 204–232.

Bussey, K., & Bandura, A. (1999). Social cognitive theory of gender development and differentiation. *Psychological Review*, **106**, 676–713.

Cappa, C., Wardlaw, T., & Morgan, R. (2011). Disparities by sex in early childhood and adolescence. *Lancet*, **378**, 1122–1123.

Chalasani, S. (2010). *The changing relationship between household wealth and child survival in India*. DHS Working Papers No. 69. Calverton, MD, USA: ICF Macro.

Chaplin, T., Cole, P. M., & Zahn-Waxler, C. (2005). Parental socialization of emotion expression: Gender differences and relations to child adjustment. *Emotion*, **5**, 80–88.

Chen, E., Matthews, K. A., & Boyce, W. T. (2002). Socioeconomic conditions in children's health: How and why do these conditions change with age? *Psychological Bulletin*, **128**, 295–329.

Chen, X., & French, D. C. (2008). Children's social competence in cultural context. *Annual Review of Psychology*, **59**, 591–616.

Cheung, Y. B. (2006). Growth and cognitive function of Indonesian children: Zero-inflated proportion models. *Statistical Medicine*, **25**, 3011–3022.

Chodorow, N. (1978). *The reproduction of mothering.* Berkeley: University of California Press.

Choi, Y., Bishai, D., & Hill, K. (2005). Socioeconomic differentials in supplementation of vitamin A: Evidence from the Philippines. *Journal of Health, Population and Nutrition*, **23**, 156–164.

Chow, E. N., Wilkinson, D. Y., & Baca Zinn, M. (Eds.). (1996). *Race, class, & gender: Common bonds, different voices. Gender & society readers.* Thousand Oaks, CA: SAGE.

Chowa, G., Ansong, D., & Masa, R. (2010). Assets and child well-being in developing countries: A research review. *Children and Youth Services Review*, **32**, 1508–1519.

Clarke-Stewart, K. A., & Allhusen, V. D. (2002). Nonparental caregiving. In M. H. Bornstein (Ed.), *Handbook of parenting Vol. 3 Status and social conditions of parenting* (2nd ed., pp. 215–252). Mahwah, NJ: Erlbaum.

Clutton-Brock, T. H. (1989). Mammalian mating systems. *Proceedings of the Royal Society of London. B. Biological Sciences*, **236**(1285), 339–372.

Clutton-Brock, T. H. (1991). *The evolution of parental care.* Princeton, NJ: Princeton University Press.

Clutton-Brock, T. H., & Vincent, A. C. J. (1991). Sexual selection and the potential reproductive rates of males and females. *Science*, **351**, 58–60.

Cohen, J. (1988). *Statistical power analysis for the behavioral sciences.* Hillsdale, NJ: Erlbaum.

Collins, D. A., Sithole, S. D., & Martin, K. S. (1990). Indoor woodsmoke pollution causing lower respiratory disease in children. *Tropical Doctor*, **20**, 151–155.

Collins, W. A., & Russell, G. (1991). Mother-child and father-child relationships in middle childhood and adolescence: A developmental analysis. *Developmental Review*, **11**, 99–136.

Collins, W. A., Maccoby, E. E., Steinberg, L., Hetherington, E. M., & Bornstein, M. H. (2001). Toward nature with nurture. *American Psychologist*, **56**, 171–173.

Collins, W. A., Madsen, S. D., & Susman-Stillman, A. (2002). Parenting during middle childhood. In M. H. Bornstein (Ed.), *Handbook of parenting (2nd ed.), Volume 3: Being and becoming a parent* (pp. 73–101). Mahwah, NJ: Erlbaum.

Coltrane, S. (1996). *Family man: Fatherhood, housework, and gender equity.* New York, NY: Oxford University Press.

Coltrane, S. (2000). Research on household labor: Modeling and measuring the social embeddedness of routine family work. *Journal of Marriage and Family*, **62**, 1208–1233.

Costa P. Jr., Terracciano, A., & McCrae, R. R. (2001). Gender differences in personality traits across cultures: Robust and surprising findings. *Journal of Personality and Social Psychology*, **81**, 322–331.

Cowan, P. A., Cowan, C. P., & Kerig, P. K. (1993). Mothers, fathers, sons, and daughters: Gender differences in family formation and parenting style. In P. A. Cowan, D. Field, D. A. Hansen, A. Skolnick, & G. E. Swanson (Eds.), *Family, self, and society: Toward a new agenda for family research* (pp. 165–195). Hillsdale, NJ: Erlbaum.

Crespi, I. (2003). Socialization and gender roles with the family: A study on adolescents and their parents in Great Britain. *Annals of the Marie Curie Fellowship Association, 3.* Retrieved from http://mariecurie.org/annals/volume3/crespi.pdf

Crouch, J. L., & Behl, L. E. (2001). Relationships among parental beliefs in corporal punishment, reported stress, and physical child abuse potential. *Child Abuse & Neglect*, **25**, 413–419.

Crowley, K., Callanan, M. A., Tenenbaum, H. R., & Allen, E. (2001). Parents explain more often to boys than to girls during shared scientific thinking. *Psychological Science*, **12**, 258–261.

Cunningham-Rundles, S., Moon, A., & McNeeley, D. F. (2008). Malnutrition and host defense. In C. Duggan, J. Watkins, & W. A. Walker (Eds.), *Nutrition in pediatrics* (4th ed., pp. 261–271). Hamilton, Ontario, Canada: Decker.

Currie, J., & Moretti, E. (2003). Mother's education and intergenerational transmission of capital: Evidence from college openings. *The Quarterly Journal of Economics*, **118**, 1495–1532.

Dammert, A. C. (2010). Siblings, child labor, and schooling in Nicaragua and Guatemala. *Journal of Population Economics*, **23**, 199–224.

Darmon, N., & Drewnowski, A. (2008). Does social class predict diet quality? *American Journal of Clinical Nutrition*, **87**, 1107–1117.

Davis, O. S. P., Haworth, C. M. A., Lewis, C. M., & Plomin, R. (2012). Visual analysis of geocoded twin data puts nature and nurture on the map. *Molecular Psychiatry*, **17**, 867–874.

de Onis, M., Blossner, M., & Borghi, E. (2012). Prevalence and trends of stunting among preschool children. *Public Health Nutrition*, **15**, 142–148.

De Silva, M. J., & Harpham, T. (2007). Maternal social capital and child nutritional status in four developing countries. *Health & Place*, **13**, 341–355.

Deater-Deckard, K. (2004). *Parenting stress*. New Haven, CT: Yale University Press.

Deater-Deckard, K., & Dodge, K. A. (1997). Externalizing behavior problems and discipline revisited: Nonlinear effects and variation by culture, context, and gender. *Psychological Inquiry*, **8**, 161–175.

Deater-Deckard, K., & Lansford, J. E. (2016). Daughters' and sons' exposure to childrearing discipline and violence in low- and middle-income countries. *Monographs of the SRCD*, **81**(1), 79–104.

Deaton, A. (2001). Counting the world's poor: Problems and possible solutions. *World Bank Research Observer*, **16**, 125–147.

Dercon, S., & Krishnan, P. (2009). Poverty and the psychosocial competencies of children: Evidence from the Young Lives sample in four developing countries. *Children, Youth and Environments*, **19**, 138–163.

Dercon, S., & Singh, A. (2013). From nutrition to aspirations and self-efficacy: gender bias over time among children in four countries. *World Development*, **45**, 31–50.

Dessy, S. E. (2000). A defense of compulsive measures against child labor. *Journal of Development Economics*, **62**, 261–275.

Dessy, S. E., & Pallage, S. (2005). A theory of the worst forms of child labour. *The Economic Journal*, **115**, 68–87.

Diener, M. L., & Lucas, R. E. (2004). Adults' desires for children's emotions across 48 countries: Associations with individual and national characteristics. *Journal of Cross-Cultural Psychology*, **35**, 525–547.

Dijkstra, A. G. (2002). Revisiting UNDP's GDI and GEM: Towards an alternative. *Social Indicators Research*, **57**, 301–338. doi: 10.1023/A:1014726207604

Dijkstra, A. G., & Hanmer, L. C. (2000). Measuring socio-economic gender inequality, towards an alternative to the UNDP gender-related development index. *Feminist Economics*, **6**, 41–75. doi: 10.1080/13545700050076106

Dorman, P. (2001). *Child labour in the developed economies.* ILO/IPEC Working Paper. Geneva: International Labour Organization. Retrieved from http://ilo-mirror.library.cornell.edu/public/english/standards/ipec/publ/policy/papers/brasil/fourth.pdf

Draper, P., & Harpending, H. (1982). Father absence and reproductive strategy: An evolutionary perspective. *Journal of Anthropological Research*, **38**, 255–273.

Dumas, C. (2007). Why do parents make their children work? A test of the poverty hypothesis in rural areas of Burkina Faso. *Oxford Economic Papers*, **59**, 301–329.

Dunn, R. R., Davies, J., Harris, N. C., & Gavin, M. C. (2010). Global drivers of human pathogen richness and prevalence. *Proceedings of the Royal Society, Biological Sciences*, **277**, 2587–2595. doi: 10.1098/rspb.2010.0340

Durik, A. M., Hyde, J. S., Marks, A. C., Roy, A. L., Anaya, D., & Schultz, G. (2006). Ethnicity and gender stereotypes of emotion. *Sex Roles*, **54**, 429–445.

Durrant, J. E. (2008). Physical punishment, culture, and rights: Current issues for professionals. *Journal of Developmental & Behavioral Pediatrics*, **29**, 55–66.

Eagly, A. H., & Wood, W. (1999). The origins of sex differences in human behavior: Evolved dispositions versus social roles. *American Psychologist*, **54**, 408–423.

Eccles, J. S., Freedman-Doan, C., Frome, P., Jacobs, J., & Yoon, K. S. (2000). Gender-role socialization in the family: A longitudinal approach. In T. Eckes & H. M. Trautner (Eds.), *The developmental social psychology of gender* (pp. 333–360). Mahwah, NJ: Erlbaum.

Edin, K., & Lein, L. (1997). *Making ends meet.* New York, NY: Russell Sage.

Edmonds, E. V. (2006). Understanding sibling differences in child labor. *Journal of Population Economics*, **19**, 795–821.

Edwards, C. P., & Whiting, B. B. (1974). Women and dependency. *Politics and Society*, **4**, 343–355.

Eisenberg, N., Cumberland, A., & Spinrad, T. L. (1998). Parental socialization of emotion. *Psychology Inquiry*, **9**, 241–273.

Eisenberg, N., Wolchik, S. A., Hernandez, R., & Pasternak, J. (1985). Parental socialization of young children's play: A short-term longitudinal study. *Child Development*, **56**, 1506–1513.

Else-Quest, N. M., & Grabe, S. (2012). The political is personal: Measurement and application of nation-level indicators of gender equity in psychological research. *Psychology of Women Quarterly*, **36**, 131–144. doi: 10.1177/0361684312441592

Ember, C. R., & Ember, M. (2005). Explaining corporal punishment of children: A cross-cultural study. *American Anthropologist*, **107**, 609–619.

Emerson, P. M., & Souza, A. P. (2007). Is *child labor harmful? The impact of working earlier in life on adult earnings.* IZA Discussion Paper No. 3027. Bonn, Germany: Iza. Retrieved from http://ftp.iza.org/dp3027.pdf

Endendijk, J. J., Groeneveld, M. G., van Berkel, S. R., Hallers-Haalboom, E. T., Mesman, J., & Bakermans-Kranenburg, M. J. (2013). Gender stereotypes in the family context: Mothers, fathers, and siblings. *Sex Roles*, **68**, 577–590. doi: 10.1007/s11199-013-0265-4

Engle, P. L., & Black, M. M. (2008). The effect of poverty of child development and educational outcomes. *Annals of the New York Academy of Sciences*, **1136**, 243–256.

Engle, P. L., Black, M. M., Behrman, J. R., Cabral de Mello, M., Gertler, P. J., Kapiriri, L., et al. (2007). Strategies to avoid the loss of developmental potential in more than 200 million children in the developing world. *Lancet*, **369**, 229–242.

REFERENCES

Ertem, I. O., Atay, G., Dogan, D. G., Bayan, A., Bingoler, B. E., Gok, C. G., et al. (2007). Mothers' knowledge of young child development in a developing country. *Child: Care, Health and Development*, **33**, 728–737.

Etaugh, C. (1993). Maternal employment: Effects on children. In J. Frankel (Ed.), *The employed mother and the family context* (pp. 68–88). New York, NY: Springer.

Evans, R. (2010). Children's caring roles and responsibilities within the family in Africa. *Geography Compass*, **4**, 1477–1496.

Fares, J., & Raju, D. (2007). *Child labor across the developing world: Patterns and correlations.* World Bank Policy Research Working Paper 4119. Retrieved from http://www-wds.worldbank.org/servlet/WDSContentServer/WDSP/IB/2007/01/25/000016406_20070125152956/Rendered/PDF/wps4119.pdf

Feitelson, D., & Goldstein, Z. (1986). Patterns of book ownership and reading to young children in Israeli school-oriented and non-school-oriented families. *The Reading Teacher*, 39, 924-930. Retrieved from http://www.reading.org/general/publications/journals/rt.aspx

Fekadu, D., Hägglöf, B., & Alem, A. (2010). Review of child labor with emphasis on mental health. *Current Psychiatry Reviews*, **6**, 176–183.

Fiadzo, E. (2004, June). *Estimating the determinants of housing quality: The case of Ghana.* Joint Center for Housing Studies, Harvard University. Paper No. W04-6.

Fisher-Thompson, D. (1993). Adult toy purchase for children: Factors affecting sex-typed toy selection. *Journal of Applied Developmental Psychology*, **14**, 385–406.

Fiske, S. T., & Stevens, L. E. (1993). What's so special about sex? Gender stereotyping and discrimination. In S. Oskamp & M. Costanzo (Eds.), *Gender issues in contemporary society. Claremont Symposium on Applied Social Psychology* (Vol. **6**, pp. 173–196). Thousand Oaks, CA: SAGE.

Fivush, R., Brotman, M. A., Buckner, J. P., & Goodman, S. H. (2000). Gender differences in parent-child emotion narratives. *Sex Roles*, **42**, 233–253.

Fivush, R., Berlin, L., McDermott Sales, J., Mennuti-Washburn, J., & Cassidy, J.(2003). Functions of parent-child reminiscing about emotionally negative events. *Memory*, **11**, 179–192.

Flinn, M. V. (1992). Paternal care in a Caribbean village. In B. S. Hewlett (Ed.), *Father-child relations: Cultural and biosocial contexts* (pp. 57–84). Hawthorne, NY: Aldine de Gruyter.

Forsythe, N., Korzeniewick, R. P., & Durrant, V. (1998). *Gender inequalities, economic growth, and structural adjustment: A longitudinal evaluation.* Paper presented to XXI Conference of the Latin American Studies Association (LASA), Washington. Available from http://www.ilo.org/wcmsp5/groups/public/--ed_emp/documents/publication/wcms_115121.pdf

French, D. C., Lee, O., & Pidada, S. U. (2006). Friendships of Indonesian, South Korean, and U.S. youth: Exclusivity, intimacy, enhancement of worth, and conflict. In X. Chen, D. C. French, & B. H. Schneider (Eds.), *Peer relationships in cultural context. Cambridge studies in social and emotional development* (pp. 379–402). New York, NY: Cambridge University Press.

Fung, H. (1999). Becoming a moral child: The socialization of shame among young Chinese children. *Ethos*, **27**, 180–209.

Gakidou, E., Cowling, K., Lozano, R., & Murray, C. J. (2010). Increased educational attainment and its effect on child mortality in 175 countries between 1970 and 2009: A systematic analysis. *The Lancet*, **376**, 959–974.

Galli, R. (2001). *The economic impact of child labour*. ILO Discussion Paper. Geneva: International Institute for Labour Studies. Retrieved from http://www.ilo.org/wcmsp5/groups/public/-dgreports/-inst/documents/publication/wcms_193680.pdf

Garcia-Coll, C., & Magnuson, K. (1999). Cultural influences on child development: Are we ready for a paradigm shift? In A. S. Masten (Ed.), *Cultural influences in child development* (pp. 1–24). Mahwah, NJ: Erlbaum.

Garside, R. B., & Klimes-Dougan, B. (2002). Socialization of discrete negative emotions: Gender differences and links with psychological distress. *Sex Roles*, **47**, 115–128.

Gauderman, W., Avol, E., Gilliland, F., Vora, H., Thomas, D., Berhane, K., et al. (2004). The effect of air pollution on lung development from 10 to 18 years of age. *New England Journal of Medicine*, **351**, 1057–1067.

Gaye, A., Klugman, J., Kovacevic, M., Twigg, S., & Zambrano, E. (2010). *Measuring key disparities in human development: The gender inequality index*. Human Development Reports Research Paper 2010/46. Retrieved from http://hdr.undp.org/sites/default/files/hdrp_2010_46.pdf

Gelman, S. A., Taylor, M. G., & Nguyen, S. P. (2004). Mother-child conversations about gender: Understanding the acquisition of essentialist beliefs. *Monographs of the Society for Research in Child Development*, **69**, vii-145.

Gershoff, E. T., Grogan-Kaylor, A., Lansford, J. E., Chang, L., Zelli, A., Deater-Deckard, K., et al. (2010). Parent discipline practices in an international sample: Associations with child behaviors and moderation by perceived normativeness. *Child Development*, **81**, 487–502.

Gibbons, E. D., Huebler, F., & Loaiza, E. (2005). *Child labour, education, and the principle of non-discrimination*. UNICEF Staff Working Papers. New York, NY: UNICEF. Retrieved from http://www.unicef.org/protection/Gibbons_Huebler_Loaiza_2005_Childlabor.pdf

Gielen, A. C., Wilson, M. E. Faden, R. R., Wissow, L., & Harvilchuck, J. D. (1995). In-home injury prevention practices for infants and toddlers: The role of parental beliefs, barriers, and housing quality. *Health Education Quarterly*, **22**, 85–95.

Goldman, J. D., & Goldman, R. J. (1983). Children's perceptions of parents and their roles: A cross-national study in Australia, England, North America, and Sweden. *Sex Roles*, **9**, 791–812.

Goodnow, J. J. (1988). Children's household work: Its nature and functions. *Psychological Bulletin*, **103**, 5–26.

Goodnow, J. J., Cashmore, J. A., Cotton, S., & Knight, R. (1984). Mothers' developmental timetables in two cultural groups. *International Journal of Psychology*, **19**, 193–205.

Goodwin, S. A., & Fiske, S. T. (2001). Power and gender: The double-edged sword of ambivalence. In R. K. Unger (Ed.), *Handbook of the psychology of women and gender* (pp. 358–366). Hoboken, NJ: Wiley.

Gottfried, A. W. (Ed.). (1984). *Home environment and early cognitive development*. Orlando, FL: Academic Press.

Gottfried, A.W., Schlackman, J., Gottfried, A. E., & Boutin-Martinez, A. S. (2015). Parental provision of early literacy environment as related to reading and educational outcomes across the academic life-span. *Parenting: Science and Practice*, **15**, 24–38.

Grantham-McGregor, S., Cheung, Y. B., Cueto, S., Glewwe, P., Richter, L., Strupp, B. et al. (2007). Developmental potential in the first 5 years for children in developing countries. *Lancet*, **369**, 60–70.

REFERENCES

Greenfield, P. M. (2009). Linking social change and developmental change: Shifting pathways of human development. *Developmental Psychology*, **45**, 401–418.

Greenfield, P. M., Brazelton, T. B., & Childs, C. P. (1989). From birth to maturity in Zinacantan: Ontogenesis in cultural context. In V. Bricker & G. Gosen (Eds.), *Ethnographic encounters in southern Mesoamerica: Celebratory essays in honor of Evon Z. Vogt* (pp. 177–216). Albany: Institute of Mesoamerican Studies, State University of New York.

Greenfield, P. M., Keller, H., Fuligni, A., & Maynard, A. (2003). Cultural pathways through universal development. *Annual Review of Psychology*, **54**, 461–490.

Griffin, P. B., & Griffin, M. B. (1992). Fathers and childcare among the Cagayan Agta. In B. S. Hewlett (Ed.), *Father-child relations: Cultural and biosocial contexts* (pp. 297–320). New York, NY: Aldine de Gruyter.

Guarcello, L., Lyon, S., & Rosati, F. C. (2008). *Child labour and education for all: An issue paper*. Working paper. Retrieved from http://ssrn.com/abstract=1780257

Gurin P., & Markus, H. (1989). Cognitive consequences of gender identity. In S. Skevington & D. Baker (Eds.), *The social identity of women* (pp. 152–72). Newbury Park, CA: SAGE.

Guryan, J., Hurst, E., & Kearney, M. S. (2008). Parental education and parental time with children. *Journal of Economic Perspective*, **22**, 23–46.

Hagemann, F., Diallo, Y., Etienne, A., & Mehran, F. (2006). *Global child labour trends 2000 to 2004*. Geneva: International Labour Organization.

Hall, A., Hewitt, G., Tuffrey, V., & de Silva, N. (2008). A review and meta-analysis of the impact of intestinal worms on child growth and nutrition. *Maternal & Child Nutrition*, **4**, 118–236.

Halle, T., Forry, N., Hair, E., Perper, K., Wandner, L., Wessel, J., et al. (2009). *Disparities in early learning and development*. Washington, DC: Child Trends.

Halpenny, C. M., Koski, K. G., Valdes, V. E., & Scott, M. E. (2012). Prediction of child health by household density and asset-based indices in impoverished indigenous villages in rural Panamá. *The American Journal of Tropical Medicine & Hygiene*, **86**, 280–291.

Harkness, S., & Super, C. M. (1986). The cultural structuring of children's play in a rural African community. In K. Blanchard (Ed.), *The many faces of play* (pp. 96–103). Champaign, IL: Human Kinetics.

Harkness, S., & Super, C. M. (2002). Culture and parenting. In M. H. Bornstein (Ed.), *Handbook of parenting. Vol. 2 Biology and ecology of parenting* (2nd ed., pp. 253–280). Mahwah, NJ: Erlbaum.

Harkness, S., Super, C. M., Moscardino, U., Rha, J.-H., Blom, M. J. M., Huitrón, B., et al. (2007). Cultural models and developmental agendas: Implications for arousal and self-regulation in early infancy. *Journal of Developmental Processes*, **2**, 5–39.

Harpham, T., Huttly, S., De Silva, M. J., & Abramsky, T. (2005). Maternal mental health and child nutritional status in four developing countries. *Journal of Epidemiology and Community Mental Health*, **59**, 1060–1064.

Hart, B., & Risley, T. R. (1995). *Meaningful differences in the everyday experience of young American children*. Baltimore, MD: Paul H Brookes.

Hausmann, R., Tyson, L. D., & Zahidi, S. (2010). *The global gender gap report 2010*. Geneva: World Economic Forum. Retrieved from http://www3.weforum.org/docs/WEF_GenderGap_Report_2010.pdf

Heady, C. (2003). The effect of child labor on learning achievement. *World Development*, **31**, 385–398.

Hendrix, L., & Johnson, G. D. (1985). Instrumental and expressive socialization: A false dichotomy. *Sex Roles*, **13**, 581–595.

Henrich, J., Heine, S. J., & Norenzayan, A. (2010). The weirdest people in the world? *Behavioral and Brain Sciences*, **33**, 61–83.

Herrin, W. E., Amaral, M. M., & Balihuta, A. M. (2013). The relationships between housing quality and occupant health in Uganda. *Social Science and Medicine*, **81**, 115–122.

Hesketh, T., & Xing, Z. W. (2006). Abnormal sex ratios in human populations: Causes and consequences. *Proceedings of the National Academy of Sciences*, **103**, 13271–13275.

Hewlett, B. S. (1988). Sexual selection and paternal investment among Aka pygmies. In L. Betzig, M. Borgerhoff Mulder, & P. Turke (Eds.), *Human reproductive behaviour: A Darwinian perspective* (pp. 263–276). Cambridge, England: Cambridge University Press.

Hewlett, B. S. (1991). *Intimate fathers: The nature and context of Aka Pygmy paternal infant care*. Ann Arbor: University of Michigan Press.

Hewlett, B. S. (Ed.). (1992). *Father-child relations: Cultural and biosocial contexts*. Hawthorne, NY: Walter de Gruyter.

Hewlett, B. S. (2004). Fathers in forager, farmer, and pastoral cultures. In M. E. Lamb (Ed.), *The role of the father in child development* (4th ed., pp. 182–195). Hoboken, NJ: Wiley.

Hill, K., & Upchurch, D. M. (1995). Gender differences in child health: Evidence from the demographic and health surveys. *Population and Development Review*, **21**, 127–151.

Hilton, J. M., & Haldeman, V. A. (1991). Gender differences in the performance of household tasks by adults and children in single-parent, two-earner families. *Journal of Family Issues*, **12**, 114–123.

Hoff, E., Laursen, B., & Tardif, T. (2002). Socioeconomic status and parenting. In M. H. Bornstein (Ed.), *Handbook of parenting Vol. 2 Biology and ecology of parenting* (2nd ed., pp. 231–252). Mahwah, NJ: Erlbaum.

Hoffman, C., & Hurst, N. (1990). Gender stereotypes: Perceptions or rationalization? *Journal of Personality and Social Psychology*, **58**, 197–208.

Hong, R., Banta, J. E., & Betancourt, J. A. (2006). Relationship between household wealth inequality and chronic under-nutrition in Bangladesh. *International Journal for Equity in Health*, **5**, 15.

Howe, L. D., Huttly, S. R., & Abramsky, T. (2006). Risk factors for injuries in young children in four developing countries: The Young Lives Study. *Tropical Medicine and International Health*, **11**, 1557–1566.

Huebler, F. (2008). *Child labour and school attendance: Evidence from MICS and DHS surveys*. Unpublished manuscript. Retrieved from http://www.childinfo.org/files/Child_labour_school_FHuebler_2008.pdf

Hurst, P. (2007). Health and child labor in agriculture. *Food and Nutrition Bulletin*, **28**, S364–S371.

Hyde, J. S. (2005). The gender similarities hypothesis. *American Psychologist*, **60**, 581–592.

Hyde, J. S. (2014). Gender similarities and differences. *Annual Review of Psychology*, **65**, 373–398.

Hyde, J. S., Lindberg, S. M., Linn, M. C., Ellis, A. B., & Williams, C. C. (2008). Gender similarities characterize math performance. *Science*, **321**, 494–495.

Inglehart, R. (1997). *Modernization and postmodernization: Cultural, economic, and political change in 43 societies* (Vol. 19). Princeton, NJ: Princeton University Press.

Inglehart, R., & Baker, W. E. (2000). Modernization, cultural change, and the persistence of traditional values. *American Sociological Review*, **65**, 19–51.

International Labour Organization (ILO). (1973). *Convention concerning minimum age for admission to employment (C138)*. Retrieved from http://www.ilo.org/dyn/normlex/en/f?p=NORMLEXPUB:12100:0::NO:12100:12100_INSTRUMENT_ID:312283:NO

International Labour Organization (ILO). (1999). *Convention concerning the prohibition and immediate action for the elimination of the worst forms of child labour (C182)*. Retrieved from http://www.ilo.org/dyn/normlex/en/f?p=NORMLEXPUB:12100:0::NO:12100:P12100_INSTRUMENT_ID:312327:NO

International Labour Organization (ILO). (2004). *Helping hands or shackled lives? Understanding child domestic labour and responses to it*. Geneva: International Labour Organization. Retrieved from http://www.unicef.org/violencestudy/pdf/2004_domestic_Helpinghands_en.pdf

International Labour Organization (ILO). (2009). *Gender equality at the heart of decent work*. Report IV of the International Labour Conference. Geneva: International Labour Organization.

International Labour Organization (ILO). (2012). What is child labour. Retrieved from http://www.ilo.org/ipec/facts/lang-en/index.htm

Jacklin, C. N. (1989). Female and male: Issues of gender. *American Psychologist*, **44**, 127–133.

Jansen, P., Raat, H., Mackenbach, J., Hofman, A., Jaddoe, V., Bakermans-Kranenburg, M., et al. (2012). Early determinants of maternal and paternal harsh discipline: The Generation R Study. *Family Relations*, **61**, 253–270.

Jensen, P., & Nielsen, H. S. (1997). Child labour or school attendance? Evidence from Zambia. *Journal of Population Economics*, **10**, 407–424.

Kashima, Y., Bain, P., Haslam, N., Peters, K., Laham, S., Whelan, J., et al. (2009). Folk theory of social change. *Asian Journal of Social Psychology*, **12**, 227–246. doi: 10.1111/j.1467-839X2009.01288.x

Kea, P. (2007). Girl farm labour and double-shift schooling in the Gambia: The paradox of development intervention. *Canadian Journal of African Studies*, **41**, 258–288.

Keller, H., Lamm, B., Abels, M., Yovsi, R., Borke, J., Jensen, H., et al. (2006). Cultural models, socialization goals, and parenting ethnotheories: A multicultural analysis. *Journal of Cross-Cultural Psychology*, **37**, 155–172.

Kieling, C., & Rohde, L. A. (2012). Child and adolescent mental health research across the globe. *Journal of the American Academy of Child & Adolescent Psychiatry*, **51**, 945–947.

Kim, E., & Hong, S. (2007). First generation Korean American parents' perceptions of discipline. *Journal of Professional Nursing*, **23**, 60–68.

Kimmel, E. B. (2000). Complicating gender. *PsycCRITIQUES*, **45**, 186–188.

Klasen, H., & Crombag, A.-C. (2013). What works where? A systematic review of child and adolescent mental health interventions for low and middle income countries. *Social Psychiatry and Psychiatric Epidemiology*, **48**, 595–611.

Klein, S. L. (2007). Sex differences in infectious and autoimmune diseases. In J. B. Becker, K. J. Berkley, N. Geary, E. Hampson, J. P. Herman, & E. Young (Eds.), *Sex difference in the brain* (pp. 329–354). New York, NY: Oxford University Press.

Knaul, F. M. (2001). The impact of child labor and school dropout on human capital: Gender differences in Mexico. In M. C. Correia (Au.) & E. G. Katz (Ed.), *The economics of gender in*

Mexico: Work, family, state, and market. *Directions in Development* (pp. 46–84). Herndon, VA: World Bank Publications.

Kolomiyets, T. (2004). *Global child labour data review: A gender perspective. Girl child labour studies (Vol. 3)*. Geneva: International Labour Organization. Retrieved from http://www.ilo.org/ipecinfo/product/viewProduct.do?productId=345

Kuo, A. A., Franke, T. M., Regalado, M., & Halfon, N. (2004). Parent report of reading to young children. *Pediatrics*, **113**(Supplement 5), 1944–1951.

Lancy, D. F. (2012a). "First you must master pain": The nature and purpose of apprenticeship. *Anthropology of Work Review*, **33**, 113–126.

Lancy, D. F. (2012b). The chore curriculum. In G. Spittler & M. Bourdillion (Eds.), *African children at work: Working and learning in growing up for life*. Zürich, Switzerland: Lit Verlag.

Lancy, D. F. (2014). "Babies aren't persons": A survey of delayed personhood. In H. Otto & H. Keller (Eds.), *Different faces of attachment: Cultural variations on a universal human need* (pp. 66–110). Cambridge: Cambridge University Press.

Lancy, D. F., & Grove, A. M. (2010). The role of adults in children's learning. In D. F. Lancy, J. C. Bock, & S. Gaskins (Eds.), *The anthropology of learning in childhood*. Walnut Creek, CA: AltaMira Press.

Lansford, J. E., Alampay, L., Bacchini, D., Bombi, A. S., Bornstein, M. H., Chang, L., et al. (2010). Corporal punishment of children in nine countries as a function of child gender and parent gender. *International Journal of Pediatrics*. doi: 10.1155/2010/672780

Lansford, J. E., Chang, L., Dodge, K. A., Malone, P. S., Oburu, P., Palmérus, K., et al. (2005). Physical discipline and children's adjustment: Cultural normativeness as a moderator. *Child Development*, **76**, 1234–1246.

Lansford, J. E., & Deater-Deckard, K. (2012). Childrearing discipline and violence in developing countries. *Child Development*, **83**, 62–75.

Lanvers, U. (2004). Gender in discourse behaviour in parent-child dyads: A literature review. *Child: Care, Health and Development*, **30**, 481–493. doi: 10.1111/j.1365-2214.2004.00443.x

Larrea, C., & Freire, W. (2002). Social inequality and child malnutrition in four Andean countries. *Pan American Journal of Public Health*, **11**, 356–363.

Larrea, C., & Kawachi, I. (2005). Does economic inequality affect child malnutrition? The case of Ecuador. *Social Science & Medicine*, **60**, 165–178.

Larson, R. W., & Verma, S. (1999). How children and adolescents spend time across the world: Work, play, and developmental opportunities. *Psychological Bulletin*, **125**, 701–736.

Larzelere, R. E. (2000). Child outcomes of nonabusive and customary physical punishment by parents: An updated literature review. *Clinical Child and Family Psychology Review*, **3**, 199–221.

Lawn, J. E., Costello, A., Mwansambo, C., & Osrin, D. (2007). Countdown to 2015: Will the Millennium goal for child survival be met? *Archives of Disease in Childhood*, **92**, 551–556.

Leaper, C. (2000a). Gender, affiliation, assertion, and the interactive context of parent-child play. *Development Psychology*, **36**, 381–393.

Leaper, C. (2000b). The social construction and socialization of gender during development. In P. H. Miller & E. Kofsky Scholnick (Eds.), *Toward a feminist developmental psychology* (pp. 127–152). Florence, KY: Taylor & Frances/ Routledge.

Leaper, C. (2002). Parenting girls and boys. In M. H. Bornstein (Ed.), *Handbook of parenting: Children and parenting* (pp. 189–225). Mahwah, NJ: Erlbaum.

REFERENCES

Leaper, C., Leve, L., Strasser, T., & Schwartz, R. (1995). Mother-child communication sequences: Play activity, child gender, and marital status effects. *Merrill-Palmer Quarterly*, **41**, 307–327.

Leaper, C., & Valin, D. (1996). Predictors of Mexican American mothers' and fathers' attitudes toward gender equality. *Hispanic Journal of Behavioral Sciences*, **18**, 343–355.

Leinaweaver, J. (2014). Informal kinship-based fostering around the world: Anthropological findings. *Child Development Perspectives*, **8**, 131–136.

Leinberger-Jabari, A., Parker, D. L., & Oberg, C. (2005). Child labor, gender, and health. *Public Health Reports*, **120**, 642–648.

Leon, I. G. (2007). Adoption losses: Naturally occurring or socially constructed? *Child Development*, **73**, 652–663.

Lerner, R. M., Hershberg, R. M., Hilliard, L. J., & Johnson, S. K. (2015). Concepts and theories of human development. In M. H. Bornstein & M. E. Lamb (Eds.), *Developmental science: An advanced textbook* (7th ed., pp. 3–41). New York, NY: Psychology Press.

Leventhal, T., & Newman, S. (2010). Housing and child development. *Children and Youth Services Review*, **32**, 1165–1174.

LeVine, R. A. (2003). *Childhood socialization*. Hong Kong: University of Hong Kong Press.

Levine, S. (2011). The race of nimble fingers: Changing patterns of children's work in post-apartheid South Africa. *Childhood*, **18**, 261–273.

Lewis, M. (1972). Parents and children: Sex-role development. *The School Review*, **80**, 229–240.

Limber, S. P., & Flekkoy, M. G. (1995). The U.N. convention on the rights of the child: Its relevance for social scientists. *Society for Research in Child Development Social Policy Reports*, **9**, 1–15.

Lindskog, P., & Lundqvist, J. (1998). *Why poor children stay sick: The human ecology of child health and welfare in rural Malawi*. Uppsala: Scandinavian Institute of African Studies.

Lott, B., & Maluso, D. (1993). The social learning of gender. In A. E. Beall & R. J. Sternberg (Eds.), *The psychology of gender* (pp. 99–123). New York, NY: Guilford Press.

Low, B. S. (1989). Cross-cultural patterns in the training of children: An evolutionary perspective. *Journal of Comparative Psychology*, **103**(4), 311–319.

Lucas, R. E. (1988). On the mechanics of economic development. *Journal of Monetary Economics*, **21**, 3–42.

Lucas, R. E., & Gohm, C. L. (2000). Age and sex differences in subjective well-being across cultures. In E. Diener & E. M. Suh (Eds.), *Culture and subjective well-being* (pp. 291–317). Cambridge, MA: The MIT Press.

Ludwig, K. M., Fernando, F., Firmino, A. F., & Joao Tadeu R.-P. (1999). Correlation between sanitation conditions and intestinal parasitosis in the population of Asses, State of Sao Paolo. *Revista da Sociedade Brasileira de Meddicina Tropical*, **32**, 547–555.

Luke, A., Omotade, O., Ayoola, O., Adeyemo, A., Brieger, W., Salami, K., et al. (2007). Stunting and underweight greater among boys than girls in rural southwest Nigeria. *The FASEB Journal*, **21**, A313.

Lutter, C. K., Chaparro, C. M., & Muñoz, S. (2010). Progress toward millennium development goal 1 in Latin America and the Caribbean: The importance of the choice of indicator for undernutrition. *Bulletin of the World Health Organization*, **89**, 22–30.

Lytton, H. (1990). Child and parent effects in boys' conduct disorder: A reinterpretation. *Developmental Psychology*, **26**, 683–697.

Lytton, H., & Romney, D. M. (1991). Parents' differential socialization of boys and girls: A meta-analysis. *Psychological Bulletin*, **109**, 267–296.
Maccoby, E. E., & Jacklin, C. N. (Eds.). (1974). *The psychology of sex differences* (Vol. 1). Palo Alto, CA: Stanford University Press.
Maccoby, E. E., & Jacklin, C. N. (1987). Gender segregation in childhood. *Advances in child development and behavior*, **20**, 239–287.
MacKenzie, M. J., Nicklas, E., Brooks-Gunn, J., & Waldfogel, J. (2011). Who spanks infants and toddlers? Evidence from the fragile families and child well-being study. *Children and Youth Services Review*, **33**, 1364–1373.
Magnuson, K. A., & Duncan, G. J. (2002). Parents in poverty. *Handbook of Parenting*, **4**, 95–121.
Mahfouz, A. A., El-Morshedy, H., Fargaly, A., & Khalil, A. (1997). Ecological determinants of intestinal parasitestic infections among pre-school children in urban squatter settlement of Egypt. *Journal of Tropical Pediatrics*, **43**, 341–344.
Mahmood, N., & Mahmood, M. A. (1995). Gender differences in child health-care practices: Evidence from the Pakistan Demographic and Health Survey, 1990–91. *The Pakistan Development Review*, **34**, 693–707.
Mankiw, N. G., Romer, D., & Weil, D. N. (1992). A contribution to the empirics of economic growth. *Quarterly Journal of Economics*, **107**, 407–437.
Marfo, K. (2011). Envisioning an African child development field. *Child Development Perspectives*, **5**, 140–147.
Mari, J. J., Patel, V., Kieling, C., Razzouk, D., Tyrer, P., & Herrman, H. (2010). The 5/95 gap in the indexation of psychiatric journals of low-and middle-income countries. *Acta Psychiatrica Scandinavica*, **121**, 152–156.
Marmot, M. (2005). Social determinants of health inequalities. *Lancet*, **365**, 1099–1104.
Martin, C. L. (2000). Cognitive theories of gender development. In T. Eckes & H. M. Trautner (Eds.), *The developmental social psychology of gender* (pp. 91–121). Mahwah, NJ: Erlbaum.
Martin, C. L., & Dinella, L. M. (2002). Children's gender cognitions, the social environment, and sex differences in cognitive domains. In A. McGillicuddy-De Lisi & R. De Lisi (Eds.), *Biology, society, and behavior: The development of sex differences in cognition* (pp. 207–239). Westport, CT: Ablex.
Martin, C. L., & Ruble, D. N. (2010). Patterns of gender development. *Annual Review of Psychology*, **61**, 353–381.
Martin, J. R. (1994). Methodological essentialism, false difference, and other dangerous traps. *Signs*, **19**, 630–57.
Martinez, M. L., Cumsille, P., & Thibaut, C. (2008). Chile. In J. J. Arnett (Ed.), *International encyclopedia of adolescence* (pp. 167–178). New York, NY: Routledge.
Martorell, R., Rivera, J., Kaplowitz, J., & Pollitt, E. (1992). Long term consequences of growth retardation during early childhood. In M. Hernandez & J. Argenta (Eds.), *Human growth: Basic and clinical aspects* (pp. 143–149). Amsterdam: Elsevier.
Masanja, H., de Savigny, D., Smithson, P., Schellenberg, J., John, T., Mbuya, C., et al. (2008). Child survival gains in Tanzania: Analysis of data from demographic and health surveys. *Lancet*, **371**, 1276–1283.
Mascaro, J. S., Hackett, P. D., & Rilling, J. K. (2013). Testicular volume is inversely correlated with nurturing-related brain activity in human fathers. *Proceedings of the National Academy of Sciences*, **110**(39), 15746–15751.

Mason, K. O., & Jensen, A.-M. (1995). *Gender and family change in industrialized countries*. Oxford, UK: Oxford University Press.

Matsumoto, D., & Fletcher, D. (1996). Cross-national differences in disease rates as accounted for by meaningful psychological dimensions of cultural variability. *Journal of Gender, Culture, and Health*, 1, 71–82.

McCall, G. J., & Simmons, J. L. (1966). *Identities and interactions*. New York, NY: Free Press.

McHale, S. M., Crouter, A. C., & Whiteman, S. D. (2003). The family contexts of gender development in childhood and adolescence. *Social Development*, 12, 125–148. doi: 10.1111/1467-9507.00225

McHale, S. M., Updegraff, K. A., Jackson-Newsom, J., Tucker, C. J., & Crouter, A. C. (2000). When does parents' differential treatment have negative implications for siblings? *Social Development*, 9, 149–172. doi: 10.1111/1467-9507.00117

McKee, L., Roland, E., Coffelt, N., Olson, A. L., Forehand, R., Massari, C., et al. (2007). Harsh discipline and child problem behaviors: The roles of positive parenting and gender. *Journal of Family Violence*, 22, 187–196. doi: 10.1007/s10896-007-9070-6

McLoyd, V. C., Aikens, N. L., & Burton, L. M. (2006). Childhood poverty, policy, and practice. In K. A. Renninger & I. E. Sigel (Eds.), W. Damon (Series Ed.), *Handbook of child psychology: Vol. 4. Child psychology in practice* (6th ed., pp. 700–775). Hoboken, NJ: Wiley.

Mead, M. (2001). *Coming of age in Samoa: A psychological study of primitive youth for Western civilisation (Perennial Classics)*. New York, NY: William Morrow.

Medhin, G., Hanlon, C., Dewey, M., Alem, A., Tesfaye, F., Worku, B., et al. (2010). Prevalence and predictors of undernutrition among infants aged six and twelve months in Butajira, Ethiopia: The P-MaMiE birth cohort. *BMC Public Health*, 10(27). doi: 10.1186/1471-2458-10-27

Mehra, R., Kurz, K., & Paolisso, M. (1992). *Child care options for working mothers in developing countries*. Washington, DC: Education Development Center. Retrieved from http://pdf.usaid.gov/pdf_docs/pnabt180.pdf

Mikulincer, M., Shaver, P. R., & Pereg, D. (2003). Attachment theory and affect regulation: The dynamics, development, and cognitive consequences of attachment-related strategies. *Motivation and Emotion*, 27, 77–102.

Miller, G. E., & Chen, E. (2013). The biological residue of childhood poverty. *Child Development Perspectives*, 7, 67–73.

Minturn, L., & Lambert, W. W. (1964). *Mothers of six cultures: Antecedents of child rearing*. New York, NY: Wiley.

Mischel, W. (1970). Sex-typing and socialization. In P. H. Mussen (Ed.), *Carmichael's manual of child psychology* (pp. 3–72). New York, NY: Wiley.

Mistry, J., Chaudhuri, J. H., & Diez, V. (2003). Ethnotheories of parenting: At the interface between culture and child development. In R. M. Lerner, D. Wertlieb, & F. Jacobs (Eds.), *Handbook of applied developmental science. Vol. I: Applying developmental science for youth and families: Historical and theoretical foundations* (pp. 233–257). Thousand Oaks, CA: SAGE.

Mitra, A. K., & Rodriguez-Fernandez, G. (2010). Latin America and the Caribbean: Assessment of advances in public health for achievement of the millennium development goals. *International Journal of Environmental Research in Public Health*, 7, 2238–2255.

Moestue, H., de Pee, S., Hall, A., Hye, A., Sultana, N., Ishtiaque, M., et al. (2004). Conclusions about differences in linear growth between Bangladeshi boys and girls depend on growth reference used. *European Journal of Clinical Nutrition*, 58, 725–731.

Moller, A. P. (2003). The evolution of monogamy: Mating relationships, parental care, and sexual selection. In C. Boesch (Ed.), *Monogamy: Mating strategies and partnerships in birds, humans, and other mammals* (pp. 29–41). Cambridge, England: Cambridge University Press.

Mondschein, E. R., Adolph, K. E., & Tamis-LeMonda, C. S. (2000). Gender bias in mothers' expectations about infant crawling. *Journal of Experimental Child Psychology*, **77**, 304–316.

Montgomery, M. R., & Hewitt, P. C. (2004). Urban poverty and health in developing countries: Household and neighborhood effects. Working Paper #184. The Population Council. Retrieved from http://www.popcouncil.org/uploads/pdfs/wp/184.pdf

Morrison, C., & Jütting, J. P. (2005). Women's discrimination in developing countries: A new data set for better policies. *World Development*, **33**, 1065–1081.

Morrow, V. (2010). Should the world really be free of "child labour"? Some reflections. *Childhood*, **17**, 435–440.

Motarjemi, Y., Käferstein, F., Moy, G., & Quevedo, F. (1993). Contaminated weaning food: A major risk factor for diarrhoea and associated malnutrition. *Bulletin of the World Health Organization*, **71**, 79–92.

Murphey, D., Cooper, M., & Forry, N. (2013). *The youngest Americans: A statistical portrait of infants and toddlers in the United States*. Washington, DC: Child Trends. Retrieved from http://www.childtrends.org/wp-content/uploads/2013/11/MCCORMICK-FINAL.pdf

Nelson, R. R., & Phelps, E. S. (1966). Investment in humans, technological diffusion and economic growth. *American Economic Review*, **56**, 69–75.

Noller, P., & Callan, V. J. (1990). Adolescents' perceptions of the nature of their communication with parents. *Journal of Youth and Adolescence*, **19**, 349–362.

Nuruddin, R., Hadden, W. C., Petersen, M. R., & Lim, M. K. (2009). Does child gender determine household decision for health care in rural Thatta, Pakistan? *Journal of Public Health*, **31**, 389–397.

Obrist, B., Iteba, N., Lengeler, C., Makemba, A., Mshana, C., Nathat, R. et al. (2007). Access to health care in contexts of livelihood insecurity: A framework for analysis and action. *PLoS Medicine*, **4**, 1584–1588.

Ochs, E. (1988). *Culture and language development*. Cambridge: Cambridge University Press.

Omokhodion, F. O., Omokhodion, S. I., & Odusote, T. O. (2006). Perceptions of child labour among working children in Ibadan, Nigeria. *Child: Care, Health and Development*, **32**, 281–286.

Orazem, P. F., & Gunnarsson, A. (2003). *Child labour, school attendance and academic performance: A review*. ILO/IPEC Working Paper. Geneva: International Labour Organization. Retrieved from http://www.ilo.org/ipecinfo/product/viewProduct.do?productId=716

Osmani, S., & Sen, A. (2003). The hidden penalties of gender inequality: Fetal origins of ill-health. *Economics and Human Biology*, **1**, 105–121.

Ouattara, M., N'Guéssan, N. A., Yapi, A., & N'Goran, E. K. (2010). Prevalence and spatial distribution of Entamoeba histolytica/dispar and Giardia lamblia among schoolchildren in Agboville Area (Côte d'Ivoire). *PLoS: Neglected Tropical Diseases*, **4**(1), e574.

Overton, W. F., & Molenaar, P. C. M. (2015). Concepts, theory, and method in developmental science: A view of the issues. In W. F. Overton & P. C. M. Molenaar (Eds.), *Theory and method*. Volume 1 of the *Handbook of child psychology and developmental science* (7th ed., pp. 1–8). Hoboken, NJ: Wiley.

Oyserman, D., & Markus, H. R. (1993). The sociocultural self. In J. M. Suls (Ed.), *The self in social perspective. Psychological perspectives on the self* (Vol. 4, pp. 187–220). Hillsdale, NJ: Erlbaum.

REFERENCES

Packer, M., & Cole, M. (2015). Culture in development. In M. H. Bornstein & M. E. Lamb (Eds.), *Developmental science: An advanced textbook* (7th ed., pp. 43–111). New York, NY: Psychology Press.

Pande, R. (2003). Selective gender differences in childhood nutrition and immunization in rural India: The role of siblings. *Demography*, **40**, 395–418.

Parke, R. D. (2002). Fathers and families. In M. Bornstein (Ed.), *Handbook of parenting: Vol. 3. Being and becoming a parent* (2nd ed., pp. 27–73). Hillsdale, NJ: Erlbaum.

Pascual, M., Bouma, M. J., & Dobson, A. P. (2002). Cholera and climate: Revisiting the quantitative evidence. *Microbes and Infection*, **4**, 237–245.

Patz, J. A., Githeko, A. K., McCarty, J. P., Hussein, S, Confalonieri, U., & de Wet, N. (2004). Climate change and infectious diseases. In A. J. McMichael, D. H. Campbell-Lendrum, C. F. Corvalán, K. L. Ebi, A. Githeko, J. D. Scheraga, & A. Woodward (Eds.), *Climate change and human health—Risks and responses* (pp. 103–132). Geneva: WHO. Retrieved from http://www.who.int/globalchange/publications/climatechangechap6.pdf

Pelletier, D. L. (1994). The relationship between child anthropometry and mortality in developing countries: Implications for programs and future research. *Journal of Nutrition*, **124**, 2047S–2081S.

Pells, K. (2010, December). *Inequalities, life chances and gender. Young lives round 3 preliminary findings*. Retrieved from http://www.younglives.org.uk/files/policy-papers/inequalities-life-chances-and-gender/view

Pells, K. (2011, September). *Poverty and gender inequalities: Evidence from young lives*. Policy paper 3. Retrieved from http://www.younglives.org.uk/files/policy-papers/yl_pp3_poverty-and-gender-inequalities

Permanyer, I. (2008). On the measurement of gender equality and gender-related development levels. *Journal of Human Development*, **9**, 87–108.

Permanyer, I. (2010). The measurement of multidimensional gender inequality: Continuing the debate. *Social Indicators Research*, **95**, 181–198.

Permanyer, I. (2013). A critical assessment of UNDP's Gender Inequality Index. *Feminist Economics*, **19**, 1–32.

Peterson, G. W., & Hann, D. (1999). Socializing children and parents in families. In M. B. Sussman, S. K. Steinmetz, & G. W. Peterson (Eds.), *Handbook of marriage and the family* (2nd ed., pp. 327–370). New York, NY: Plenum.

Pettit, G. S., Laird, R. D., Dodge, K. A., Bates, J. E., & Criss, M. M. (2001). Antecedents and behavior problem outcomes of parental monitoring and psychological control in early adolescence. *Child Development*, **72**, 583–598. doi: 10.1111/1467-8624.00298

Pinderhughes, E. E., Dodge, K. A., Bates, J. E., Pettit, G. S., & Zelli, A. (2000). Discipline responses: Influences of parents' socioeconomic status, ethnicity, beliefs about parenting, stress, and cognitive-emotional processes. *Journal of Family Psychology*, **14**, 380–400. doi: 10.1037/0893-3200.14.3.380

Pinheiro, P. S. (2006). *Report of the independent expert for the United Nations study on violence against children*. United Nations General Assembly. Retrieved from http://www.unicef.org/violencestudy/reports/SG_violencestudy_en.pdf

Pinzas, J. (2008). Peru. In J. J. Arnett (Ed.), *International encyclopedia of adolescence* (pp. 764–773). New York, NY: Routledge.

Pleck, J. H. (2010). Why could father involvement benefit children? Theoretical perspectives. *Applied Developmental Science*, **11**, 196–202.

Pleck, J. (2012). Integrating father involvement in parenting research. *Parenting; Science and Practice*, **12**, 243–253.

Podewils, L. J., Mintz, E. D., Nataro, J. P., & Parashar, U. D. (2004). Acute, infectious diarrhea among children in developing countries. *Seminars in Pediatric Infectious Diseases*, **15**, 155–168.

Pokhrel, S., & Sauerborn, R. (2004). Household decision-making on child health care in developing countries: The case of Nepal. *Health Policy and Planning*, **19**, 218–233. doi: 0.1093/heapol/czh027

Pomerleau, A., Bolduc, D., Malcuit, G., & Cossette, L. (1990). Pink or blue: Environmental gender stereotypes in the first two years of life. *Sex Roles*, **22**, 359–367.

Population Reference Bureau. (2013). *2013 world population data sheet*. Washington, DC: Population Reference Bureau. Retrieved from http://www.prb.org/pdf13/2013-population-data-sheet_eng.pdf

Prosser, G. V., Hutt, C., Hutt, S. J., Mahindadasa, K. J., & Goonetilleke, M. D. J. (1986). Children's play in Sri Lanka: A cross-cultural study. *British Journal of Developmental Psychology*, **4**, 170–186.

Putnam, S. P., Sanson, A. V., & Rothbart, M. K. (2002). Child temperament and parenting. In M. H. Bornstein (Ed.), *Handbook of parenting. Vol I: Children and parenting*. London: LEA.

Putnick, D. L., & Bornstein, M. H. (2015). Is child labor a barrier to school enrollment in low- and middle-income countries? *International Journal of Educational Development*, **41**, 112–120. doi: 10.1016/j.ijedudev.2015.02.001

Putnick, D. L., & Bornstein, M. H. (2016). Girls' and boys' labor and household chores in low- and middle-income countries. *Monographs of the SRCD*, **81**(1), 105–123.

Quinn, N. (2005). Universals of child rearing. *Anthopological Theory*, **5**, 477–516.

Quinn, N., & Holland, D. (1987). Culture and cognition. In D. Holland & N. Quinn (Eds.), *Cultural models in language and thought* (pp. 3–42). Cambridge: Cambridge University Press.

Quinn, P. C., Yahr, J., Kuhn, A., Slater, A. M., & Pascalis, O. (2002). Representation of the gender of human faces by infants: A preference for female. *Perception*, **31**, 1109–1122.

Quiroz, B. G., Snow, C. E., & Zhao, J. (2010). Vocabulary skills of Spanish-English bilinguals: Impact of mother-child language interactions and home language and literacy support. *International Journal of Bilingualism*, **14**, 379–399.

Raley, S., & Bianchi, S. (2006). Sons, daughters, and family processes: Does gender of children matter? *Annual Review of Sociology*, **32**, 401–422.

Regalado, M., Sareen, H., Inkelas, M., Wisso, L., & Halfon, N. (2004). Parents' discipline of young children: Results from the National Survey of Early Childhood Health. *Pediatrics*, **113**, 1952–1958.

Reid, P. T., & Comas-Diaz, L. (1990). Gender and ethnicity: Perspectives on dual status. *Sex Roles*, **22**, 397–408.

Rendall, M. (2012). Structural changes in developing countries: Has it decreased gender inequality? *World Development*, **45**, 1–16.

Ricci, J., & Becker, S. (1996). Risk factors for wasting and stunting among children in Metro Cebu, Philippines. *American Journal of Clinical Nutrition*, **63**, 966–975.

Risman, B. J. (2001). Necessity and the invention of mothering. In R. Satow (Ed.), *Gender and social life* (pp. 26–31). Needham Heights, MA: Allyn & Bacon.

Roberts, L., Chartier, Y. Chartier, O., Malenga, G., Toole, M., & Rodka, H. (2001). Keeping clean water clean in a Malawi refugee camp: A randomized clinical trial. *Bulletin of the World Health Organization*, **79**, 280–287.

Robinson, C. C., & Morris, J. T. (1986). The gender-stereotyped nature of Christmas toys received by 36-, 48-, and 60- month-old children: A comparison between nonrequested vs. requested toys. *Sex Roles*, **15**, 21–32.

Robinson, J. A., Little, C., & Biringen, Z. (1993). Emotional communication in mother-toddler relationships: Evidence for early gender differentiation. *Merrill Palmer Quarterly*, **39**, 496–517.

Roggero, P., Mangiaterra, V., Bustreo, F., & Rosati, F. (2007). The health impact of child labor in developing countries: Evidence from cross-country data. *American Journal of Public Health*, **97**, 271–275.

Rohner, R. P. (1994). Universals in youths' perceptions of parental acceptance and rejection: Evidence from factor analyses within eight sociocultural groups worldwide. *Cross-Cultural Research*, **28**, 371–383.

Rohner, R. P., & Rohner, E. C. (1982). Enculturative continuity and the importance of caretakers: Cross-cultural codes. *Behavior Science Research*, **17**, 91–114.

Rubin, J., Provenzano, F., & Luria, Z. (1974). The eye of the beholder: Parents' view of sex of newborns. *American Journal of Orthopsychiatry*, **43**, 720–731.

Ruble, D. N., Martin, C. L., & Berenbaum, S. A. (2006). Gender development. In W. Damon (Series Ed.) & N. Eisenberg (Vol. Ed.), *Handbook of child psychology* (6th ed., Vol. **3**, pp. 858–932). New York, NY: Wiley.

Rushton, L., & Elliott, P. (2003). Evaluating evidence on environmental health risks. *British Medical Bulletin*, **68**, 113–128.

Russell, A., & Saebel, J. (1997). Mother-son, mother-daughter, father-son, and father-daughter: Are they distinct relationships? *Developmental Review*, **17**, 111–147.

Sadowski, L. S., Hunter, W. M., Bangdiwala, S. E., & Munoz, S. R. (2004). The World Studies of Abuse in the Family Environment: A model of a multi-national study of family violence. *Injury Control and Safety Promotion*, **11**, 81–90.

Sagar, A. D., & Najam, A. (1998). The human development index: A critical review. *Ecological Economics*, **25**, 249–264.

Sahn, D. E., & Stifel, D. C. (2000). Poverty comparisons over time and across countries in Africa. *World Development*, **28**, 2123–2155.

Schenck-Gustafsson, K., DeCola, P. R., Pfaff, D. W., & Pisetsky, D. S. (Eds.). (2012). *Handbook of clinical gender medicine*. Basel: Karger.

Schkolnik, M. (2004). ¿Por qué es tan increíblemente baja la tasa de participatión de las majeres en Chile? *Documentos En Foco*. Santiago: Expansiva. Retrieved from http://www2.expansiva.cl/media/en_foco/documentos/06102004132738.pdf

Schuette, C., & Killen, M. (2009). Children's evaluations of gender-stereotypic household activities in the family context. *Early Education and Development*, **20**, 693–712.

Seavey, C.A., Katz, P.A., & Zalk, S.R. (1975). Baby X: The effect of gender labels on adult responses to infants. *Sex Roles*, **1**, 103–110.

Seedat, S., Scott, K. M., Angermeyer, M. C., Berglund, P., Bromet, E. J., Brugha, T. S., et al. (2009). Cross-national associations between gender and mental disorders in the World Health Organization World Mental Health Surveys. *Archives of General Psychiatry*, **66**, 785–795.

Sen, A. (1989). Development as capability expansion. *Journal of Development Planning*, **17**, 41–58.
Shields, S. A. (1975). Functionalism, Darwinism, and the psychology of women: A study in social myth. *American Psychologist*, **30**, 739–754.
Shields, S. A. (2007) Passionate men, emotional women: Psychology constructs gender difference in the late 19th century. *History of Psychology*, **10**, 92–110.
Sidorowicz, L. S., & Lunney, S. G. (1980). Baby x revised. *Sex Roles*, **6**, 67–73.
Smith, P. K., & Drew, L. M. (2002). Grandparenthood. In M. H. Bornstein (Ed.), *Handbook of parenting Vol. 3 status and social conditions of parenting* (2nd ed., pp. 141–172). Mahwah, NJ: Erlbaum.
Social Watch. (2009). *Gender Equality Index 2009*. Retrieved from http://www.socialwatch.org/sites/default/files/GEI2009-VALUES.pdf
Starrels, M. (1994). Gender differences in parent-child relations. *Journal of Family Issues*, **15**, 148–165.
Steinberg, L. (1987). Recent research on the family at adolescence: The extent and nature of sex differences. *Journal of Youth and Adolescence*, **16**, 191–197.
Stevenson, M. R., & Black, K. N. (1988). Paternal absence and sex-role development: A meta-analysis. *Child Development*, **59**, 793–814.
Stewart, A. J. (1998). Doing personality research: How can feminist theories help? In B. M. Clinchy & J. K. Norem (Eds.), *The gender and psychology reader* (pp. 54–68). New York, NY: New York University Press.
Stewart, A. J., & Mcdermott, C. (2004). Gender in psychology. *Annual Review Psychology*, **55**, 519–544.
Straus, M. A., Hamby, S. L., Findelor, D., Moore, D. W., & Runyan, D. (1998). Identification of child maltreatment with the Parent-Child Conflict Tactics Scales: Development and psychometric data for a national sample of American parents. *Child Abuse and Neglect*, **22**, 249–270.
Straus, M. A., & Stewart, J. H. (1999). Corporal punishment by American parents: National data on prevalence, chronicity, severity, and duration, in relation to child and family characteristics. *Clinical Child and Family Psychology Review*, **2**, 55–70.
Streiner, D. L. (2003). Being inconsistent about consistency: When coefficient alpha does and doesn't matter. *Journal of Personality Assessment*, **80**, 217–222.
Super, C. M., & Harkness, S. (1986). The developmental niche: A conceptualization at the interface of child and culture. *International Journal of Behavioral Development*, **9**, 545–569.
Svedberg, P. (1990). Undernutrition in Sub-Saharan Africa: Is there a gender bias? *The Journal of Development Studies*, **26**, 469–486.
Sweeney, J., & Bradbard, M.R. (1989). Mothers' and fathers' changing perceptions of their male and female infants over the course of pregnancy. *Journal of Genetic Psychology*, **149**, 393–404.
Tenenbaum, H. R., & Leaper, C. (2003). Parent-child conversations about science: The socialization of gender inequities? *Developmental Psychology*, **39**, 34–47.
Thabet, A. A., Matar, S., Carointero, A., Bankart, J., & Vostanis, P. (2010). Mental health problems among labour children in the Gaza Strip. *Child: Care, Health and Development*, **37**, 89–95.
Tomlinson, M., Bornstein, M. H., Marlow, M., & Swartz, L. (2014). Imbalances in the knowledge about infant mental health in rich and poor countries: Too little progress in bridging the gap. *Infant Mental Health Journal*, **35**, 624–629.

Tomlinson, M., & Swartz, L. (2003). Imbalances in the knowledge about infancy: The divide between rich and poor countries. *Infant Mental Health Journal*, **24**, 547–556.

Trivers, R. L. (1972). Parental investment and sexual selection. In B. Campbell (Ed.), *Sexual selection and the descent of man 1871–1971* (pp. 136–179). Chicago, IL: Aldine.

UNESCO. (2005). *EFA global monitoring report 2005*. Paris, France: Author.

United Nations. (2000). *United Nations Millennium Declaration, Resolution 55/2*. Retrieved from http://www.un.org/millennium/declaration/ares552e.pdf

United Nations. (2005). *Progress towards the millennium development goals*. Author. Retrived from http://millenniumindicators.un.org/unsd/mdg/Host.aspx?Content=Products/Progress2005.htm

United Nations. (2011a). *Millennium development goals: Progress chart 2011*. Retrieved from http://unstats.un.org/unsd/mdg/Resources/Static/Products/Progress2011/11-31330%20(E)%20MDG%20Report%202011_Progress%20Chart%20LR.pdf

United Nations. (2011b). *The millennium development goals report. addendum: Goal 1*. Retrieved from http://unstats.un.org/unsd/mdg/Resources/Static/Products/Progress2011/Addendum_ G1.pdf

United Nations Children's Fund (UNICEF). (2006). *Multiple Indicator Cluster Survey manual 2005: Monitoring the situation of children and women*. New York, NY: Author. Retrieved from http://www.childinfo.org/files/Multiple_Indicator_Cluster_Survey_Manual_2005.pdf

United Nations Children's Fund (UNICEF). (2007a). *Progress for children: A world fit for children statistical review* (Vol. 6). New York, NY: Author. Retrieved from http://www.unicef.org/publications/files/Progress_for_Children_No_6_revised.pdf

United Nations Children's Fund (UNICEF). (2007b). *The state of the world's children 2007: Women and children. The double dividend of gender equality*. New York, NY: Author.

United Nations Children's Fund (UNICEF). (2009). *Human development report 2009. Overcoming barriers: Human mobility and development*. Retrieved from http://hdr.undp.org/sites/default/files/reports/269/hdr_2009_en_complete.pdf

United Nations Children's Fund (UNICEF). (2011). *Boys and girls in the life cycle: Sex-disaggregated data on a selection of well-being indicators, from early childhood to young adulthood*. New York, NY: Author. Retrieved from http://www.unicef.org/media/files/Gender_hi_res.pdf

United Nations Children's Fund (UNICEF). (2012). *Appendix Five: Anthropometric techniques*. Retrieved from http://www.childinfo.org/files/MICS3_Appendix_5_-_Anthropometric_Techniques_060525.pdf

United Nations Children's Fund (UNICEF). (2014). *The state of the world's children 2014: Every child counts: Revealing disparities, advancing children's rights*. New York, NY: Author.

United Nations, Department of Economic and Social Affairs, Population Division. (2011). *Sex differentials in childhood mortality* (United Nations publication, ST/ESA/SER.A/314).

United Nations Development Programme (UNDP). (1995). *Human development report 1995. Gender and human development*. New York, NY: Palgrave Macmillan. Retrieved from http://hdr.undp.org/en/reports/global/hdr1995/chapters/

United Nations Development Programme (UNDP). (2008). *Human development indices: A statistical update*. Retrieved from http://www10.iadb.org/intal/intalcdi/PE/2009/03143.pdf

United Nations Development Programme (UNDP). (2011). *Human development report 2011. sustainability and equity: A better future for all*. New York, NY: Palgrave Macmillan. Retrieved

from http://hdr.undp.org/sites/default/files/reports/271/hdr_2011_en_complete.pdf
United Nations Development Programme (UNDP). (2013). *Human development report 2013. The rise of the south: Human progress in a diverse world.* Retrieved from http://hdr.undp.org/sites/default/files/reports/14/hdr2013_en_complete.pdf
United Nations General Assembly. (1989). *Convention on the rights of the child.* New York, NY: United Nations.
United Nations General Assembly. (2006). *Convention on the rights of the child: General comment No. 7.* New York, NY: United Nations.
United Nations General Assembly. (2015). *Transforming our world: The 2030 Agenda for Sustainable Development.* New York, NY: United Nations. Available from http://www.un.org/ga/search/view_doc.asp?symbol=A/70/L.1&Lang=E
Valenzuela, M. (1997). Maternal sensitivity in a developing society: The context of urban poverty and infant chronic undernutrition. *Developmental Psychology,* **33**, 845–855.
van IJzendoorn, M. H., Moran, G., Belsky, J., Pederson, D., Bakermans-Kranenburg, M. J., & Kneppers, K. (2000). The similarity of siblings' attachments to their mother. *Child Development,* **71**, 1086–1098.
Vygotsky, L. (2005). Interaction between learning and development. In M. Gauvain & M. Cole (Eds.), *Readings on the development of children* (4th ed., pp. 34–42). New York: Worth. (Reprinted from *Mind in society: The development of higher psychological processes,* pp. 71–91, by M. Cole, V. John-Steiner, S. Scribner, & E. Souberman (Eds.), 1978, Cambridge, MA: Harvard University Press.)
Wachs, T. D. (2008). Commentary: Mechanisms linking parental education and stunting. *Lancet,* **371**, 280–281.
Wachs, T. D. (2015). Assessing bioecological influences. In M. H. Bornstein & T. Leventhal (Eds.), *Ecological settings and processes in developmental systems.* Volume 4 of the *Handbook of child psychology and developmental science* (7th ed., pp. 811–846). Hoboken, NJ: Wiley.
Wagstaff, A., Bustreo, F., Bryce, J., Claeson, M., & WHO-World Bank Child Health and Poverty Working Group. (2004). Child health: Reaching the poor. *American Journal of Public Health,* **94**, 726–736.
Wallen, K. (1996). Nature needs nurture: The interaction of hormonal and social influences on the development of behavioral sex differences in rhesus monkeys. *Hormones and Behavior,* **30**, 364–378.
Wamani, H., Åstrøm, A. N., Peterson, S., Tumwine, J. K., & Tylleskär, R. (2007). Boys are more stunted than girls in Sub-Saharan Africa: A meta-analysis of 16 demographic and health surveys. *BMC Pediatrics,* **7**, 17.
Wamani, H., Tylleskär, T., Åstrøm, A. N., Tumine, J. K., & Peterson, S. (2004). Mothers' education but not fathers' education, household assets or land ownership is the best predictor of child health inequalities in rural Uganda. *International Journal of Equity in Health,* **3**, 9.
Wang, L. (2003). Determinants of child mortality in LDCs: Empirical findings from demographic and health surveys. *Health Policy,* **65**, 277–299.
Webbink, E., Smits, J., & de Jong, E. (2010). *Hidden child labour: Determinants of housework and family business work of children in 16 developing countries.* NiCE Working Paper 10-110. Retrieved from http://www.ru.nl/publish/pages/516298/nice_10110.pdf

Weisner, T. S. (1984). Ecocultural niches of middle childhood: A cross-cultural perspective. In W. A. Collins (Ed.), *Development during middle childhood: The years from six to twelve* (pp. 335–369). Washington, DC: National Academy of Sciences.

Weisner, T. S., & Gallimore, R. (1977). My brother's keeper: Child and sibling caretaking. *Current Anthropology*, **18**, 169–190.

Weisner, T. S., Garnier, H., & Loucky, J. (1994). Domestic tasks, gender egalitarian values and children's gender typing in current and nonconventional families. *Sex Roles*, **30**, 23–54.

West, M. M., & Konner, M. J. (1976). The role of father: An anthropological perspective. In M. E. Lamb (Ed.), *The role of the father in child development* (pp. 185–217). New York, NY: Wiley.

White, H. (1997). *Patterns of gender discrimination: An examination of the UNDP's gender development index*. The Hague: Institute of Social Studies.

Whiteman, S. D., Becerra, J. M., & Killoren, S. E. (2009). Mechanisms of sibling socialization in normative family development. In L. Kramer & K. J. Conger (Eds.), *Siblings as agents of socialization. New directions for child and adolescent development*, Vol **126**, pp. 29–43. San Francisco: Jossey-Bass.

Whiting, B. B. (1963). *Six cultures: Studies of child rearing*. Oxford, England: Wiley.

Whiting, B. B. (1986). The effect of experience on peer relationships. In E. C. Mueller & C. R. Cooper (Eds.), *Process and outcome in peer relationships* (pp. 79–99). Orlando, FL: Academic Press.

Whiting, B., & Edwards, C. P. (1973). A cross-cultural analysis of sex differences in the behavior of children aged 3 to 11. *Journal of Social Psychology*, **91**, 171–188

Whiting, B. B., & Edwards, C. P. (1988). *Children of different worlds: The formation of social behavior*. Cambridge, MA: Harvard University Press.

Whiting, B. B., & Whiting, J. W. (1975). *Children of six cultures: A psycho-cultural analysis*. Oxford, England: Harvard University Press.

WHO. (1997). *WHO global database on child growth and malnutrition*. Retrieved from http://www.who.int/nutgrowthdb/en/

WHO. (2006). *WHO child growth standards: Length/height-for-age, weight-for-age, weight-for length, weight-for-height and body mass index-for-age: Methods and development*. Geneva, Switzerland: WHO Press. Retrieved from http://www.who.int/childgrowth/standards/Technical_report.pdf

WHO. (2011). *Child growth standards. Special SPSS macros*. Retrieved from http://www.who.int/childgrowth/software/macros_special_spss/en/index.html

WHO & UNICEF. (2008). *Progress on drinking water and sanitation: Special focus on sanitation*. Geneva, Switzerland: WHO Press. Retrieved from http://www.who.int/water_sanitation_health/monitoring/jmp2008.pdf

WHO & UNICEF. (2009). *WHO child growth standards and the identification of severe acute malnutrition in infants and children. A Joint Statement by the World Health Organization and the United Nations Children's Fund*. Retrieved from http://www.who.int/nutrition/publications/severemalnutrition/9789241598163_eng.pdf

Wilcox, B., & Kline, K. K. (Eds.). (2013). *Gender and parenthood: Biological and social scientific perspectives*. New York, NY: Columbia University Press.

Williams, J. E., & Best, D. L. (1982/1990). *Measuring sex stereotypes: A multination study* (Rev. ed., 1990). Newbury Park, CA: SAGE.

Wood, D., Bruner, J. S., & Ross, G. (1976). The role of tutoring in problem solving. *Journal of Child Psychology and Psychiatry*, **17**, 89–100.

Wood, W., & Eagly, A. H. (2012). Biosocial construction of sex differences and similarities in behavior. *Advances in Experimental Social Psychology*, **46**, 55–123.

Woodhead, M. (1999). Combating child labour: Listen to what the children say. *Childhood*, **6**, 27–49.

Woolf, A. D. (2002). Health hazards for children at work. *Clinical Toxicology*, **40**, 477–482.

World Bank. (2000). *World development report 2000/01: Attacking poverty*. Washington, DC: World Bank.

World Bank. (2001). *Engendering development: Through gender equality in rights, resources, and voice*, World Bank Policy Research Report No. 21776 New York, NY: Oxford University Press.

World Bank. (2012). 2012 world development indicators. Washington, DC: Author. Retrieved from http://data.worldbank.org/sites/default/files/wdi-2012-ebook.pdf

World Bank. (2014). *How we classify countries*. Washington, DC: Author. Retrieved from http://data.worldbank.org/about/country-classifications

Xie, J., & Dow, W. (2005). Longitudinal study of child immunization determinants in China. *Social Science & Medicine*, **61**, 601–611.

Zadeh, Z. Y., Farnia, F., & Ungerleider, C. (2010). How home enrichment mediates the relationship between maternal education and children's achievement in reading and math. *Early Education and Development*, **21**, 568–594.

Zahn-Waxler, C. (2000). The development of empathy, guilt, and internalization of distress: Implications for gender differences in internalizing and externalizing problems. In R. Davidson (Ed.), *Wisconsin Symposium on Emotion: Vol. 1. Anxiety, depression, and emotion* (pp. 222–265). Oxford, England: Oxford University Press.

Zentner, M., & Mitura, K. (2012). Stepping out of the caveman's shadow: Nations' gender gap predicts degree of sex differentiation in mate preferences. *Psychological Science*, **23**, 1176–1185.

Zukow-Goldring, P. (2002). Sibling caregiving. In M. H. Bornstein (Ed.), *Handbook of parenting Vol. 3: Status and social conditions of parenting* (2nd ed., pp. 253–286). Mahwah, NJ: Erlbaum.

ACKNOWLEDGMENTS

This article is part of the issue "Gender in Low- and Middle-Income Countries," Bornstein, Putnick, Lansford, Deater-Deckard, and Bradley (Issue Authors). For a full listing of articles in this issue, see: http://onlinelibrary.wiley.com/doi/10.1111/mono.v81.1/issuetoc.

This research was supported by the Intramural Research Program of the NIH, NICHD. We thank UNICEF and participating countries for collecting the data.

Corresponding author: Marc H. Bornstein, Child and Family Research, National Institute of Child Health and Human Development, National Institutes of Health, Suite 8030, 6705 Rockledge Drive, Bethesda MD 20892-7971; email: Marc_H_Bornstein@nih.gov.

DOI: 10.1111/mono.12231

© 2015 The Society for Research in Child Development, Inc.

COMMENTARY

CONTEXT AND THE ADVANCEMENT OF A GLOBAL SCIENCE OF HUMAN DEVELOPMENT: A COMMENTARY

Kofi Marfo, Ph.D.

> This article is part of the issue "Gender in Low- and Middle-Income Countries," Bornstein, Putnick, Lansford, Deater-Deckard, and Bradley (Issue Authors). For a full listing of articles in this issue, see: http://onlinelibrary.wiley.com/doi/10.1111/mono.v81.1/issuetoc.

United Nations agencies mandated to address the needs of children around the developing (Majority) world, routinely create large global data sets mostly for purposes of surveillance and strategic planning of development aid. UNICEF's Multiple Indicator Cluster Surveys (MICS) have produced one of the largest sources of internationally comparable data on women and children. This monograph creatively and elegantly harnesses MICS data on 41 low- and middle-income countries to shed light on risk and protective factors associated with growing up a boy or girl in the developing world. In this commentary, I assess the monograph's contribution to the progress that our field must make toward greater geo-ecological and cultural inclusiveness of its knowledge base. I do so in the context of scholarship that is increasingly and justifiably questioning the relevance of mainstream developmental science outside the Euro-American world. I conclude that notwithstanding the limitations inherent in the data set, Bornstein, Putnick, Lansford, Deater-Deckard, and Bradley have done our field a great service by moving us further on a trajectory toward a more global science.

Corresponding author: Kofi Marfo, Professor and Founding Director, Institute for Human Development, Aga Khan University, P. O. Box 30270, Nairobi, Kenya; email: kofi.marfo@aku.edu
  DOI: 10.1111/mono.12232
  © 2015 The Society for Research in Child Development, Inc.

COMMENTARY

Significant contributions toward understandings of human development in cultural contexts have been made at the intersection of fields such as anthropology, developmental psychology, cross-cultural psychology, cultural psychology, and indigenous psychology (Bronfenbrenner, 1979; Cole, 1996; Kağitçibaşi, 2007; LeVine et al., 1994; Nsamenang, 1992; Rogoff, 2003; Shweder, 1991; Super & Harkness, 1986; Valsiner, 2000). Nevertheless, the core of so-called mainstream developmental psychology is increasingly seen as very much remaining a science built around studies of limited samples within rather small segments of the world's population (Arnett, 2008; Henrich, Heine, & Noreyanzepam, 2010). With the field drawing its study samples preponderantly from the rich and industrialized Euro-American world—and from restricted demographic populations even within that world—the field's knowledge base, critics argue, is not global enough to be broadly relevant in, and/or applicable to, populations and contexts outside the Euro-American world (Arnett, 2008).

Implicit in past and contemporary cultural critiques of our field is a call for a more global science of human development. In sharp contrast to the trend toward globalization of the Euro-American status quo, I define a global science of human development as a science with broader global content and relevance. Such a science would draw not only from multiple disciplines and methodologies as we now know them, but also from multiple conceptions and constructions of developmental phenomena as grounded in worldviews and idea systems across the world's diverse cultures. From this standpoint, our field has a long way to go on a trajectory toward an authentically global science with broader global content and relevance. The work presented in this monograph offers a piece of the bridge to that global science.

FRAMING REQUIREMENTS FOR ADVANCING A GLOBAL SCIENCE

In this section, I place my commentary in the context of three conditions for progress toward that *global science* of human development with broader content and relevance across geographic and cultural contexts. The first condition is representativeness of samples *within investigations* aiming for broader generalizability across populations. The second is shared representation of measured constructs and their underlying cultural meanings *across the sampled populations*. The third is representativeness of worldviews and idea systems *within the disciplinary knowledge base*. The first condition is much more easily attained. Large-scale international nomothetic studies generally aspire to meet this condition through careful selection and inclusion of diverse representative samples from different clearly delineated contexts. For at least two reasons, attaining the second condition is relatively more challenging. First, much of our science privileges the search for developmental universals

173

over considerations of context-specific mechanisms and outcomes (Arnett, 2008; Pence, 2011; Pence & Nsamenang, 2008; Serpell & Marfo, 2014). Second, it is practically easier and expedient to adopt existing measures than to develop and validate new ones for particular populations. For these reasons, cross-context comparative research tends to overlook contextual biases.

The third condition, perhaps, the farthest away from where our field needs to be to warrant claims of a global knowledge base, is premised on the proposition that there is significant diversity in the world views, idea systems, and ethno-theories that shape conceptions, representations, and meanings of developmental phenomena across cultures (Henrich et al., 2010; Marfo, 2011; Shweder, 1991). Consequently, the field's knowledge base must be inclusive of multiple worldviews and traditions across societies. Such openness to other worldviews would ensure that diverse paradigmatic perspectives and value systems drive the complex enterprise of advancing knowledge with complementary considerations of (1) the culturally situated nature of human functioning and (2) the biological and cultural universals that account for behavioral similarities across cultures (Marfo, 2011; Wiredu, 1996). Context-analytic inquiry yielding knowledge on alternative and complementary conceptions of developmental constructs across cultures is necessary if comparative research is to appropriately meet the standard of shared representation of measured constructs (condition 2) (e.g., Nsamenang, 1992, 2006; Serpell, 1996, 2011).

In framing the three conditions presented here, my intention is not to score this monograph on each of the conditions. Rather, I use them to guide a broader discussion of the monograph's contributions to the field and to highlight some of the challenges that our field faces if attainment of global cultural/contextual inclusiveness within our knowledge base is an aspirational goal.

OVERVIEW OF THE STUDIES

Countering the near-neglect of Majority World populations in large-scale child development research, Bornstein, Putnick, Lansford, Deater-Deckard, and Bradley draw from existing population-level data to shed insights on aspects of child development in parts of the world and cultural contexts that are poorly represented in our developmental knowledge base. The data for the analyses reported in the monograph are drawn from UNICEF's Multiple Indicator Cluster Surveys (in this case MICS3), which, since the mid-1990s, have produced, perhaps, one of the largest sources of internationally comparable data on women and children (http://mics.unicef.org/about). Four studies are reported, each benefitting from a large nationally representative probability sample and each addressing two primary questions: (1) inter-country differences on indicators of child growth/development or caregiving/socialization and (2) and relationships between measures of the latter and two country-level variables: gender policy and socio-economic development. The substantive areas under study were early growth and mortality/survival (Chapter III), parental caregiving (Chapter IV), methods of discipline used by adults (Chapter V), and children's work within and outside home and family (Chapter VI).

The monograph authors have described the MICS3 data set as "a unique resource that could not be built even by a large research team on its own" (p. 103). This is a fitting observation, but what the researchers have undertaken here is a rather bold adventure that is not without risk. Even as they do their very best to acknowledge and address the limitations that the nature of the data imposes on conceptualization, analysis, and interpretation, there are simply no remedies for inherently incurable shortcomings in a database established for a different purpose and made available for independent analyses by scholars far removed from both the intended use of the data and the design and implementation of the originating surveys.

As consolation prize, however, the authors have the benefit of the opportunity to demonstrate how population-based data intended mainly for global surveillance of health, education, and well-being can, within reasonable limits, be harnessed for developmental science insights. They have accomplished this elegantly, and in so doing, they have pointed the way for developmental and behavioral scientists—and the professional bodies to which they belong—to cultivate collaborative partnerships that position developmental researchers to embed context-rich investigations into the gathering of surveillance and policy-driven data by international multilateral agencies like UNICEF and WHO.

A focus on such a large number of Majority World societies in any one study is rare in the human development literature. It is these large samples—and the questions and survey administration—that have made it possible for the authors to bring such highly sophisticated statistical tools to the analysis. It is important to note, however, that although certainly necessary, methodologically sound sampling across a diverse range of populations and physical contexts alone would not guarantee that the resulting knowledge would have global appeal in terms of content and relevance. It is possible to have broad sample or population representativeness and still leave other threats to generalizability unaddressed (Ceci, Kahan, & Braman, 2010). For example, unless there is shared meaning around the constructs being measured, items might represent different things to different respondents and, hence, the data generated would be difficult to interpret, if not altogether invalid. This is the predicament that psychological and other behavioral sciences face in an era of proliferating interest in international studies of developmental interventions. Bornstein's (1995) conceptual analysis of the relationship between activity (form) and meaning (function) in cultural comparisons sheds illuminating insights on this challenge.

As alluded to earlier, the conceptual lenses by which developmental phenomena are experienced and expressed at both the individual and social levels are shaped by worldviews, ethno-theories, and knowledge traditions with deep cultural underpinnings. What may be salient, important, or meaningful in one cultural context may not be so in another setting (Marfo, 1999; Zimba, 2002). Valued developmental milestones and outcomes—and the socialization processes that prime them—could also vary to differing degrees across cultures. In effect, comparing nationally or culturally representative samples on constructs and measures with no comparable meaning or relevance is problematic.

What implications do the issues raised above have for assessment of the evidence reported in this monograph? The MICS3 surveys employed standard questions and administration protocols. However, the data analyzed in the monograph are not derived from standardized normative measures generated and validated in one cultural setting and applied to all others. For this reason, threats to validity at the superficial survey item level might be rather innocuous. Potentially problematic, however, are (1) the decontextualized nature of the data and (2) the appearance of culture-blindness with regard, in particular, to the caregiving and children's work data. It is to these two issues that I turn next.

CONTEXT MATTERS: TWO ILLUSTRATIVE EXAMPLES

In discussing findings throughout the monograph, the authors have been consistent and forthright in acknowledging limitations stemming from the decontextualized nature of the MICS3 data. In the remainder of my commentary, I speak to these limitations with particular reference to the caregiving and "child labor" data.

Implicit Cultural Models of Caregiving

Across cultures, parents have primary responsibility for caregiving. However, in societies outside the Euro-American world, this responsibility may be shared widely across the extended family, and hence, beyond mothers and fathers. This *distributed system of socialization* (Marfo, 2011; Weisner, 1987, 2014) is likely the dominant model of caregiving in the 39 countries providing the dataset for the analysis of parental caregiving. Very young children have the benefit of receiving culturally normative developmental caregiving from older siblings and significant other members of the extended family, such as grandparents, living in the same household (Harkness & Super, 1992; Marfo, 2011; Weisner, 1984, 1987). Indeed, in cultures with distributed systems of socialization, social responsibility (Serpell, 2011) as expressed through care for younger siblings may be seen as a dimension of intelligence.

The manner of data collection on the six MICS3 caregiving activities, on the other hand, projects a dyadic, parent-centered model of socialization. Respondents were asked about what parents did with their children in the three days preceding the survey: taking the child outside; playing with the child; singing to the child; engaging in naming, counting and drawing with the child; telling stories to the child; and reading with the child. It strikes me that what is (and should be) important in the analysis of the six caregiving activities is not just who provides the exposure to these activities but also, and perhaps even more important, the degree to which the child is exposed to these activities. In many family contexts within the 39 nations in the analyses, older siblings under age 15 are perhaps as likely (if not more so) to engage the target child in each of the six activities than adults. The activity entailing the least "involvement" of parents was reading with the child—22% of mothers and 9% of fathers. This is also the activity most likely to require parents to be school-educated, and with close to one-third of the parents in the study described as having no more than pre-school education, it is not surprising that if children under 5 are read to, it would likely be by others, including older siblings.

By limiting caregiving activities to those provided by parents (biological or surrogate), the MICS3 survey may have underestimated the amount and depth of socio-emotional and cognitive caregiving available to children in the participating cultures. For this reason, in interpreting the percentages of mothers or fathers who engage their children in any of the six activities, value judgments conveying inferences about levels of deprivation, whether within the LMIC samples or between the LMIC populations in this monograph and any other population, must be made with extreme caution. One ramification of this problem is the potential to undercut the validity and meaningfulness of any future analyses exploring relational or predictive associations involving the caregiving measures. As a hypothetical illustration, in future analyses exploring long-term impacts of early caregiving, a finding of an absence of a predictive relationship between any aspect of parental caregiving and later school performance would be spurious simply because the measures of caregiving would not have sufficiently sampled the actual range of children's caregiving experiences.

Conceptions of Child Labor

In the chapter on children's work as well, the authors make a commendable effort to provide nuanced interpretations of their findings. But here too, there is a lot to be learned about how methods, tools, and measures are at best reflections of the cultural values, beliefs, and theoretical understandings researchers bring to the framing of human behavior in eco-cultural contexts. In this case, the authors of this monograph had no control over the choice of methods and measures. One inherent challenge with the measurement and/or analysis of child labor in this monograph is the possible conflation of children's eco-culturally relevant and "valid" work with child labor. Within the international community, there is increasing realization of the need to distinguish between children's work and child labor on the grounds, in part, that "it cannot be assumed that all children's work is incompatible with child welfare and development" (ILO/IPEC SIMPOC, 2007, p. 5). The MICS3 household questionnaire appears to reflect the need for this distinction, and the data coding in this monograph further separates children's work outside the home (ostensibly paid or unpaid economic activity) from children's work occurring within the confines of family. The coding further distinguishes between family work (e.g., farm or business activity) and household chores. However, there is nothing in the data set to help place in context the amount of time children spent engaging in the various forms of work.

Globally, the stakes are so high on this subject that analysis of data that is devoid of information on the circumstances and likely determinants of children's work is at best problematic. In the rather terse exploration of the literature on why children engage in work outside the home, the authors cite some of the reasons that children from a number of developing countries (including Nigeria, Bangladesh, and Nicaragua) give for their involvement in paid word outside the family. The responses converged around the need to earn money to support family, pay for school, or learn a trade.

A central concern about children's work, especially work undertaken outside the realm of the family, is that it threatens access to educational opportunities. There is nothing in the study reported in this monograph to validate or dispute this central concern. To underscore the complexity of the linkage between children's work and the pursuit of educational opportunities, consider the following responses extracted from a study of 14- to 17-year-old children working at an artisanal gold mine in Ghana (Okyere, 2012, pp. 85–86):

CHILD A: *"My father and I used to work on people's farms at first but one day he decided it will be good if I attended school instead. He cannot always afford to give me school money so I come here to earn some money which I save for school."*

CHILD B: *"I want to be a nurse when I grow up because I can earn enough to take care of myself and my family. I know if I don't go to school, I can never become a nurse… Things are difficult but if I stop school, I will only stay in the village doing nothing and waste my life so I will keep working."*

CHILD C: *"If I did not have to work, I will have finished school a long time ago . . . I have had to quit school sometimes for a couple of months so I can save money and go back to continue. By that time, all my mates will have completed that level and I have to start again with a new batch of students."*

These responses illustrate some of the nuances often lost in statements linking children's work to lost educational opportunities or other life benefits emanating from education. Child C's response affirms the traditional view that outside work can have disruptive effects on schooling, but it does, on the other hand, also underscore two themes that cut across all three responses, namely (1) that the desire to pursue educational opportunities could indeed, be one reason for children's work outside the home, and (2) when children engage in paid work outside the home, it may not necessarily be the case that parents put them to that work; many children choose to work out of a sense of social responsibility to take care of self and, sometimes, family. This second insight is particularly important because it balances the picture one gets from sections of the chapter on child labor that much of the labor might be driven by parental desire or need to supplement family resources.

Finally, let me place this discussion in the contemporary context of the United Nations Convention on the Rights of Children and the growing recognition of the imperative for societies all over the world to protect those rights with explicit governmental policies. It can be argued that for many of the millions of preadolescent children whose educational opportunities are routinely jeopardized by resource constraints within their families, the ability to engage in outside or family work for remuneration might, quite paradoxically be a necessary condition for realization of their rights to education and self-advancement (Okyere, 2012)—the very rights that global and national child labor laws are intended to protect.

There is no justification for children's work that places a child's life, education, and well-being in jeopardy. However, in low- and middle-income societies, scholars and lay persons alike consider children's work in their part of the world as a poorly understood phenomenon in the Euro-American world. The global discourse on this subject suggests that there is danger in lumping all forms of children's work into an amorphous, undifferentiated indicator of "child labor." This is because it muddies the waters on a complicated and controversial subject, and it has the potential to undermine necessary and legitimate interventions to eliminate the worst forms of out-of-home child labor. For this and other reasons, scholars pursuing research on this topic need to approach their work with clear awareness of the implications of their work for public discourse that is, at this point, still in need of evidence and clear delineation of what does and does not constitute child labor with potential deleterious consequences.

The authors may not have produced explanatory data on the various forms of children's work, but they have been prudent in ensuring that their analysis of the composite index was preceded by separate analyses of the three individual work categories making up the composite index. In so doing, they have offset potentially ambiguous interpretations of their data. Their cautious and nuanced discussion of the findings is wise.

CONCLUSION

In the last few years, the Society for Research in Child Development has invested in the advancement of interdisciplinary, international, and cultural understandings of developmental phenomena through collaborative intellectual activities undertaken by its members with modest funding support provided in furtherance of the society's strategic goals. The society has also been forging formal collaborative partnerships with international multilateral agencies with defined missions and mandates around the well-being of children around the world. These linkages are exceedingly important for at least three reasons. First, they have the potential to increase the contributions of developmental scientists to population-level data gathering activities undertaken under the auspices of these international agencies. Second, they facilitate, where possible and meaningful, the post hoc harnessing of developmental knowledge from the resulting databases. Third, and flowing from the preceding benefit, they have the potential to advance cultural and other contextual understandings in a field that acknowledges cultural contributions to human development but remains largely entrapped in Euro-American conceptions of development.

Bornstein et al. have demonstrated in this monograph that notwithstanding their limitations, such databases do have scientific value and could become a gateway through which our field can begin to cultivate greater representation of Majority World data in our existing developmental knowledge base. As I have argued, however, increasing the representation of Majority World samples is only the first step. Measures on which comparisons are made must have shared meaning across samples or else there is no common metric for comparative analyses. This, in turn, requires increased openness to, and deliberate advancement of, context-analytic research exploring variations and similarities in developmental constructs across cultures. These directions could have the effect of extending existing conceptions of norms, variability, and comparability within our field. When they do, they will signal that our field has made additional strides on a trajectory toward a more global science of human development. Bornstein, Putnick, Lansford, Deater-Deckard, and Bradley have provided in this monograph a piece of the bridging edifice.

REFERENCES

Arnett, J. J. (2008). The neglected 95%: Why American psychology needs to become less American. *American Psychologist*, **63**, 602–614.

Bornstein, M. H. (1995). Form and function: Implications for studies of culture and human development. *Culture & Psychology*, **1**, 123–137.

Bronfenbrenner, U. (1979). *The ecology of human development*. Cambridge, MA: Cambridge University Press.

Ceci, S. J., Kahan, D. M., & Braman, D. (2010). The WEIRD are even weirder than you think: Diversifying contexts is as important as diversifying samples. *Behavior and Brain Sciences*, **33**, 87–88.

Cole, M. (1996). *Cultural psychology: A once and future discipline*. Cambridge, MA: Belknap Press of Harvard University Press.

Harkness, S., & Super, C. M. (1992). Shared child care in East Africa: Socio-cultural origins and developmental consequences. In M. E. Lamb, K. J. Sternberg, C. P. Hwang, & A. G. Broberg (Eds.), *Child care in context: Socio-cultural perspectives* (pp. 441–459). Hillsdale, NJ: Erlbaum.

Henrich, J., Heine, S. J., & Norenzayan, A. (2010). The weirdest people in the world. *Behavioral and Brain Sciences*, **33**, 61–135.

Kağitçibaşi, C. (2007). *Family, self, and human development across cultures: Theory and applications* (2nd ed.). (Mahwah, NJ: Erlbaum.

ILO/IPEC SIMPOC. (2007). *Towards an internationally accepted statistical definition of child labor: Children's activities and their definitions*. Geneva: International Labor Organization/International Program on the Elimination of Child Labor's Statistical Information and Monitoring Program on Child Labor. Retrieved from: http://www.ilo.org

LeVine, R. A., Dixon, S., LeVine, S., Richman, A., Leiderman, P. H., Keefer, C. H. et al. (1994). *Child care and culture: Lessons from Africa* Cambridge, UK: Cambridge University Press.

Marfo, K. (1999). Disability research in cultural contexts. Beyond methods and techniques. In B. Holzer, A. Vreede, & G. Weigt (Eds.), *Disability in different cultures: Reflections on local concepts* (pp. 314–322). Bielefeld, Germany: Transcript Verlag.

Marfo, K. (2011). Envisioning an African child development field. *Child Development Perspectives*, **5**, 140–147.

Nsamenang, A. B. (1992). *Human development in cultural context: A third world perspective*. Newbury Park, CA: SAGE.

Nsamenang, A. B. (2006). Human ontogenesis: An indigenous African view on development and intelligence. *International Journal of Psychology*, **41**, 293–297.

Okyere, S. (2012). Are working children's rights and child labor abolition complementary of opposing realms? *International Social Work*, **56**, 80–91.

Pence, A. (2011). Early childhood care and development research in Africa: Historical, conceptual, and structural challenges. *Child Development Perspectives*, **5**, 112–118.

Pence, A., & Nsamenang, B. (2008) *A case for early childhood development in sub-Saharan Africa*. Working Paper No. 51. The Hague, The Netherlands: Bernard van Leer Foundation.

Rogoff, B. (2003). *The cultural nature of human development*. New York, NY: Oxford University Press.

Serpell, R. (1996). Cultural models of childhood in indigenous socialization and formal schooling in Zambia. In C. P. Hwang, M. E. Lamb, & I. E. Siegel (Eds.). *Images of childhood* (pp. 129–143). New York, NY: Psychology Press.

Serpell, R. (2000). Intelligence and culture. In R. J. Sternberg (Ed.). *Handbook of Intelligence* (pp. 549–579). Cambridge: Cambridge University Press.

Serpell, R. (2011). Social responsibility as a dimension of intelligence, and as an educational goal: Insights from programmatic research in an African society. *Child Development Perspectives*, **5**, 126–133.

Serpell, R., & Marfo, K. (2014). Some long-standing and emerging research lines in Africa. In R. Serpell & K. Marfo (Eds.), *Child development in Africa: Views from inside. New directions for child and adolescent development*. Vol. **146**, pp. 1–22.

Shweder, R. A. (1991). *Thinking through cultures: Expeditions in cultural psychology*. Cambridge, MA: Harvard University Press.

Super, C. M. & Harkness, S. (1986). The developmental niche: A conceptualization at the interface of child and culture. *International Journal of Behavioral Development*, **9**, 545–569.

Valsiner, J. (2000). *Culture and human development: An introduction*. Thousand Oaks, CA: SAGE.

Weisner, T. S. (1984). A cross-cultural perspective: Ecocultural niches of middle childhood. In A. Collins (Ed.), *The elementary school years: Understanding development during middle childhood* (pp. 335–369). Washington, DC: National Academy Press.

Weisner, T. S. (1987). Socialization for parenthood in sibling caretaking societies. In J. B. Lancaster, J. Altman, A. S. Rossi, & L. R. Sherrod (Eds.), *Parenting across the lifespan: Biosocial dimensions* (pp. 237–270). Hawthorne, NY: Aldine de Gruyter.

Weisner, T. S. (2014). The socialization of trust: Plural caregiving and diverse pathways in human development. In H. Otto & H. Keller (Eds.), *Different faces of attachment: Cultural variations on a universal human need* (pp. 263–277). Cambridge, UK: Cambridge University Press.

Wiredu, K. (1996). *Cultural universals and particulars: An African perspective*. Bloomington: Indiana University Press.

Zimba, R. F. (2002). Indigenous conceptions of childhood development and social realities in southern Africa. In H. Keller, Y. P. Poortinga, & A. Scholmerish (Eds.), *Between cultures and biology: Perspectives on ontogenetic development* (pp. 89–115). Cambridge, UK: Cambridge University Press.

CONTRIBUTORS

> This article is part of the issue "Gender in Low- and Middle-Income Countries," Bornstein, Putnick, Lansford, Deater-Deckard, and Bradley (Issue Authors). For a full listing of articles in this issue, see: http://onlinelibrary.wiley.com/doi/10.1111/mono.v81.1/issuetoc.

Marc H. Bornstein, Ph.D., is Senior Investigator and Head of Child and Family Research at the *Eunice Kennedy Shriver* National Institute of Child Health and Human Development. He has published in experimental, methodological, comparative, developmental, and cultural science as well as neuroscience, pediatrics, and aesthetics.

Robert H. Bradley, Ph.D., is Professor and Director of the Family and Human Dynamics Research Institute at Arizona State University. His research focuses on family environments, child care and early education, with emphasis on how each is implicated in children's development. He is also involved in developing measures of the home environment.

Kirby Deater-Deckard, Ph.D., is Professor and Director of Developmental Science in Psychology at Virginia Tech. He conducts research on the intergenerational transmission and development of social-emotional and cognitive attributes, with emphasis on parenting and gene-environment processes.

Jennifer E. Lansford, Ph.D., is Research Professor in the Center for Child and Family Policy at Duke University. Her research focuses on the development of aggression and other behavior problems in children and adolescents, with an

---

Corresponding author: Marc H. Bornstein, Child and Family Research, *Eunice Kennedy Shriver*, National Institute of Child Health and Human Development, National Institutes of Health, Suite 8030, 6705 Rockledge Drive, Bethesda MD 20892-7971; email: Marc_H_Bornstein@nih.gov.
DOI: 10.1111/mono.12233
© 2015 The Society for Research in Child Development, Inc.

emphasis on how family, peer, and cultural contexts contribute to or protect against these outcomes.

Diane L. Putnick, Ph.D., is a researcher and statistician with the Child and Family Research Section of the *Eunice Kennedy Shriver* National Institute of Child Health and Human Development. Her research interests include child and family processes across cultures.

Kofi Marfo is Professor and Founding Director, Institute for Human Development, Aga Khan University (East Africa, South-Central Asia, and United Kingdom). His scholarly interests include developmental science and practice, advancement of a global science of human development, and philosophical issues in behavioral science and education research. He co-leads an African child development research capacity enhancement initiative, co-convenes the African Child Development Scholars Workshop series, and has most recently co-edited Child Development in Africa: Views from inside (Serpell and Marfo, 2014), a volume in New Directions for Child and Adolescent Development.

STATEMENT OF EDITORIAL POLICY

The SRCD *Monographs* series aims to publish major reports of developmental research that generates authoritative new findings and that foster a fresh perspective and/or integration of data/research on conceptually significant issues. Submissions may consist of individually or group-authored reports of findings from some single large-scale investigation or from a series of experiments centering on a particular question. Multiauthored sets of independent studies concerning the same underlying question also may be appropriate. A critical requirement in such instances is that the individual authors address common issues and that the contribution arising from the set as a whole be unique, substantial, and well integrated. Manuscripts reporting interdisciplinary or multidisciplinary research on significant developmental questions and those including evidence from diverse cultural, racial, and ethnic groups are of particular interest. Also of special interest are manuscripts that bridge basic and applied developmental science, and that reflect the international perspective of the Society. Because the aim of the *Monographs* series is to enhance cross-fertilization among disciplines or subfields as well as advance knowledge on specialized topics, the links between the specific issues under study and larger questions relating to developmental processes should emerge clearly and be apparent for both general readers and specialists on the topic. In short, irrespective of how it may be framed, work that contributes significant data and/or extends a developmental perspective will be considered.

Potential authors who may be unsure whether the manuscript they are planning wouldmake an appropriate submission to the SRCD *Monographs* are invited to draft an outline or prospectus of what they propose and send it to the incoming editor for review and comment.

Potential authors are not required to be members of the Society for Research in Child Development nor affiliated with the academic discipline of psychology to submit a manuscript for consideration by the *Monographs*. The significance of the work in extending developmental theory and in contributing new empirical information is the crucial consideration.

Submissions should contain a minimum of 80 manuscript pages (including tables and references). The upper boundary of 150–175 pages is more flexible, but authors should try to keep within this limit. Manuscripts must be double-spaced, 12pt Times New Roman font, with 1-inch margins. If color artwork is submitted, and the authors believe color art is necessary to the presentation of their work, the submissions letter should indicate that one or more authors or their institutions are prepared to pay the substantial costs associated with color art reproduction. Please submit manuscripts electronically to the SRCD *Monographs* Online Submissions and Review Site (Scholar One) at http://mc.manuscriptcentral.com/mono. Please contact the *Monographs* office with any questions at monographs@srcd.org.

The corresponding author for any manuscript must, in the submission letter, warrant that all coauthors are in agreement with the content of the manuscript. The corresponding author also is responsible for informing all coauthors, in a timely manner, of manuscript submission, editorial decisions, reviews received, and any revisions recommended. Before publication, the corresponding author must warrant in the submissions letter that the study has been conducted according to the ethical guidelines of the Society for Research in Child Development.

A more detailed description of all editorial policies, evaluation processes, and format requirements can be found under the "Submission Guidelines" link at http://srcd.org/publications/monographs.

Monographs Editorial Office
e-mail: monographs@srcd.org

Editor, Patricia J. Bauer
Department of Psychology, Emory University
36 Eagle Row
Atlanta, GA 30322
e-mail: pjbauer@emory.edu

Note to NIH Grantees

Pursuant to NIH mandate, Society through Wiley-Blackwell will post the accepted version of Contributions authored by NIH grantholders to PubMed Central upon acceptance. This accepted version will be made publicly available 12 months after publication. For further information, see http://www.wiley.com/go/nihmandate.

SUBJECT INDEX

Page numbers in *italics* represent figures.

agricultural work, 105, 107–108, 120. *See also* child labor
Albania
    mother–father agreement, 70, 71
    quality of housing, 48
anthropometry. *See* child growth
anxiety, 108, 121
armed conflict, 105
attachment research, 13

Bangladesh
    child labor benefits, 106, 178
    childrearing discipline questionnaire, 83
    cooking facilities, 38–39
    growth and mortality, 35
    play (caregiving practice), 72
    take outside (caregiving practice), 72
Belarus
    household chores, 118
    quality of housing, 48
beliefs, patterns of, 16
Belize, mortality, 47
bioecological theory, 15–17, 23
biology and gender differences, 11, 99
Bosnia and Herzegovina
    height-for-age and stunting, 46
    household chores, 118
    name, count, draw (caregiving practice), 72
    play (caregiving practice), 72
    quality of housing, 48
    sing songs (caregiving practice), 72
    take outside (caregiving practice), 72

Botswana, childcare, 62
Brazil, child labor age of entry, 107
Burkina Faso
   household material resources, 50
   play (caregiving practice), 72
   take outside (caregiving practice), 72
   weight-for-height and wasting, 47
Burundi
   child labor, 114, 120
   childrearing discipline questionnaire, 83
   household chores, 118

Cameroon
   household material resources, 49, 50, 51, 56
   work outside the home, 115
caregiving. *See* parenting/caregiving
Central African Republic
   childcare, 62
   family work, 115
   take outside (caregiving practice), 72
child abuse/neglect, 17, 144
child growth
   capital assets and —, 33–59
   child labor and health/well-being, 104
   data, 40, 43
   explanatory models, 47–51
   gender and country, 45–47
   gender similarities/differences, 35, 51, 52, 53, 53, 124–136, 138
   health care, 17, 142, 144
   height-for-age and stunting, 33–59, 125
   home environment, 37–40, 125
   indicators, 7, 34–35, 125
   nutrition, 17, 21, 33–35, 36, 54, 55, 107, 142, 144
   research study, 26, 40–53, 57–59, 174
   sociocultural impact on health and behavior, 12
   sources of gender similarities/differences, 35–37
   weight-for-age and underweight, 33–59, 125
   weight-for-height and wasting, 33–59, 125, 134
child labor
   age, 107, 110, 113, 121–122
   benefits and costs, 107–108
   childcare, 106, 109, 126, 129, 131
   conceptions of, 177–180

descriptive statistics, 110, *111–112*
divisions of, 16–17, 18
eco-cultural contexts, 178
eldercare, 109
family work, 104, 105, 109, 126, 129, 133, 178
gender differences, 104, 106, 108–109, 119–120, 126, 127, 129–132, 134, 138
government policies, 105–106, 122
household chores, 20–21, 104, 105, 107, 109–122, 126, 129–130, 133, 134, 142, 178
index, 113, 114–115
indicators, 7
"loaning," 120
poverty and —, 106–107
reasons for, 106, 142
reporting, 136
research study, 26, 109–122, 175
types of, 105
work outside the home, 105, 107, 108–109, 109–122, 126, 129–130, 132, 134, 179
work vs. play, 106, 177–178
child mortality. *See* mortality, child
childrearing strategies. *See* parenting/caregiving
child rights, 17
child trafficking, 105
China
   caregiver behavior, 81
   child autonomy, 128
   gender preference, 55
climate conditions, 57
cognitive social learning theory, 10
Colombia, caregiver behavior, 81
context and bioecological theory, 15
Convention on the Rights of the Child (CRC), 17
cooking facilities, 38–39, 43–44
Côte d'Ivoire
   name, count, draw (caregiving practice), 72
   play (caregiving practice), 72
   take outside (caregiving practice), 72
   weight-for-height and wasting, 47
cultural traditions, 9, 16, 127, 139, 144
   caregiving, 128, 176–177
   child growth and mortality, 36, 39

child labor, 120, 122, 127, 177–180
childrearing discipline, 79–80, 129
gender preference, 55, 58
rites of passage, 127
customs, patterns of, 16

depression, 108, 121
diarrhea, 38, 54, 56
discipline, childrearing, 22, 125
　child age, 82, 83, *83*, 87, 99
　country-level correlates, 98–99, 132
　descriptive statistics, 85–87, *86*, *88–97*, 98–99
　education and —, 143
　frequency/timing, 102
　gender differences, 80–82, 83, *83*, 87, *98*, 99–103, 125–126, 129, 130–132, 134, 138, 139
　indicators, 7, 18
　national and cultural variations, 79–80
　reporting, 136
　research study, 26, 83–103, 175
　rewarding/punishing, 79–80, 87, 99
　siblings, 102
　statistical associations, *83*
　See also socialization; violence/nonviolence
diseases and gender differences, 36
Djibouti
　mortality, 47
　take outside (caregiving practice), 72
drug trafficking, 105
durable goods, 39–40

education
　aspirations, 133
　child, 22, 58, 60–61, 77, 142–143, 177
　child labor and —, 104, 107, 121–122, 142, 179
　double-shift schooling, 120
　female, 128, 142
　gross enrollment in school, 28, 30, 140, 142
　Human Development Index, 31
　maternal, 13, 39, 46, 56, 59, 66, 67, 70, 76, 82, 83, *83*, 87, 99, 109, 110, 114, 142
　parental, 82, 142
　rights to, 179
　universal, 23

electricity, 39
El Salvador, child labor benefits, 106
emotion, parental ideas, 8
empowerment, gendered, 28, 30
environmental conditions, 16, 17. *See also* bioecological theory
  child growth and mortality, 36
  gendered patterns of behavior, 99
Ethiopia
  child labor benefits, 106, 108, 122
  growth and mortality, 35, 36, 56
evolutionary theory, 10–11

farm work. *See* agricultural work
food, 22
  allocation, 131
  contamination, 38
  storage and refrigeration, 38, 44

Gambia
  child labor, 120, 122
  family work, 115
gender, bioecological perspective, 15–17, 23
gender discrimination, 35, 36
gender equality
  child growth and mortality, 135, 143
  child labor, 109, 110, 118, 119–120, 134
  disadvantaged, 28
  indices, 28, *29*, 30
  national indicators, 16–17, 134–140
  parenting practices, 66, 73–74, *74*
  See also gender similarities/differences
gender in low- and middle-income countries
  bioecological perspective on child gender, 15–17
  child growth and mortality, 33–59
  child labor, 104–122
  childrearing discipline, 78–103
  described, 8–10
  gender research and international development science, 18–22
  gender research topics, 17–18
  gender theory and gender similarities/differences, 10–15
  parenting practices, 60–77
  research study, general methods, 24–32
  study reflections, limitations, directions, implications, 123–144

191

gender segregation, 127
gender similarities/differences, 7
   behavior, 80, 129
   biological, 23
   child growth and mortality, 34–59, 125, 131, 135, 138
   child labor, 104–122, 126, 127, 129–132, 133, 138
   childrearing discipline, 80–82, 87, *88–98*, 98–103, 125, 129, 130–131, 134
   domains, 13–14
   gender theory, 10–15, 123–124
   home environment, 8
   "hypothesis," 143
   parenting practices, 60–77, 131, 138
   social construction, 11, 13, 18–22
   sources of — in child growth and mortality, 35–37
   stereotypes, 18–21, 123–124, 141
   studies of, 18–22
   treatment with family, 9
   within-gender variability, 19
gender theory, 10–15, 123–124
gendered parenting. *See* parenting/caregiving
genetic disposition, 35–37, 54–55, 58, 128
Georgia
   child labor, 120
   household material resources, 50
   mother–father agreement, 70, 71
   quality of housing, 48
geographic factors, 39
Germany, child autonomy, 128
Ghana
   child labor and poverty, 107
   education and child labor, 178
   name, count, draw (caregiving practice), 72
Great Britain, gender differences, 8
Guatemala, child labor benefits, 106
Guinea-Bissau
   quality of housing, 48
   storytelling (caregiving practice), 73
   take outside (caregiving practice), 71, 72
Guyana
   family work, 115
   household material resources, 50
   storytelling (caregiving practice), 73

health care, 54, 55, 58, 82. *See also* child growth
home environment and bioecological theory, 15
  data, 43
  impact on child growth and mortality, 37–40
household chores. *See* child labor
household material resources, 21, 34, 36, 131, 142
  explanatory models, 49–51
  indicators, 43–44, 45, 54, 56, 58, 125
housing, quality of, 34, 37, 39–40, 45
  construction materials, 39
  dwelling floor, 43, 44
  explanatory models, 47–49
  indicators, 43–44, 54, 56, 58, 125
human development, global science, 172–180
Human Development Index (HDI), 8, *28*, 30–31, 51

immunizations, 39
income, estimated earned, 28
India
  child autonomy, 128
  gender preference, 55
  growth and mortality, 35, 36
  parenting practices, 77
industrial work, 105, 109. *See also* child labor
Iraq
  height-for-age and stunting, 46
  name, count, draw (caregiving practice), 72
  play (caregiving practice), 72
  read books (caregiving practice), 73
  sing songs (caregiving practice), 72
  storytelling (caregiving practice), 73
  take outside (caregiving practice), 72
  weight-for-height and wasting, 46
  work outside the home, 115
Italy, caregiver behavior, 81

Jordan, caregiver behavior, 81

Kazakhstan
  childrearing discipline, 85
  mother–father agreement, 70
Kenya, caregiver behavior, 81
Kyrgyzstan, household material resources, 49, 50, 51, 56

labor. *See* child labor
labor market, 30
language, 77
Laos
   mother–father agreement, 70, 71
   sing songs (caregiving practice), 72
   storytelling (caregiving practice), 73
   weight-for-height and wasting, 46
life expectancy, 28, 30
literacy rate, 28, 30, 56, 140
living standards. *See* socioeconomic conditions
low- and middle-income countries (LMIC), 7, 21
   child labor, 104–122, 142
   childrearing discipline, 78–103
   gender differences, 9, 24–32
   gender equality indices, 28, *29*, 30
   parenting practices, 60–77
   social contexts, 14–15
   study reflections, limitations, directions, implications, 123–144

Macedonia
   household chores, 118
   mother–father agreement, 70
   sing songs (caregiving practice), 72
Malawi, provisions for water, 38
Mauritania
   childrearing discipline questionnaire, 83
   household material resources, 50
   weight-for-height and wasting, 47
mental health problems, 108
Mongolia
   childrearing discipline questionnaire, 83, 98
   weight-for-height and wasting, 46
Montenegro
   family work, 115
   household material resources, 50
mortality, child
   capital assets and —, 33–59
   child labor, 107
   data, 43
   gender similarities/differences, 18, 35–37, 54–57, 125, 128, 131, 134–135, 138, 143
   home environment, 37–40

indicators, 7, 34–35, 125
infant, 23
life expectancy, 140
rates of, 36
research study, 26, 40–53, 58–59, 175
sources of gender similarities/differences, 35–37
See also child growth
Mozambique
childrearing discipline questionnaire, 83
household material resources, 50
storytelling (caregiving practice), 73
weight-for-height and wasting, 47
Multiple Indicator Cluster Survey (MICS), 7, 18, *22*, 23, 24–28, 69, 110, 113, 124–134, 135–140, 172

name, count, draw (caregiving practice), 71, 72, 74, 75, 133, 135, 137, 141, 177
natural selection, 10
Nepal, growth and mortality, 37
Nicaragua, child labor benefits, 106, 178
Nigeria
child labor benefits, 106, 178
childrearing discipline questionnaire, 83
growth and mortality, 35
household material resources, 49, 50
take outside (caregiving practice), 72
nutrition. *See* child growth

Pakistan, growth and mortality, 35
parenting/caregiving
age of parent, 67
–child interactions, 15
childrearing strategies, 17, 18
cultural models, 128, 176–177
daughters and sons, 63–65
death of parent, 12
evolutionary theory, 10–11
fathers' investments, 75
gender and context, 65–66
gender equity and economic factors, 66, 75–76, 135–136
gender gaps, 75
gendered, 18, 20–21, 62–65
group differences by parent and child gender, 71–73, *71*

indicators, 7
  investment, 10
  mother–father agreement, 70–71
  mothers and fathers, 62–63, 75, 125, 177
  mothers and fathers, daughters and sons, 65, 136
  nurturing, 17
  practices, 8–9, 58, 60–77, 131, 133–134, 141–142
  research study, 67–75, 175
  role models, 64, 129–130
  scaffolding activities, 64, 130
  survival value, 12
  See also discipline, childrearing; education
Peru, growth and mortality, 36
pesticides. *See* toxin exposure
Philippines
  caregiver behavior, 81
  child labor benefits, 106
  cooking facilities, 39
  growth and mortality, 36
play (caregiving practice), 13, 70–71, 72, 75, 107, 129, 130, 131, 133, 137, 177.
  See also toys
poverty, 21, 53
  child labor and —, 106–107, 142
  eliminating, 23
process and bioecological theory, 15
prostitution, 105

read books (caregiving practice), 71, 73, 75, 76–77, 133, 135, 141, 177
religious traditions, 9, 16
reproductive health, 28, 140
research study, 31–32
  caregiver report, 135–136
  child labor, 109–122
  childrearing discipline, 82–99
  data collection, 31–32
  implementation, 27–28
  methods, 40–45, 83–85
  parenting practices, 67, 69–70, 76–77
  participating countries, 25, *25*, 26, 40, *41–42*
  procedures and measures, 40, 69–70, 110, 113
  questionnaire content, 26–27, 136–137
  questionnaire timing, 137
  reflections, limitations, directions, implications, 123–144

respondents, 26, 67, 69, 83, 110
  sampling, 27, 30, *68–69*, 137–138
respiratory problems, 39, 56

sanitation facilities, 36, 37, 54, 82
school. *See* education
self-esteem, 121, 133
self-reliance, 20
Serbia
  play (caregiving practice), 72
  weight-for-age and underweight, 46
  weight-for-height and wasting, 47
service work, 105, 108. *See also* child labor
siblings, 20, 102, 129, 132, 133, 138, 176
Sierra Leone
  read books (caregiving practice), 73
  weight-for-height and wasting, 47
sing songs (caregiving practice), 71, 72, 75, 133, 177
slavery, 105
socialization
  childrearing discipline, 79–80, 99, 101, 125
  distributed system, 176
  gender differences, 80–82, 99, 129–130, 138, 141, 144
  male mobility, 16
  parental, 21, 128, 142, 177
  parenting practices, 13, 16, 60–61, 124, 131–132
  psychological, 9
  social contexts of LMIC, 14–15
  women's power, 16
sociocultural theory, 10–12
socioeconomic conditions, 9, 16, 132, 134–135
  capital assets in mortality and growth, 33–59
  child labor, 118, *118*
  childrearing discipline, 82
  growth, 23
  living standards, 21
  parenting practices, 66, 73–74, *74*, 75
  siblings, 129
Somalia
  childrearing discipline questionnaire, 83
  household chores, 120
  household material resources, 50
  take outside (caregiving practice), 72

weight-for-age and underweight, 46
weight-for-height and wasting, 46
Sri Lanka, gender differences, 8
storytelling (caregiving practice), 71, 73, 75, 133, 141, 177
stunting, 36, 37, 38, 43, 45–59, 125. *See also* child growth
Suriname, household material resources, 50
Sweden
    caregiver behavior, 81
    gendered inequality, 30
Syrian Arab Republic
    household material resources, 50
    take outside (caregiving practice), 72
    weight-for-height and wasting, 47
    work outside the home, 115

Tajikistan, mother–father agreement, 70, 71
take outside (caregiving practice), 70, 71–72, 75, 129, 133, 135, 177
Tanzania, child mortality, 55
tell stories. *See* storytelling
Thailand
    caregiver behavior, 81
    childrearing discipline questionnaire, 83
    name, count, draw (caregiving practice), 72
    play (caregiving practice), 72
    read books (caregiving practice), 73
    sing songs (caregiving practice), 72
    weight-for-height and wasting, 46
time and bioecological theory, 15
Togo, household material resources, 50
toilet facilities, 43, 44. *See also* sanitation facilities
toxin exposure, 105, 107
toys, 8, 13, 64, 131
Trinidad and Tobago, household chores, 118

Uganda, household material resources, 56
underweight, 43, 45–59. *See also* child growth
United States
    caregiver behavior, 81
    child autonomy, 128
Uzbekistan
    childrearing discipline questionnaire, 83
    household chores, 118
    mother–father agreement, 70–71

values, patterns of, 16
Vanuatu
  childrearing discipline questionnaire, 83
  household material resources, 50
  mortality, 47
  quality of housing, 48
Vietnam
  child labor, 120
  growth and mortality, 36
  violence/nonviolence, 7, 78–103, 125–126
  work outside the home, 115
violence/nonviolence, 7, 78–103, 125–126, 132, 134, 138

wasting, 30, 36, 37, 43, 45–59, 125, 134. *See also* child growth
water
  contamination, 38
  provisions, 38
  safe drinking, 21, 36, 37, 43, 44, 54, 82
  storage, 38

Yemen
  childrearing discipline, 85
  gendered inequality, 30
  mortality, 47
  take outside (caregiving practice), 71
  work outside the home, 115

CURRENT

Gender in Low- and Middle-Income Countries —*Marc H. Bornstein, Diane L. Putnick, Jennifer E. Lansford, Kirby Deater-Deckard, and Robert H. Bradley* (SERIAL NO. 320, 2016)

A Longitudinal Study of Infant Cortisol Response During Learning Events—*Laura A. Thompson, Gin Morgan, and Kellie A. Jurado* (SERIAL NO. 319, 2015)

Studies in Fetal Behavior: Revisited, Renewed, and Reimagined—*Janet A. DiPietro, Kathleen A. Costigan and Kristin M. Voegtline* (SERIAL NO. 318, 2015)

The Role of Parents in The Ontogeny of Achievement-Related Motivation and Behavioral Choices—*Sandra D. Simpkins Jennifer A. Fredricks and Jacquelynne S. Eccles* (SERIAL NO. 317, 2015)

Sleep and Development: Advancing Theory and Research—*Mona El-Sheikh and Avi Sadeh* (SERIAL NO. 316, 2015)

The Relation of Childhood Physical Activity to Brain Health, Cognition, and Scholastic Achievement—*Charles H. Hillman* (SERIAL NO. 315, 2014)

The Adult Attachment Interview: Psychometrics, Stability and Change From Infancy, and Developmental Origins—*Cathryn Booth-LaForce and Glenn I. Roisman* (SERIAL NO. 314, 2014)

The Emergent Executive: A Dynamic Field Theory of the Development of Executive Function—*Aaron T. Buss and John P. Spencer* (SERIAL NO. 313, 2014)

Children's Understanding of Death: Toward a Contextualized and Integrated Account— *Karl S. Rosengren, Peggy J. Miller, Isabel T. Gutiérrez, Philip I. Chow, Stevie S. Schein, and Kathy N. Anderson* (SERIAL NO. 312, 2014)

Physical Attractiveness and the Accumulation of Social and Human Capital in Adolescence and Young Adulthood: Assets and Distractions—*Rachel A. Gordon, Robert Crosnoe, and Xue Wang* (SERIAL NO. 311, 2013)

The Family Life Project: An Epidemiological and Developmental Study of Young Children Living in Poor Rural Communities—*Lynne Vernon-Feagans, Martha Cox, and FLP Key Investigators* (SERIAL NO. 310, 2013)

National Institutes of Health Toolbox Cognition Battery (NIH Toolbox CB): Validation for Children Between 3 and 15 Years—*Philip David Zelazo and Patricia J. Bauer* (SERIAL NO. 309, 2013)

Resilience in Children With Incarcerated Parents—*Julie Poehlmann and J. Mark Eddy* (SERIAL NO. 308, 2013)

The Emergence of a Temporally Extended Self and Factors That Contribute to Its Development: From Theoretical and Empirical Perspectives—*Mary Lazaridis* (SERIAL NO. 307, 2013)

What Makes a Difference: Early Head Start Evaluation Findings in a Developmental Context—*John M. Love, Rachel Chazan-Cohen, Helen Raikes, and Jeanne Brooks-Gunn* (SERIAL NO. 306, 2013)

The Development of Mirror Self-Recognition in Different Sociocultural Contexts—*Joscha Kärtner, Heidi Keller, Nandita Chaudhary, and Relindis D. Yovsi* (SERIAL NO. 305, 2012)

"Emotions Are a Window Into One's Heart": A Qualitative Analysis of Parental Beliefs About Children's Emotions Across Three Ethnic Groups—*Alison E. Parker, Amy G. Halberstadt, Julie C. Dunsmore, Greg Townley, Alfred Bryant, Jr., Julie A. Thompson, and Karen S. Beale* (SERIAL NO. 304, 2012)

Physiological Measures of Emotion From a Developmental Perspective: State of the Science—*Tracy A. Dennis, Kristin A. Buss, and Paul D. Hastings* (SERIAL NO. 303, 2012)

How Socialization Happens on the Ground: Narrative Practices as Alternate Socializing Pathways in Taiwanese and European-American Families—*Peggy J. Miller, Heidi Fung, Shumin Lin, Eva Chian-Hui Chen, and Benjamin R. Boldt* (SERIAL NO. 302, 2012)

Children Without Permanent Parents: Research, Practice, and Policy—*Robert B. McCall, Marinus H. van IJzendoorn, Femmie Juffer, Christina J. Groark, and Victor K. Groza* (SERIAL NO. 301, 2011)

I Remember Me: Mnemonic Self-Reference Effects in Preschool Children—*Josephine Ross, James R. Anderson, and Robin N. Campbell* (SERIAL NO. 300, 2011)

Early Social Cognition in Three Cultural Contexts—*Tara Callaghan, Henrike Moll, Hannes Rakoczy, Felix Warneken, Ulf Liszkowski, Tanya Behne, and Michael Tomasello* (SERIAL NO. 299, 2011)

The Development of Ambiguous Figure Perception—*Marina C. Wimmer and Martin J. Doherty* (SERIAL NO. 298, 2011)

The Better Beinnings, Better Futures Project: Findings From Grade 3 to Grade 9—*Ray DeV. Peters, Alison J. Bradshaw, Kelly Petrunka, Geoffrey Nelson, Yves Herry, Wendy M. Craig, Robert Arnold, Kevin C. H. Parker, Shahriar R. Khan, Jeffrey S. Hoch, S. Mark Pancer, Colleen Loomis, Jean-Marc B´el anger , Susan Evers, Claire Maltais, Katherine Thompson, and Melissa D. Rossiter* (SERIAL NO. 297, 2010)